Stand by your Beds!

A Wry Look at National Service

David Findlay Clark

Cualann Press

ISBN 0 9535036 6 6

First Edition October 2001

British Library Cataloguing in Publication Data. A catalogue record of this book is available at the British Library.

Printed by Bell & Bain, Glasgow

Published by:
Cualann Press, 6 Corpach Drive, Dunfermline, KY12 7XG, Scotland
Email: cualann@btinternet.com
Website: http://users.ouvip.com/cualann/

Author's Note

Half a century after the first of the conscripts under the terms of the National Service Act of 1948 (which was enacted with effect from 1st January 1949), few ordinary people in the UK, other than those who served as National Servicemen themselves, will remember much about it or the effect it had on so many young men. The bibliography is not wide. For example, when the author keyed in the term 'National Service' on his local Aberdeen University and Aberdeenshire Library Service computers in an attempt to establish useful references, nothing came up but 'National Health Service' references.

To redress that apparent imbalance, this record attempts to capture something of the impressions of one of these National Servicemen and to make more general comment, where appropriate, on what must have been the experiences of many others. It would be unfair, and unrealistic, to suppose that what follows is necessarily typical of the experience of all. What it does purport to do is to try to capture some of the atmosphere and experiences which will be remembered by most who underwent it.

This is a book about Service life. A brief caveat is perhaps necessary. It features young men of extremely varied backgrounds flung together in situations which were often highly stressed and almost always entirely male. The traditions of the barrack-room and the battlefield are 'macho' and harsh. In consequence, habits of speech are far removed from the drawing room or the academic debate. The same speech habits may be found in nearly all prisons, some large factories or in football crowds.

The writer has therefore not shrunk from using in this book the spontaneously coarse and profane language which was so characteristic of the barrack-room. To do otherwise would have been to reduce verisimilitude and to distort and unnaturally 'clean up' the true atmosphere into which young men of the time were plunged. It was impossible to stop it, one simply had to adapt to it. For those whose earlier background had not already desensitised them, it was just another of the adjustments that National Service forced its recruits to make. The author regrets if some readers may be offended but can reassure those that the habit need not persist and the vast majority of us who were immersed in it were able to unlearn the habit easily enough on our discharge.

Contents

Acknowledgements

The author is indebted to many people, some who may recognise themselves, and others who have been given fictional names and will, for a variety of reasons, never be mentioned by their own names in this book. These include his RAF friends and colleagues who shared the exigencies of these two years and made some of the worst moments tolerable, most days and nights interesting and some utterly hilarious.

Trevor Royle's *The Best Years of their Lives* was the original stimulus which spurred the writer to produce this volume and the author is very much indebted to Mr Royle for his courtesy and support in writing the Preface, as well as for permitting some quotation from his work.

Similar acknowledgment is due to a number of authors from whose work several references have been drawn. They include Peter Chambers and Amy Landreth, Norman Gelb, Arthur Marwick and Len Woodrup. The Readers' Digest Association is also thanked for permission to quote briefly from *The World at Arms* as are Wordsworth Editions for their permission to use a quotation from their *Collected Works of Wilfred Owen.*

Illustrations have been drawn from sources as diverse as Hulton's *Picture Post*, now Hulton-Getty, (Plates 1 and 4), *Aeroplane* magazine (Plate 10), the Ministry of Defence (main picture from front cover and Plates 11 and 13), a wartime cigarette card (Plate 7), Roy Conyers Nesbit's *Illustrated History of the RAF from 1918* (Plate 8), Forbes Law (Plate 9), Paul Crossley (Plate 16) and Andy Thomas (Plate 18). One other illustration (Plate 5) is included by courtesy of Trevor Royle and Mr D McNeill who originally made it available to Mr Royle. Where possible, formal acknowledgement is made to authors and suppliers of illustrations for permission to use material but if, in spite of all reasonable effort, specific and personal acknowledgment cannot be made, the author would still wish to express his gratitude and recognise the rights of the original authors in the matter.

If there should still remain features in the book which have not been acknowledged explicitly, or if there are errors of fact which may have crept in because the author has for any reason been unable to research them in detail or have occurred simply due to the caprice of memory after half a century, then this, though certainly unwitting, is the writer's responsibility.

List of Plates

Preface

For an episode which lasted eighteen years and involved over two million young men, National Service has been strangely neglected by the historians. In most accounts of the post-war period, it attracts little more than a brief mention and although there is a reasonable amount of literature from the period, most notably in novels by Leslie Thomas and David Lodge, there is an acute shortage of lively memoirs.

Now David Clark has done his bit to remedy that omission by writing his own account of his National Service days in the Royal Air Force in the early 1950s. Flattered though I was by being asked to read it in manuscript, my one regret is that I did not meet Dr Clark some dozen years ago while I was researching my history of post-war conscription. It would certainly have added to my understanding for it seems to me that he has produced an account which every former National Serviceman will recognise instantly. In so doing, he has added to our knowledge of that period – the aim of every good historical writer.

As conscription came to an end in 1963, several generations have grown up without knowing what it was like to wear uniform and to have the honour of serving one's sovereign and country. As a result, the armed forces have become smaller and there is a gap between civilian and military life which would have been unthinkable only a few decades ago. Even the sight of men and women in uniform is rare. At a time when the Services are more conscious of security, Dr Clark's description of travelling home in Service dress seems to come from another, and perhaps more idealistic, age.

Few National Servicemen felt that their lives had not been changed by two years' service in the armed forces. Some believed that it was a waste of time but, as the author argues with some force, those who got most out of the experience were those who were prepared to make something of it. As a result they emerged as different people, boys who had become men, more disciplined and more likely to accept responsibility.

And then there was the sense of togetherness. During basic training – the period which no National Serviceman will ever forget – the barrack-room was the nation in microcosm where boys from every type of background, social and educational, found that they had to sink or swim. The vast majority swam, often with a little help from friends whom they might never have met but for the intensity of their shared experience. Where in today's world is that university of life?

They are growing older now, those men who spent what many still insist were the best (or at least the most unforgettable) years of their lives in uniform. Their story deserves to be told in all its richness and variety: by deciding to commit his own memories to print, David Clark has done just that.

Trevor Royle

CHAPTER 1

Prologue

'Stand still! Wot d'ye think yer doin', you 'orrible little man?' If that 100 decibel repetitious command and question sounded once in the ears of a National Serviceman, it sounded a hundred times. Many of us did stand still, in more ways than one, for a couple of years. Many of us did often wonder what we were doing. Some of us look back wryly, a few wistfully and most perhaps with an odd mixture of affection and disaffection. There is an awareness of a bond with all those who did see it through and a sense that, in the end, in spite of some of our feelings at the time, we were probably quite glad that we did it. For most, the memories are fragmentary and variable in their intensity. One has to ask, however, why had so many of these recollections clung, like strands of seaweed, to the trawl net of memory. For those of us who have lived through a childhood and adolescence of wartime, a protracted university education and several major changes in job, relationships, domicile, professional and other responsibilities, there is still an intensity and clarity about these two years which mark them as especially significant and different in quality from any other two years in one's life.

Nearly fifty years on, the vast bulk of the British population, neither at first hand nor through reading and listening, has any real awareness of National Service as a phenomenon. Some will have enjoyed Leslie Thomas's *The Virgin Soldiers*, Arnold Wesker's *Chips with Everything* or Trevor Royle's more documentary analysis in *The Best Years of Their Lives*. They may not have realised fully that the lads, alert for snipers, cutting their way through the Malaysian jungle and living it up on leave in Kuala Lumpur or Singapore were, a few months before, looking to complete an apprenticeship, find a job in the local Woolworth's or train to be lawyers before they were rudely whisked away for a couple of years of widely varying stresses and experiences. Royle's book is richly enlivened by many contributions, letters and the verbatim comments of men from all the Services. Some of these saw active combat. Others found for the first time an ordered and interesting life, maybe even the beginnings of a trade. Others again were bored to tears or resentful of the waste of time. Very few indeed have forgotten everything about it. So what was it like?

The National Service Act of 1948 took effect from 1st January 1949. Between that date and 1960, approximately 2,000,000 young men between the ages of eighteen and twenty-three or thereabouts were conscripted into one of the three main fighting Services. Amongst those of us involved, it is probable that few then appreciated that the vast majority (over 1,130,000) served in the Army. Fewer served in the RAF, as did the writer, and fewer still in the Royal Navy. The recruitment ratios were such that for every Navy Serviceman there would have been twelve in the RAF and thirty-three in the Army. In the early days, eighteen months serving King and country were deemed sufficient. However, a variety of exigencies, combined with the outbreak of the Korean war, found that period extended in 1950 to two years.

So far as this writer was concerned, deferment to complete a first degree at university meant that he had matured to a sturdy twenty-one years of age before starting his two years of National Service in 1951. Although there were several advantages about this which he did not at first appreciate and which will be touched on later, disadvantages seemed at the time to preponderate. Having already lived through the Second World War just before university, he was less than enthusiastic about the prospect of what then may well have seemed to be two wasted years. As people rejoiced in the post-war years, a new, fresh, liberalised world with exciting career prospects for many outside the Services beckoned. To many of us, the need for massive military forces to defend the interests of a rapidly declining empire was not immediately obvious and unless one of the Services could use our new-found skills constructively (something which on hearsay evidence at the time seemed highly unlikely), National Service promised to take a frustrating chunk out of many young lives. A further significant fact was that during the period in which National Service was sustained, there were more than a dozen active conflicts around the world. In the course of these, some National Servicemen were seriously wounded or lost their lives, so such service might also have brought a premature end to the young lives of several more amongst the less fortunate of us.

Gratitude to Winston Churchill for his outstanding wartime leadership did not outlast the end of the war. Much of what had happened to many men from all sorts of social, racial and economic origins led them to look for a better and more egalitarian world on their return from the struggle. It was not surprising then that a great resurgence of enthusiasm for Labour should have followed the end of World War Two. Hopes were high for a 'brave new world' in which there would be much more equality of opportunity at least and in which the prospects of reconstructing the physical and the social structures of the country boded well for the many rather than the few.

By the second post-war election in 1951, however, the Conservatives were re-elected with a majority of only twenty. Labour then actually polled more votes than did the Conservatives but the tricky 'first past the post' style of the British electoral system led to this result. Some contemporary historians thought that there was not so much an undercurrent of deep dissatisfaction with the immediate post-war socialist government as just the effects of an ageing Labour leadership, some members of it worn and perhaps wearied by their part in the wartime coalition government. Perhaps too, the development of the ill-understood Korean war from 1950 to 1953 had also led to an uneasy feeling of insecurity amongst many too soon after the war years.

There were no great differences then, as indeed now at the time of writing, between the policies of the Tory and Labour governments. Arthur Marwick, a historian of these years, pointed out in *Britain in our Century* that:

' ... *a factor which in the sixties and seventies became quite significant in Britain's economic decline made its early appearance: the uncertainty created in the business and investment worlds by the habit of incoming governments of sharply reversing important policies of their predecessors. After the Korean war international terms of trade swung in Britain's favour: primary products cost less, manufactured products commanded higher prices. The post-war growth in international trade continued.'* (p 149)

As a result, individual prosperity improved. In 1951, we celebrated with the then Millennium equivalents of the Skylon and the South Bank Exhibition. People began to sport new possessions such as non-utility clothes, domestic appliances, bigger cars and, after years of austerity, to anticipate a better general standard of living. However, Marwick reminded us that the government was still indulging in a series of 'stop/go' economic policies and there was still much in Britain, in spite of the development of comprehensive schooling following the Butler Education Act of 1944, and better funding for university students, of the old parochial ways. Attitudes to class, especially in England, hierarchical attitudes in the management of industry and pressure to hang on to the last shreds of imperial power in spite of having ceded independence to many former colonies, meant that we were still a 'tight little island'.

True, these features were beginning to break down. There were for the first time, in England, as distinct from Scotland where educational policies had always been more egalitarian anyway, working class kids who had been through grammar schools and a wider range of late teenagers were finding their way into universities. There, for a few years from the late forties, they would mix, willy-nilly, with men and women five or six years their senior who had seen at first hand some of the most gruelling horrors of war, who had developed critical and auto-critical faculties far beyond anything that an eighteen-year-old might imagine.

The bitter, the disillusioned, the fresh young aspirants and the very goal-directed were thus all flung together in a completely new way. There were those who had seen more than enough of Service life and wanted nothing more of it. There were those who saw nothing but glamour and excitement in Service life and could not wait to experience it. Most of all, however, was the great mass of ambivalent young men who were well aware in the late 1940s and early 1950s that National Service was still, like food rationing, a harsh reality, and that it was compulsory. Wars were still being fought elsewhere in the world, relatively serious ones in Malaya and Korea in particular, and National Servicemen were being caught up in these distant and little understood conflicts, some to have their lives cruelly ended all too prematurely and others to be damaged in a variety of ways before they could return to a more normal existence.

The National Service Act of 1948, which both post-war governments had allowed to stand until it was repealed in 1960, meant that approximately 160,000 young men between the ages of eighteen and the early twenties were called up each year to undergo basic military training, followed by service for what remained of the two years and in certain cases, a further three and a half years part-time in the Reserves. Temporary deferment was allowed for students, as in the case of the writer, and others to complete a tertiary educational qualification, such as a completed trade apprenticeship or a first degree at university, but thereafter every male had to do his stint. As remarked above, the vast majority served in the Army. Rather fewer found their way into the Royal Air Force and fewer still into the Royal Navy. The latter, even then, preferred volunteers. Some young men became 'Bevin Boys' and were sent down the mines.

In spite of the fact that numbers of National Servicemen found their way into theatres of war in, for example, Eritrea, Somaliland, Malaya and Korea, many did find it to be two years wasted and of little relevance to the kinds of career or lifestyle to which they aspired. For those who had left school at fifteen and had begun to train in a trade or other occupation, the period from eighteen to twenty was simply a gross intrusion into their occupational development. For those who had deferment until later, like the writer, the career disruption was probably less than each of us imagined, though it seemed harsh at the time, and the widening of experience these two years afforded may well have been to the later advantage of many whose lives would otherwise have been rather circumscribed. As Professor Marwick put it:

'While it is probably true that once a Teddy boy had been called up, he probably ceased forever to be a Teddy boy, it is hard to say whether National Service really served as a force for social control (as latter-day right-wing advocates of its restoration have maintained) or whether, by breaking family links, disrupting apprenticeships, opening new horizons, imposing new, and sometimes brutal, stresses, it was a potential agent of social dislocation.' (p 153, *Britain in Our Century*)

One hears, even now, periodic calls for the return of National Service as a specific treatment or even prophylaxis for much juvenile delinquency and other more general laxities among modern youth. A number of factors in the contemporary scene militate against this proposal, not the least of which is the fact that the modern, technical armed Services no more want to be bothered with trouble-makers, drug addicts and layabouts than does the rest of society. Another factor is that the very eighteen to twenty-year-olds who cause so much mayhem in the civilian world are psychologically damaged persons who simply would not respond to orders and structure in a military setting but would simply finish up in detention barracks, doing nothing useful and costing the country as much as they would if left among the rest of us. Even in the fifties, the ethos in the Services, in spite of a wealth of wry comment and a few mini-rebellions, was one of service to the country and a spirit of general cooperation and goodwill among all ranks. In his 1993 book *Training for War Games*, Len Woodrup puts the point neatly:

'Today, advocates of the short sharp shock treatment for delinquents suggest the government should re-introduce National Service to instil some discipline into the youth of today. The majority of National Servicemen were not delinquents and they were serving King and Country and later Queen and Country, and many of them died defending the peace. They served their country, not a custodial sentence.' (p 9)

The preoccupations of some commentators with the life of a National Serviceman were evidenced by Peter Chambers and Amy Landreth in *Called Up* (1955) when they remarked that they found it 'difficult to estimate to what extent National Servicemen take advantage of the freedom from parental control to gain sexual experience. Certainly a young man unversed in the 'facts of life' will very soon learn the repertoire of sexual possibilities from the conversation of his comrades. If he is posted abroad, he may visit a brothel for the first time in his life, but that does not mean he will avail himself of the opportunities provided by the establishment ... On the other hand, the moral climate of Service life tends to impel the soldier towards sexual adventures, and if he leaves the Army inexperienced in this field, then it is likely to be for moral or psychological reasons, not for lack of opportunity.'

This rather odd preoccupation on the part of some journalists and academics with the sexual aspects of National Service may have reflected a Puritanical ideal, deeply ingrained in some of the middle classes just after what may have, to them, seemed the sexual liberties, even excesses, of wartime. The 'Swinging Sixties' were yet to come.

It was not, however, the primary concern of the vast majority of National Servicemen known to the writer. Of far greater import was the disruption of normal career prospects among the older entrants and the forced removal from the simple securities of home among the younger. In the case of the writer, he had just graduated from university and was the proud and aspiring holder of a First Class Honours degree, departmental and class prizes and a competitive scholarship to fund doctoral studies in a choice of two or three much sought-after American universities. The 'Men from the Ministry' were not, however, to be moved from their view that no further deferment could be allowed and the call to arms was an immediate imperative. The scholarship, tenable only that year and the next, had therefore to be forfeited, and fell, inevitably, to a female student next in line. It was a significant disappointment and rankled for a year or two. No doubt there were others up and down the length of the country who could quote similar tales of woe. However, although it could not be foreseen at the time, it simply delayed a later doctorate and, in due course, visits to various American universities to report on personal research rather than to do it.

Governmental policies in regard to the Armed Forces were in something of a flux in these immediate post-war years. Over centuries, the British had depended on volunteer recruits to all the main arms and, broadly speaking, conscription to the colours had never been deemed appropriate so long as a steady supply of good volunteers continued to present itself. The change of attitudes heralded by the end of the war led to a sudden drop in such 'natural recruitment' and it became apparent that more serious measures would be required to maintain forces commensurate with the role of a victorious nation (and diminishing Empire) in the world as a whole. To some extent, therefore, National Service could be seen as a relatively cheap way of remedying this deficit. The trouble was that the remaining Regular soldiers, seamen and airmen saw their status and role being apparently diminished by the influx of these callow and unenthusiastic boys. There remained, as a result, a good deal of enmity between the Regular staffs who trained them and the body of National Servicemen being trained. Moreover, in spite of quite strenuous efforts to persuade National Servicemen to sign on for a longer period of service than the statutory two years (and several incentives, such as the prospect of special training or a commission were offered) only relatively few did so. There was thus further irritation felt by the Regulars that all the training inculcated in these conscripts would be wasted if they served only for the statutory two years. These undercurrents played a significant part in explaining much of the often unnecessary harshness suffered by National Service trainees, especially in the first months of their service.

Some commentators have suggested that these rivalries and petty jealousies between National Servicemen and Regulars were a feature mainly in the barracks among other ranks. It seems to have been especially marked in Sergeants' messes. There, newcomers, for example in the RAEC (Royal Army Educational Corps) and REME (Royal Electrical and Mechanical Engineers), would suddenly arrive with a good deal more specialist expertise than their Regular Forces' colleagues and three stripes on their arms by dint of their technical or academic qualifications achieved before their Army days. It was probably least observed among the officers, be they holders of National Service Commissions or fully-fledged Sandhurst or Cranwell products.

It was the case that the selection process for officers, whether National Service or Regular, was a very tough one for all. And once selection had been completed, there was an equally tough physical, academic and psychological process of training to be survived. In the latter too, there was always, regardless of in which arm of the Services one served, the repeated inculcation of the ethos of living up to the model of 'Officer and Gentleman' which held in every Service, every officers' mess, ship, regiment or squadron. In this writer's experience, only a few diehards from the war years ever expressed any real resentment of National Service officers sharing their Mess. Of course, there was always within the Mess a lot of light-hearted banter about the difference but it was superficial. When it came to the crunch in many Service situations, all officers of similar rank 'carried the same cans', solved the same problems and were, to all intents and purposes, treated as equals. Obviously, rank and experience counted, but amongst equals in respect of the former, no differences in how one's day-to-day life was pursued would have been apparent even to careful observers.

Young trainee officers, freshly hatched from OCTU (Officer Cadet Training Unit) very quickly learned the tricks of the trade from their colleagues of greater experience. The writer was once told by a senior RAF Officer visiting his first operational unit, that if he wanted to manage a difficult situation (on the ground at least), then the best thing he could do would be to ensure that he made friends of, and sought advice from, the most experienced of the Sergeants, or Flight Sergeants, 'Chiefies' as they were called. They, being almost always Regulars, were wise in the ways of the Service world beyond their specific RAF responsibilities and would always come up trumps either in their direct actions or by way of good advice. This was confirmed many times over. Naturally one had to be circumspect about this and take a little time to weigh up the calibre of one's Station NCOs before making a premature approach. Moreover, the respect had to be mutual. This only applied to matters once one had been through the training mill. Later experience taught this witness that the personal style and calibre of Recruit Training NCOs was substantially different from NCOs on an operational unit.

Indeed, most National Servicemen found that once the dreaded initial training, the 'square bashing', had been completed, then, both the technical training, for those lucky enough to be awarded it, and placement eventually on a Service unit, were much more relaxed and free of spit and polish, irksome and pointless duties and slavish commitment to rules and regulations.

A characteristic, however, of both early training and later experiences in a billet or Mess was that friendships were formed which in many cases would last for a lifetime. There was something about the sharing of privation, stress and sometimes odd pleasures within a context of forced equality, but sometimes extreme heterogeneity of upbringing and past experience, which gave these Service affiliations a strength and quality never experienced in civilian life. Most National Servicemen will recall with great pleasure the events, pleasures and hardships they shared with particular pals – their quirks, their strengths, their resilience, their humour and, above all, their openness, honesty and sense of mutual acceptance. Some will have kept up these contacts over many years until death or distance, of time or place, sees an end to them. Others, who have remembered friendships equally well, will endlessly regret that they did not maintain the contacts after demobilisation. As Trevor Royle in *The Best Years of their Lives* remarks:

'As the years rolled by after demob it was all too easy to forget to reply to letters or to lose forwarding addresses as men married, had children and bent their minds to domestic matters. Also men changed quickly on their return to civilian life, and incidents which had seemed all consuming or just plain humorous in the services soon began to pale.' (p 109)

Especially in the case of the first call-ups during the early fifties, recruits were living in a world which young men of the last decade of the twentieth century would hardly recognise. The initial journey from home would have been by public transport – a local, fairly clapped-out post-war bus, followed by a long and wearisome journey in a none too clean steam train. One needs to recognise that in 1951 there were then far fewer families with cars and fewer still young men with their own vehicle, unless it might have been an old motorbike. In any case, there was nothing like the present system of motorways to make travel throughout the Kingdom simple and direct. Even trunk roads were relatively narrow, poorly graded, sometimes with dangerous bends, and they passed through the centre of every town and village rather than bypassing them. Even in 1953, the last year of the writer's full-time National Service, there was only a tiny ten-mile strip of dual carriageway on the A1 between, for example, Leicester and Scotland, and single-track roads with occasional narrow passing places were the norm northwest of the Great Glen.

If the initial journey of recruits to their first base was therefore boring and uncomfortable, it was not helped by the fact that most were also relatively poor financially at that stage in their young lives. Some of us who, like the writer, had sustained ourselves at university for three or four years already on a bursary and/or grant of about £100 per annum had already learned to live frugally. Even so, we had also learned that any little extras like a new jacket and slacks or other small personal items had to be funded by extra cash, hard earned in the course of holiday work on farms or in factories.

We thus travelled light in terms of cash and would have had no more than a few shillings (80p or 90p in modern terms) in our pockets as we left home. Pay in the Services was meagre. As rankers, recruits were paid well under £2 per week and there would have been deductions even from that paltry sum for National Insurance, a small clothing allowance and a sum for 'barrack damages' whether such damages occurred or not! Some of us eventually discovered that a Regular aircraftman was paid nearly twice as much for doing essentially the same job. Their defence of this apparent injustice was that they had signed up to do it for much longer.

These conditions were probably more likely to hurt the lads who had completed a trade apprenticeship and had had some time as journeyman tradesmen before their service. At that time in the early fifties, such skilled men would have expected to earn around £10 per week. It came as no surprise to any of us when we found out that the NAAFI sold only beer and never spirits. That was reasonably cheaply priced (a few pence per pint) but even so, few recruits could raise the price of significant debauchery without serious saving. By the time the second year of service was reached, pay rose a bit by dint of Servicemen having by then been awarded trade qualifications or flying pay. Very few recruits indeed were married on call-up so marriage allowances did not apply.

The various arms of His Majesty's Services were therefore augmented, in the early fifties particularly, by thousands of callow, brash, anxious or rebellious young men with little or no money, and a simmering resentment, in many cases, that they had to be there at all. They were usually far from home, in a harsh and strange 'working' environment, pushed around and shouted at by men who seemed to have come from a different planet, whom they did not, at first at least, respect, and with whom, in the ordinary way, they would have had only the slightest of affiliations. What was really remarkable was that by the time the two years were up and it was all turned over in memory, 'emotion recollected in tranquillity', most of these thousands were able to claim that the experience had held something of value for them.

Many made deep and lasting friendships, born of adversity perhaps, which normal life would have kept from them. Some travelled to parts of the world which they would normally have only gazed on as variously coloured sections in a school atlas and a few experienced adventures which thrilled them at the time but which looked pretty 'hairy' in retrospect. They had gained regard, and even affection, for the particular Force, Squadron, Regiment or ship in which they had served and a sense of both corporate and personal achievement which few would have anticipated at the outset.

CHAPTER 2

Initiation

My own entry into His (as it was then) Majesty's Royal Air Force was not auspicious. About the end of October 1951, shortly after 0600 hours, as Services time is designated, a weary and somewhat bedraggled figure padded in his 'brothel-creepers' across the threshold of a kind of concentration camp, known as RAF Padgate in rainy Lancashire. Lest sensitive readers be alarmed, 'brothel-creepers' was the name given to the then fashionable suede shoes with thick squelchy crepe rubber soles. Mine were a faded navy blue and went, I thought, rather well with the wide padded shoulders and broad lapels of my double-breasted suit – a snazzy little number in Lovat coloured hopsack. It had seen me through many a varsity dance or post-athletics field-day thrash so there seemed to be no way that it would not do for my call to arms.

I had set out from home in Banff the night before. Bus to Aberdeen, then a night (no sleeper) jammed among other sweaty bodies in the train as we trundled down through Perth, Glasgow and Preston, trying at first – and vainly – to sleep, then latterly to keep awake – also vainly – until the train juddered to a stop in Warrington, a town previously unknown to most of us, where we had been instructed to disembark. At 04:45 hours none of us was exactly over-enthusiastic about this sprawling gem of the Lancashire industrial heartlands. We waited disconsolately at a bus stop in the drizzle for a couple of years – or was it hours? – until the first double-decker taking the early shift workers loomed through the murk and we scrambled aboard, incongruously glad of the shelter and a seat in spite of the fact that we had sat all night. Few of us spoke. It came to our notice later that, had we but waited for another hour or so at the railway station, RAF trucks would have arrived to pick us up and deposit us inside the gates of the base.

In the bus, however, most of us were dozing, partly with fatigue, partly with boredom and perhaps a little with apprehension about what awaited us. Tired fingers rubbed anxiously at our greasy and stubbly faces. Prickly eyes and dishevelled locks spoke of a restless night. A shower and a toothbrush would have worked wonders.

I was quietly amazed at the perkiness of the few early shift workers who shared the bus with us. They were animated Lowry manikins, headscarves over their curlers (at least in the case of the women) flat caps and boiler suits smelling of oil and swarf. Metal-capped boots vied with wooden clogs for a space on the damp slatted floor of the bus. There had not been sufficient traffic so far for the slats to have gathered their customary garnish of fag ends, bits of orange peel and the usual other less salubrious particles. Stained and over-used wartime gasmask cases over shoulders allowed the tops of Thermos flasks to declare the intention of their owners to lunch frugally from the tin sandwich boxes alongside. They obviously all knew each other and the unselfconscious vulgar chat reflected the ribaldry and the familiarity of the mine and of the factory floor. None of them paid the slightest attention to us dreary expatriates. At home, such people would have had to 'place us', to find out who we were, where we'd come from and what we were doing there. Here, in an alien culture, our anonymity was secure, – a bit too secure, I thought – more like our identity had been eroded. Little did we realise how much more of it was to be more systematically eroded in the course of the next few months.

At the huge air force blue sign proclaiming RAF PADGATE, a dozen or so of us disembarked and it was apparent that we were all bound for the same destination. Even then, caught up morosely in our own anticipations and anxieties, we were, every man, islands sufficient unto ourselves. The others had disappeared by the time my first little seminar with the Corporal concluded.

There was a lot of shouting going on as I entered these noble portals. I gawped at the statutory, clapped-out old Spitfire, (or was it a Lancaster?), bolted down to a concrete pad at the gates. What ignominy for a thing of such grace and power to suffer, bereft of its natural element, shorn of its noble history, a dead symbol in a place of moribund initiatives! The little attention I was at that ungodly hour capable of was turned to the various posses of blue-grey humanoids which could be seen making their way about a huge expanse of tarmac. Around this desert, there clustered grey nondescript huts and some larger buildings of unknown purpose. Happily, they seemed to have taken down the searchlights and machine gun turrets at the corners of the encampment though the high barbed-wire fence around it remained. The cracking of whips and moans of the tortured were, however, amazingly subdued. My spirits rose fractionally at this observation, only for my attention to be drawn to one of the little groups of more Lowry manikins which seemed to comprise a motley of young men with what looked like Parkinson's disease. They stumbled and scratched their way forward in three irregular lines abreast and some sixteen long.

I was later to discover that they were trying to march. A World War One ditty about 'Bless 'em all, bless 'em all; the long and the short and the tall' flashed through what remained of my consciousness after a night in the train from Aberdeen. The marchers seemed to be a walking textbook of neurological anomalies. Such arms as were unencumbered with impediments swung or flopped in glorious incoordination, feet fought for a grip on the loose dirt of the tarmac desert and every now and again, bits fell off. These bits turned out to be elements of new kit which had to be retrieved or lost forever. I could not restrain a guffaw of delight, wonderment and pity. It was my first mistake.

There fell on my ears a stentorian 'Airman!' Naturally, I paid no great attention. The term, after all, was one I had previously associated with Icarus, the Wright brothers or possibly Richard Hillary. Certainly the epithet hardly fitted my ego-identity at that time. However, it turned out that I had become 'The Last Enemy' of a bristling little Corporal now bearing down on me, every cell in his body obviously at pains to disengage from any other, centrifugal with ire, as he strode relentlessly in my direction. In the next three months or so I was destined to revise completely my notion of sin. My first impromptu tutorial dwelt on the necessity of regarding all corporals, all sergeants and most of higher rank as only fractionally junior in authority to the Deity. Agnosticism would not be tolerated – and, more importantly, laughing at His Majesty's airmen, no matter how risible or inept they might be, was clearly a sin. It also seemed important to STAND STILL! I was reminded of this several times a minute at a high level of decibels.

It also seemed that from the moment I entered the gates, I too had joined the ranks of the airmen and, even without a number, had become subject to military law and discipline. In due course, the intense, if one-sided, tutorial came to an end. The Corporal, reassured of his station in life, strode off, preening himself at his violent and (as I was to discover later) much rehearsed loquacity to take up his duties with 'the ragged-arsed, God-forsaken, witless and (seemingly) fatherless 'orrible little men' he was lumbered with for the week.

No recruit remained in Padgate for more than a week. Either you were despatched to your provincial origins as being unfit for military duty or to a Recruit Training Camp in some other choice, but inevitably rainy, cold and insalubrious corner of this green and pleasant land. The first of these options was occasionally sought by the weak, the feckless or the ultra-sophisticated among us.

The one successful case in our Flight (as we were now described) was a poor myope with a First Class Honours degree in English who was both purblind and incoordinate. He suffered partly from the fact that his spectacles, like beer-bottle bottoms, left him largely sensorily deprived of the visual environment, but his major disqualification from Service life was that he marched like a camel. Your average recruit, indeed your average citizen, can be seen to swing arms and legs contralaterally when walking or marching. Philip had the odd propensity, from which no amount of bawling or other indignity heaped on him by the Corporal could budge him, of marching so that when his left leg came forward, so did his left arm. The symmetrical perfection so sought after by the military in a body of men on the move was thus compromised and after one week, he retired perhaps to complete a leisurely Ph.D. in the groves of Academe. Until recently, I had thought that cases of such neuromuscular incoordinations as Philip demonstrated were rare. However, Len Woodrup, who was called up a month before this writer, has quoted another case (of 'Malcolm') who appeared to the DIs to suffer the same anomaly – only to have demonstrated at the end of training that he could march normally after all!

National Service had for me, and many others, been deferred beyond the age of eighteen in the cause of allowing us to complete some tertiary education. In consequence, each intake of recruits to two years in the service of the Crown comprised a majority of callow eighteen year olds, many of whom had never ventured far beyond their home town or village, and a much smaller percentage who had reached the ripe maturity of twenty-one or twenty-two, and were the proud possessors of a degree or trade qualification. In spite of this, the heterogeneity of physiques and personalities thus flung almost randomly together was staggering. At that time, some 600 bodies a week passed through the Padgate sieve.

No longer amused, I cast about for someone to instruct me as to where I could have my needs for both input and output properly serviced. It turned out that one of the large grey buildings on the left would serve both purposes. Having 'washed my hands' as the English are wont to put it, I lined up before the servery of a cavernous and echoing 'cookhouse' with a few other latecomers to the trough. Breakfast was memorable. It must have been, because I have never forgotten it! Into a scratched and none too clean dixie-tin (for we had not so far been issued with kit and KFS (knife, fork and spoon) went two pieces of Weetabix, rapidly detumescing in the juice of a spoonful of cold, stewed prunes (we were obviously not regulars!) and a cold kipper. Two slices of white bread and a mug of cool tea from a near empty urn at the side of the Mess hall completed the meal. Still, a man's got to live, so down it went, though others more squeamish than myself preferred to starve. It turned out that they had made their first mistake in so far as no further sustenance would be forthcoming until midday. The blessed NAAFI was not yet open to us.

It is impossible in the hazy retrospect of nearly fifty years to un-jumble the exact sequence of the events of that week. Among the first of these to follow that famous breakfast was the issue of kit. We queued in alphabetical order. His Majesty's Services seemed to have an overweening preoccupation with only two variables determining the human condition – our surname initial and our height. All others such as intelligence, friendliness, humour, meanness, weight, literacy or aggressiveness were totally ignored or seen as irrelevant. The first alphabetical queue was for us to be awarded our sSrvice number, ('Engrave it on yer 'eart, laddie. They shoot you if you forget it!') then, to be issued with uniforms, greatcoat with plenty of brass buttons to polish, denims, PT kit, boots, Plimsolls, the aforementioned KFS, underwear and pyjamas, tie, towels, socks, all topped off by tin hat, rifle, bayonet, gas mask and a tangle of webbing harness with brass attachments which would have looked well on a Shetland pony at a horse show but which became the very symbol of tedium (because of the necessity of 'blanco-ing' it daily).

Grotesquely overloaded with ill-fitting garments and the rest, the recruits, now airmen, but with very clipped wings, were shepherded to a long trestle table where sets of stencils, black paint, indelible fabric pencils and metal number dies and mallets awaited our efforts. The rules were simple. They had to be. The heterogeneity remarked on earlier extended also to IQ, though it was our proud boast that the lowest IQ admitted to the RAF was still ten points higher than that accepted by the other more senior services. I never discovered whether that particular tale was apocryphal or not.

Rule 1 stated that you first put your name, rank and number on your canvas kit bag. Rule 2 told you then to put each item therein as you numbered it and so on. Hammer, hammer, hammer went the mallets as knives, forks and spoons took on the magic symbols. Dab, dab, dab went the paint over the stencils. 'F**k, f**k, f**k!' went the expletives as some poor idiot got the digits mixed up – his error permanently enshrined, and corrected, in the space left. An hour of such endeavours persuaded me that 2536746 was not so hard to learn. Indeed, once you got your number, you were allowed the intimacy on such occasions as pay parades, of responding to the 'last three' digits only. I was now '746 Clark' for the next three months until at OCTU (Officer Cadet Training Unit) where one became a 'Mister' and lived in a limbo between the '746 Clark' of an AC2 (aircraftman, second class) and the 'Sir' of the officer class.

Pay parades were then, incidentally, weekly events at which one marched up to the Pay Officer, with his acolytes, the Pay Sergeant and an Accounts' Clerk, all of whom emanated total ennui. One saluted, collected a small packet containing a couple of banknotes and a few coins, stepped back a pace, as if receiving a regal honour, saluted again and marched back to the billet to gloat over the twenty-eight shillings per week (about £1.40 nowadays) an AC2 was paid. We were paid at what was essentially a daily rate, presumably so that not too much would be owed to our dependents were we to have the misfortune to succumb, early in the week, to a stray bullet, a dropped hand grenade on the range, or to the sadistic ministrations of a PTI (Physical Training Instructor) at the double on the battle training course.

In tens and twenties we then shuttled back and forth from the tailor's shop to the barber's (spelt 'barbarous'!) and then to the photographer's. That sequence ensured that the worst excesses of mass production could be removed, at least from the outer garments of our uniforms. It was clear that this had nothing to do with our *amour propre* but everything to do with presenting a uniform appearance, so to speak, on the parade ground. One Drill Sergeant was much distressed to see me being kitted out in a wartime model blouson jacket rather than the slightly more fitted blouson acquired by those of more orthodox shape in the queue before and after me. Having vainly trained for a period of my university athletics' life as a pole-vaulter, I had acquired a 44" shoulder measurement and the only blouson to fit me had to be the wartime model. In a Flight of marching airmen, this sartorial anomaly was enough to produce a close approximation to a fit of *grand mal* proportions in a DI. However, in the billet, and in our own time, any necessary adjustments, and there were many, were made to denims and other garments by ourselves. It wasn't pretty but it was functional.

Plate 1: A freshly done 'short back and sides' is already cleaning his rifle while two other recruits with proudly trained and cosseted locks await their fate at Sweeney Todd's (Hutton-Getty)

Over at Sweeney Todd's, four maniacs with power clippers grabbed us like Aussie sheep shearers competing for a gallon of beer. In a trice, the lank, dank hanks from over our ears we had so carefully nurtured as students, fell limp on to the ankle-deep mass of locks on the floor. Those of us not 'in the chair' lined up around the walls of this less than salubrious salon of mad trichologists and watched morosely as the first damp snowflakes of winter began to spatter hesitantly on the golden glow of sodium lighting outside on the roadway. Conversation was encouraged neither by the circumstances nor by the limited articulacy of my compatriots. There seemed to be only one concession to style. Those with the longest hair to start with finished with the shortest 'back and sides' ever seen, prior to Kojak. In spite of all protests, the artistic was sacrificed to the functional. No Samsons would be pushing over the odd temple for a month or two after that little exercise, I thought. It must have been as much a symbolic shearing of power as an attempt to achieve the longed-for uniformity and tonsorial hygiene so beloved of the military mind.

By this time, all within the day, most were in uniform and the Lovat hopsack suit and brothel-creepers were in the kit bag to be parcelled up later and sent home. That signified that the umbilical cord was then really cut.

The photographers ran a slick production line, even if some of the eighteen-year-olds thought they were in for an interrogation by the Gestapo. In a plain wooden hut, an SAC (Senior Aircraftman) confronted one with 'Wot's yer number, laddie?' and even before the incantation was complete, he had chalked the seven digits on an oblong piece of blackboard which was then thrust into your hands to be held just under the chin. He would then unconsciously select any one of the phrases, 'No smilin'!', 'Shut yer face; you mental or sutthin'?' or 'Wipe that f****** grin off yer face, Airman!' while gesturing to a plain wooden chair facing two glaring photofloods. Reassuring ourselves that it bore no electrodes or straps to fix our arms and legs, we then faced the camera and SAC (Photographic Section) No 2. His only vocal repertoire consisted of 'Hold up the board! Sit still and look at the camera.' A click, and it was all over. No officer would ever say again, 'I know the number, but I can't put a face to it!'

All this was in the interests of reconstructing our identities. The most important single item in that process was the issuing of a '1250', an RAF Identity Card bearing the Sing Sing-like portrait and number together with one's full name and rank. This, we were told, you would 'carry on your person at all times', produce immediately to any person with a right to see it and lose it on pain of a Court Martial. Suitably impressed, but a bit uncomfortable where spikes of shorn hair had infiltrated between neck and the hard collar of a new blue shirt, we were then marched off to collect 'biscuits'. This was the most enthusiastic bit of marching we had so far engaged in. Perhaps there would also be a cup of tea. That fond notion quickly evaporated when we were marched into an ill-named Decontamination Centre where each was told he could select three biscuits from piles on the concrete floor. These were 30" square mini-mattresses of canvas filled (almost) with straw (and, as it turned out, fleas). Decontamination had been less than complete. With these, we separated the wire frame of our beds from the sheet and three blankets we had also been issued with there. Several of us were to wish that we hadn't.

Overloaded with these symbols of near domesticity, we finally lined up in the sleet and darkness and were marched to our billet for the week we would be resident at RAF Padgate. Fifty wire-framed bare beds were promptly appropriated (alphabetical order again!) and we dumped our new possessions onto them with something approaching relief. The cookhouse would be open by the time we had our gear sorted out into our lockers and the beds made in regulation fashion. We were bawled at to 'Stand by your beds!'. We did. We were treated to another noisy homily about the importance of 'Standing still!' and doing so promptly. We listened wearily. The bustling little Corporal dismissed us and spun out of the hut like a genie disappearing back into his lamp. Inconsequentially, somebody muttered 'F*** me!' and we all slumped onto our biscuits. It had been quite a day.

A couple of well-filled days later, a second visit to the Decontamination Centre introduced us to the RAF medical staff. First came an FFI. This was the jargon for a physical examination to ensure we were 'free from infection'. Nobody seemed to care if we were carrying typhoid or gibbering with cerebral malaria. All they cared about was whether or not we had venereal disease (VD). Since we had not so far enjoyed our lecture on the evils of casual sex with the natives (some of whom could be glimpsed of an evening dawdling about, just beyond the perimeter fence), the infections were assumed to be any permutation of the commoner venereal diseases. The jaunty young MO Flt. Lt. addressed us on the more gruesome symptoms of syphilis and gonorrhoea (AIDS was then unknown) before reminding us that our willies were best left buttoned up (zips were then also unknown on trousers, at least in the military) behind our trouser flies except when there were less threatening calls of nature. He then dashed off to sharpen his injection needles against the concrete wall.

Like condemned Jews in the Holocaust we were instructed to strip entirely naked and leave our clothes on benches along the wall. Several hundred pale bodies varying in physique from young Charles Atlases, hairy frames a-ripple with muscle, to anxious and cowering boy-children, scrawny and nipped-in, with sharp corrugations of ribs on which one might have played the xylophone, lined up. We formed a snake, writhing around the bare, cold hall as we moved forward, one by one, to where a white-coated MO and a medical orderly or two, one with a three-foot length of cane, carried out the inspection. Arriving at point X, one was required to stand, legs astride, in front of the inspectors, one of whom might, from time to time, use the cane to move aside a flaccid but obstructing penis in order to ascertain that the spots were no more than the flea bites from yesterday's 'biscuits'. Then one had to do an about turn and bend over while the other orifice was scrutinised at a safe distance.

While some were picked out for more detailed diagnosis and had to disappear into an inner sanctum, a few of us capable of either systematic thought or whispered conversation in this unreal, even Kafka-esque, charade speculated on whether the personal barrack-room kudos to be gained from a noisy fart at the crucial bend-over could compensate for the unnamed and unknowable punishments hidden deep in King's Regulations for such an insult in the face of authority (literally) that might ensue. We had already discovered that these very Regulations contained a phrase about 'behaviour prejudicial to good order and discipline in His Majesty's Forces' which could apparently be invoked in almost any circumstances within the imagination of man.

When my turn came, the incipient smirk induced by the foregoing fantasy was smartly wiped from my features when I was appalled to see that my nether regions were a mass of raised red spots. Some of my less respectable fantasies might well have warranted these signifying the worst, but the reality was altogether more mundane. The orderly crouched down for a closer look, and, to my great relief, pronounced, with all the authority of a Harley Street Consultant, to the white coat and stethoscope, 'Flea bites, Sir! – Next!' and I padded off to find my clothes. It was like a reprieve.

Warming up after the FFI was achieved by a fearsomely stern and utterly authoritarian Drill Sergeant starting us out drilling on the parade ground. There was the usual ponderous lecture on learning to know right from left, front from rear, standing to 'attention', 'at ease' and 'easy' – the last of these we took to as ducks to water. Wisely, the Drill Sergeant worked us first without rifles and settled only for repeated descriptions of our individual and corporate incompetence, deafness and parentless existence, all at the usual 100 decibels. We had no right of reply, it seemed, but the beginnings of a common bond of hatred were becoming apparent among us. In the cookhouse that day, the fight for slices of white bread, heaped at intervals along the tables, was less violent and animal and one or two even fetched mugs of tea for each other from the urn. A subtle bonding process was at work.

Come afternoon, however, a second strip-off, only the top half this time, was called for and in batches of two hundred we were more carefully medically examined – though even that is a relative term. Four digits were scrawled on each medical record as a result of this, ranging from A1 G1 down to an A6 G6. As it happens, I never saw anyone with an A6 G6 rating, presumably they would not even have been warm and vertical. 'A' stood for Air, or one's fitness for flying duties and 'G' for Ground duties only. A few, myself included, turned out to be A1 G1 and were whisked away at a later date to give innumerable urine samples, be whirled in a centrifuge – yes, us, as well as the urine samples – to blow up mercury in tubes and do reaction time tests and other show-ground capers.

After the physical examinations, we then were lined up in the by now familiar snake of bodies, again in alphabetical order, and filed past a table. On this was draped, as on a ritual altar, a grubby off-white cloth which when flicked away with a fine flourish, revealed, on a slightly less grubby white cloth, a number of stainless steel kidney dishes containing iodine and several fairly wide bore injection needles, a steaming sterilizer, large boxes of phials and a dozen or so syringes. Two upright chairs were placed in front of the table and a couple of fairly junior MOs in white coats shuffled record cards or squirted the last air bubbles out of the solutions in the syringes. Such a sight was sufficient to scare some of the young laddies (and a few of the older ones) into a dead faint. They were then dragged out of the column, had a pint or so of cold water flung in their faces, and were stood up at the end of the queue. Some had this happen two or three times during the afternoon. It would have been more rational to bring them round and to put them at the top of the queue, but 'Common sense is not so common!' as I think G K Chesterton had it.

The theory was that two airmen at a time would sit on the chairs, extend their arms across the table so that, at one and the same time, the needle bearers would shove a couple of subcutaneous needles into the front of each lower arm (for a Schick test and another I could not identify) while others gave one simultaneously a vaccination in one deltoid and another did an intramuscular of triple antigen into the other. It seemed the same needles had been used all week for previous intakes of recruits and were now so blunt and barbed that they actually tore the skin as they were withdrawn. Mine made a distinct 'pop' as it came out and several of us bled a bit as a result. The staff simply injected, flung the used needle into the bath of iodine and fished out another while the first was soaking and hopefully disinfecting. However, we were, all 600 of us, run through, so to speak, in just over an hour.

As a distraction, we were treated to another hour of drill on the parade ground, this time with rifles all the while. The idea was that it might prevent us noticing how stiff and sore our arms were becoming. Thereafter, we were bussed off at His Majesty's expense to a theatre in Blackpool where we watched the incomparable Kay Kendall as our arms stiffened and two of our number had fits – nothing to do with Kay Kendall! A third, the so-called Senior Man (because he had a moustache) in our hut, had a major one when we got back to base and indeed had to be taken to the Sickbay. For myself, I enjoyed the play less than might have been expected but found it hard to discern whether the various aches and pains I was experiencing were due to the injections, to throwing a rifle around without dropping it (there is no worse misdemeanour in the Services!) or to several nights minor gymnastics trying to avoid the fleas and find a comfortable sleeping position on the 'biscuits'. Whatever, the visit to the theatre was the only sign of any sort of human understanding and sympathy we ever found all the way through our recruit training period.

The bus was a bit subdued. We were all being especially careful not to jostle or nudge our mates – especially about the arms and shoulders. It was dark and we did not know anything about the back roads of west Lancashire. They were suddenly unconscionably bumpy. The Sergeant driver from the Regular MT Section was sympathetic and tried to jolly us along by keeping up a running commentary on the great range of sexual outrages these girls from Blackpool would, in due course, visit upon us, perhaps not tonight, he added thoughtfully, but later in our stay. We'd see the Blackpool Lights and the Winter Garden. We'd savour the Blackpool beer in copious amounts until we pee'd it into our boots back in the billet because we'd be 'too f****** pissed to go to the bogs' and we'd learn to 'keep our f****** eyes peeled for the Whitecaps' (Military Police). Up till now most of us thought we'd completed our tertiary education. How wrong we were.

During our first week, we were allocated to huts on what appeared, as did so much in the Services, to be a chance basis. I suddenly became that statistician's delight, one of a random cross-section of the young male general population – ego identity at last! This was a salutary learning experience. Each of us was to discover the true meaning of heterogeneity, although only a select few could spell the word. Physically, the long, the short and the tall could be properly arranged by a command from the Corporal, 'In single rank – Size!' Bawling this at us resulted in a general mêlée whereby the only six-and-a-half footer shot to one end of the row, the only four-and-a-half footer scampered to the other and the rest of us shouldered and levered and kicked our way past each other trying to decipher whether we looked down on, or looked up, to our neighbour till we found our rightful place in the order of things, a true microcosm of the English class struggle. Perhaps that was why the Scots among us seemed to find it harder to do.

The analogous ordering by personal qualities, and perhaps IQ, was achieved later in yet another of the mysterious grey buildings, but in the non-privacy of our lovely home in the huts we were to find as motley a crew of young humans as any experimental ethologist could wish. For the first time in my life, I was asked by a contemporary, one or two beds down the billet, 'What school did you go to, old chap?'

Unaware of the deep implications this seemed to have for the questioner, I was able to say, wondering at his concern, 'Banff Academy'.

'Is that a public school?'

'Oh yes. That's where we all went in Banff.'

'Good God, how remarkable! I went to Rugby'.

Why should I bother to tell him that we would have considered the latter to be a private rather than a public school? Turning to the chap on the other side of the billet with the same question, he got a dustier answer.

'Public School? I just coom out o' a f****** Approved School, mite, an' I learned a f****** sight more of use to me 'ere than you f****** did, I betcha!'

In point of fact, there was little to choose between them when it came to surviving Ground Combat Training or the finely honed sadism of the Drill Corporals.

Nevertheless, characters emerged, even in these first traumatic few days. A cheery little motor mechanic from Manchester afforded us one of the highlights of a taxing week. Once in a while, at our early morning parade before the Corporal, it would be necessary for him to address a specific recruit by name if for no better reason than to put him on a Charge ('a Fizzer' or 'in jankers'). Our wee mechanic rejoiced in the name of ('Doughy') Balls. I never discovered his Christian name. As the pompous ass of a corporal bawled, 'Balls!', with one voice, fifty-seven recruits bawled back 'And balls to you too, Corporal!'. It was the high point of our day, though in retrospect, seeming too juvenile to be true. We later discovered that the Corporal was the owner of a clapped-out old car which he hoped young Doughy could breathe on, or otherwise bring some new life to the rattling old rust heap.

The relationships of that first week were, however, transient and slight. Introspection, born of uncertainty about our respective futures, was enhanced by the need to get to grips with the harsh realities of protecting our kit from predators and ensuring that the last of the cash from home was efficiently spent in the NAAFI on Blanco, tins of Duraglit wadding or Brasso, razor blades, boot polish, a light bulb for the ablutions and a spare stopper for the bath. The two last-named were absolute necessities. Nobody ever knew why the originals were so inevitably stolen, but any recruit who, like me, had to achieve a bath by stuffing the plug hole with lavatory paper and holding the soggy wad in place with a heel while soaping one's grubby frame in complete darkness, soon learned that proud possession of one's own plug and 60 watt bulb was the nearest to luxury that could be achieved in any Recruit Training Camp. Showers were at that time reserved for Gas Decontamination Centres and Officers' Quarters. But time for a move was at hand.

CHAPTER 3

Square-bashing

At the end of that momentous week, 600 recruits were shipped out of Padgate to their various recruit training bases. These seemed to be scattered about parts of England (mostly, we weren't sure whether Herefordshire counted as England or Wales) and were apparently graded by certain knowing recruits, who perhaps had had brothers already in the Services, in terms of how harsh were the Drill Corporals, how remote they, both camps and Corporals, were from civilisation (in the form of beer, women, dance halls and cinemas) or whether they housed a large or small number of MPs (the kind with riot batons, pistols, and white covers over their caps; not the kind with maces, pinstripes and a pad in Westminster!)

Thus it was that just over 100 of us draped our various webbing harnesses, ammunition pouches and haversacks over our bodies, shouldered our kit bags and rifles and marched, yes, marched rather than slouched, down to the railway station to entrain for our new home at RAF Kirkham. This was, like Padgate, an ominously well-fenced and secure laager. No one who had ever endured a few months there during the early fifties could ever be surprised by the fact that in later years it was upgraded to become one of the toughest Borstals in England. While there, we were firmly of the view that it already was. The train wheezed its way through the grey and dripping industrial backcloth of Lancashire, through Chorley to Lytham St Annes where we were transferred to lorries for the final stage of the trip. In the rain, (and it was always raining in Kirkham) the camp looked even more miserable than Padgate.

It was mid-afternoon, and parties of airmen were galloping about in PT kit. Others were marching with a mixture of fear and dedication on the drill square under the eagle gaze of a formidable Drill Sergeant who wielded a brass trimmed wooden pace stick as if he had just drawn Excalibur from the rock. His intelligence was unknowable, his power was infinite and his expression was cast in bronze, a harsh metallic rigidity of mien from which cold, laser-beam eyes scanned every minutest detail of the posture, uniform, features, equipment and motion of every recruit under his command. These paragons of the drill square ordered their lives and thoughts by the Drill Manual. If it was not in there it did not exist and God help any ''orrible little man' who might challenge this dogma.

'… But I thought, Sergeant … '

'You ain't paid to think, laddie. You're paid to do wot you're bloody well told. Shut up – and STAND STILL!'

A hundred little blue men with white faces reflected from the burnished and sparkling brass fittings on his pace stick. We were standing still. A pace stick is no more than a hardwood pair of compasses about three feet long with brass points at the end of each leg and a quadrant with adjustable milled screw near the top hinge which, if necessary, could be opened to, say, a distance of 27" at the points. This could then be swivelled from point to point as one marched, the instructor's feet falling alongside the pace stick points so as to ensure a regular pace of 27" steps. The pace stick was, however, more than that. It was a symbol of power and authority second only to a Field Marshall's baton. I never saw one wielded by any rank other than a Drill Sergeant or Warrant Officer and I only once saw one used in the orthodox way. More often, pace sticks were used as if they were cattle prods or batons – on recalcitrant AC2s who could neither stand still nor keep to a 27" pace. Psychoanalysts would have had a ball considering the sexual and other symbolism of this long straight rod on which so much obvious care and affection was lavished by their over-macho owners.

The Kirkham grey-green wooden huts stretched in serried ranks linked by narrow paths and a line of poles bearing black clad water or steam pipes, power and telephone lines. The (structural) similarities to Auschwitz and Bergen-Belsen were all too apparent to most of us. But amidst all the cloud, a silver lining began to appear. Casual talk among the newcomers nearest in line revealed that at least some of us were no ordinary batch of recruits. Some homogeneity at last became apparent. Camplin, Cawthorpe, Clark and Clayton (all in adjacent beds in the hut to which we had been allocated) discovered that at least we all had endured the privileges, pleasures and purgatories of a tertiary education. Various ancient universities had regurgitated a linguist, a geographer, an architect and a psychologist. Along the walls of that squalid shed of a place were ranged fifty or so egg-heads dredged from the awful miscellany of Padgate to be beaten into shape before being sent off to various establishments where any special aptitudes that might be of especial use to the Service would be probed for by other psychologists, personnel officers and an Officer Selection Panel.

It was only then that we suddenly remembered how, weeks before, and not long after our graduation ceremonies, we had been invited to the local RAF recruiting centre, in my case in Aberdeen, where we had undergone preliminary psychological testing and some wearisome interviewing about our possible futures in the RAF. This must have been the end result of that.

A bouncy, aggressive, red-haired Corporal leapt into the midst of us, like a trapeze artist in a circus swinging down from the Big Top, to advise us with undisguised scorn that we were POMs – Potential Officer Material. (It sounded like some sort of ectoplasm or potato substitute!). He went on to advise us that such a classification must have been bestowed upon us by some lunatic at HQ for we, sure as 'eggs was eggs', looked like as feeble, ignorant and feckless a shower of wankers as ever disgraced the face of this earth! Flight 58A, as we were known, thereafter became immediately better identified, not only to the Drill Corporals, but also to all the other Flights of more ordinary mortals as 'The F***ing Professors'.

In his first seconds of existence, for us, Corporal Corral leapt on to the nearest table with a brisk athleticism, which we admired wanly, and began to harangue us with a vigour, if not with a grammar, which was impressive in its intensity.

'Gather round and STAND STILL, you 'orrible little men. My name's Corral, Corporal C-O-R-R-A-L. You don't call me Sir – that's for hofficers! You don't call me Mister – that's for civilians. You call me Corporal. What do you call me?'

'Corporal, Corporal!' we chorused, in mystified unison.

'While you're 'ere you ain't got no rights – and you ain't got no privileges. You can't go whinin' to yer Mams and you can't go writin' to yer M f******Ps. You do wot yer told and you don't argue and you do it NOW! While you're 'ere I'm yer mother, yer father, yer uncle, yer brother, yer cousin, yer neighbour and Jesus Christ 'isself! You don't do nuthin' I don't know about. You only do wot I tells you or the Sergeant there. There's bloody nuthin' we can't sort out between us, and we'se watchin' you all the time, so it's no use runnin' to the bloody hofficers. Half o' them don't know their arse from their f****** elbow anyway!'

Then followed a litany of rules about the running of the hut.

He leapt from the table, swivelled his all-seeing eyes around our blank and wondering faces, snapped his cane into his oxter with a vehemence and accuracy that made us wince, clicked his shining heels together and finally bawled, 'STAND BY YOUR BEDS!'

Plate 2: Sunday morning in the Kirkham billet (November 1951). The author (left foreground) writes home while, under the blankets, one of the most assiduous womanisers in the hut sleeps it off after a night in Blackpool (author)

We shuffled off to take our posts at attention, each at the foot of his bed. Corral marched briskly to the door at the end of the hut, spun on his heel in a perfect about turn to fix us again with his steely gaze. (We were, after all, in the land of clichés). 'And don't any one of you pansy boys forget a single f****** syllable of wot I told you. Dissssmissssss!' The outside door banged shut and we slumped on our beds to assimilate the lessons of the day.

One of the first tasks in the hut involved the completion of little buff cards which were to be fixed to the wall above our beds. These cards bore our name, rank (Aircraftmen 2nd class, abbreviated to AC2) and number and, so that they would know how to bury us appropriately in the event of our unforeseen demise at the hands of the enemy, or more likely, by what has become subsequently known oxymoronically, as 'friendly fire', our religion. Amid the plethora of C of Es and RCs, casually announced with the repetitious thoughtlessness of the uncritical believer, we numbered a few agnostics, a Theosophist, a Buddhist and a couple of Jews. King's Regulations were explicit about the RCs and Jews.

They were the ones who, at every weekly Church Parade, were marched down to the parade ground or even to the Station chapel but were then bawled at, 'Fall out, Roman Catholics and Jews!' Too late did many of us discover that had we, when we were filling out our buff cards, but claimed addiction to the rosary or to a minor operation in childhood, we could have successfully avoided the worst excesses of falsely chatty sermonising and military religiosity at the hands of the Station padre. Since there was nothing in KRs about Theosophists, Buddhists or agnostics, the Corporal promptly treated our honest declarations of unfaith as the purest evidence that we were only 'a shower of f****** chancers', autocratically scored out these terms on our cards and promptly substituted 'C of E' on all of them. That had to be my fastest conversion course ever, although my subsequent lapse into habitual agnosticism coincided exactly with demobilisation two years later.

Whether or not in the pursuit of religious metaphor, our first week at RAF Kirkham could undoubtedly be described as purgatorial. Because our Corporals saw us as Messiahs due for a second coming as Pilot Officers in an unspecified number of months, and therefore likely to find ways of getting our own back, we were awarded the scruffiest, foulest, old hut on the Station. It had been due for renovation and re-equipping and the best that the Maintenance Section had been able to do before our arrival had been to paint the ceiling white. The linoleum on the floor had therefore a Christmassy look, flecked with a million snowflakes of hard dried paint which offended the Corporal's aesthetic sensitivities. The latter were never terribly well defined, but he did like to see a hut floor 'wot 'as a shine on it so's you could f****** shave youssell jus' lookin' at it!' To that noble end, our whole week was directed. Most of us were instructed to purchase a packet of safety razor blades at the NAAFI at tea break that afternoon. Broken in half longitudinally, these were to be used, not to shave while gazing Narcissus-like at the floor, but to scrape, one by one, every particle of hard dried paint from the linoleum, all 3,600 square feet of it! Some of us, even less fortunate, were allocated the task of renovating a large chunk of scrap iron, deeply rusted, which some careless idiot had left right in the middle of the floor. This turned out to be our stove – not only the sole source of heat for the whole hut, but the focus of all social life and community activity during our three months of 'square-bashing'.

Plate 3: Some of the members of Flight 58A, RAF Kirkham, November 1951. The author is on extreme right of the middle row (author)

Every night of that first week was declared a 'bull-night'. Nobody could escape to the camp cinema or the NAAFI, or even the gym. All were confined to the hut under the Corporal's eagle eye – truly corralled! In the ordinary way, there might be a 'bull-night' once a week. That is the night when special efforts are made to blanco every piece of webbing, polish every brass buckle, bone, and spit and polish every boot till the toecap seemed carved from high gloss ebony. We had to pull-through (with '4 by 2' – a piece of soft flannel of exactly those dimensions in inches, soaked in light oil and tied to a lead weighted piece of string) and oil every rifle, clean and sharpen every bayonet and darn every holed sock or shirt. Not only had our personal kit to be impeccably well prepared, but the whole hut had to be spotlessly clean and tidy as well.

In order to retain the high gloss of polish we had established on the floor and elsewhere, by the sweat of our brows, any movement over the floor had to be undertaken with the aid of squares of old blanket which lay piled at the doorway. Woe betide any punter who carelessly wandered in on to the hallowed linoleum with his boots on! As soon as a foot crossed the threshold, it would be carefully placed on a square of blanket, the other foot would follow on another and thereafter the airman would slide over the floor to his destination, i.e. bed, locker or rifle rack, secure in the knowledge that every step was renewing the high gloss of the polish.

The latter had been initially achieved by many hours of working 'bumpers' over the floor to rub down the previously spread polish. 'Bumpers' were simply brush shafts on a piece of wood like a brush head fixed in turn to a heavy lead or iron weight weighing about 16–20 lb under which even more squares of old blanket were attached. There were times when the casual observer might have thought he had mistakenly gate-crashed a ballet school or a figure skating championship such were the various lithe and flowing postures, *pas de deux* and arabesques assumed by a group of airmen going about their rightful business on their woollen 'skates'.

All was inspected with a meticulousness just short of using an electron microscope the following morning. It was all extremely tedious, dirty and time-consuming and was usually accompanied by a steady commentary of such awe-inspiring profanity and obscenity so that stray mice or nearby wandering dogs fled, shifty-eyed and tails adroop, from the vicinity. The 'f-word' has been quoted in various contexts in this record already. Such repetition is not a permanent feature of the writer's normal social vocabulary, but to have omitted it entirely would have been to have traduced the harsh actuality of life in these circumstances. Anyone who has gone through it during these first months in the Services, that particular word and every possible variant of it, together with many other old and well-worn obscenities interlarded the vocabulary of all of us a hundred times more frequently than they ever will in this little piece.

For those keen readers whose minds drop out of gear until some strange term has its derivation clarified, it should be explained that a 'bull-night' has nothing to do with the sanguinary activities of a summer evening in Valencia, nor with artificial insemination (or otherwise) in the byres of Britain's farmers. It is simply a shortened form to describe a night when Servicemen are committed to an activity known as 'Bullshit'. In all of Her Majesty's Services there is an axiom, 'Bullshit baffles brains!' This is the Drill Corporal's supreme defence against the criticism of his seniors. 'Bullshit' is a term given to any activity the essence of which is extreme apparent correctness and industriousness but which has no real purpose or useful outcome. The best is planned to produce an immediate dazzle of superficial brilliance while being created only by mind-dulling tedium and unoriginality. Outside the Services, the writer has only found good examples of this phenomenon among advertising executives, car salesmen and some university lecturers.

So far as recruit training was concerned, however, a 'bull-night' was simply one when normal human pleasures were denied us in favour of endless cleaning, polishing and blanco-ing of our persons, our equipment and our humble dwelling. Coming as they did, after long, hard days on the square, route marching or on the firing range, they were seen as a punishment rather than as a necessity – a punishment presumably for the harsh and aggressive thoughts we directed, occasionally in speech but perpetually in fantasy, toward our mentors. There were few occasions when our actual behaviour really warranted punishment. The trouble was that the Sergeant and Corporal could, between them, fabricate misdemeanours on our part.

Mornings were especially tough at Kirkham, partly because it was so damned dark at the time of year we were there and partly because we had been worked so hard all day on the square and range and all night 'bulling' in the billet. No sooner had one, it seemed, dropped off to sleep than wretched 'Reveille' (always pronounced 'revalley') would blast through the Tannoy at the end of the hut and the Corporal would be in shouting at us to 'Show a leg!' There was a story that went around, probably apocryphal, to the effect that in military law, one could not be held responsible for what one did within the first minute of being suddenly awakened from a deep sleep. None of us really tested this out by slugging the noisy little man as he bent over your bed and bawled in your ear at 0530 hours on a cold sleety morning, but lots of plans were laid, and savoured, as we blearily made our way to the ablutions.

One bitterly cold and wet morning, we were mustered outside the hut at 0600 hours and formed up for inspection in the dark and pouring rain. A favourite trick was for the Corporal to sneak quietly up behind some pallid wee mouse of an eighteen-year-old who would inevitably be standing rigidly to attention and bawl, an inch from his ear, 'Stand s-t-i-l-l!' On this occasion, however, the gimlet-eyed Drill Sergeant had elected, probably quite at random, our hero for the treatment.

'Wot's yer name and last three, laddie?'

'746 Clark, Sergeant.'

'You clean yer cap badge this morning, laddie?'

'Yes, Sergeant.'

'Corporal Corral, does this look like a clean cap badge to you?'

'No, Sergeant.'

'Right, Corporal. Take this man's name for making a false statement and 'ave 'im report to me at 1830 hours. You hear that, laddie? A cap badge like that tomorrow an' ye're on a charge!' ('In jankers' was the barrack-room terminology.)

So it happened that all of that evening, in my so-called free time, I learned what it is like to tear one's fingers to mince with the backs of broken razor blades, the sharp edges of which were being used to scrape a thick layer of black bitumen paint from the outer surface of a coke bin while at the same time harbouring the direst of murderous thoughts towards the source of this gross injustice. The fact that several men had seen me polish the bloody cap badge that very morning before going on parade made no difference to the Sergeant who simply hoped to impress his will and power on at least some of the 'F****** Professors'. The bin was then to be polished with Brasso supplied at my own expense, inside and out – a major task, since the wretched thing was about three feet by two feet by two feet in size – and then (by this time, nearly 11 o'clock at night) shown to the Sergeant, who had spent the evening over beer and darts in the Sergeants' Mess. The swine then glanced at the gleaming *chef d'oeuvre* before kicking it into a big muddy puddle where it would accumulate enough rust in the next few days to make it worth while torturing some other poor sod from the next Flight who would have to scrape and polish it all over again.

The arbitrary imposition of this kind of needless harshness was all too common in several arms of the Services during the early 1950s. It even reached the stage whereby one Corporal regularly boasted to his current Flight, standing rigidly to attention in the rain and gloom of an early winter morning while he harangued them, that he had made things so tough for his recruits in previous Flights that two of them had committed suicide because of it. Professionally, I recognised all the signs of a psychopath in the Corporal in question but we took it at first that this was yet another attempt at intimidation on his part and probably untrue. We had heard that, weeks before, one young eighteen-year-old, never previously away from home, had quietly hanged himself at the back of the ablutions.

There is little doubt that for many recruits the deliberate provocations imposed on us daily could become virtually unbearable. In all the Services, one of the first things one was taught was that there was only ONE way – the RIGHT WAY! – to make one's bed and lay out one's kit for inspection every morning. I often thought that the role of DI would have been perfect for poorly socialised obsessionals, but, unfortunately, I was not then in the business of vocational guidance. Anyway, while it was not too difficult to remember the correct lay-out for all the items to be laid out on the bed for scrutiny, there were often difficulties in achieving the exactitude sought by those in authority in folding one's sheets and blankets just so. Each item was removed from the bed each morning and folded meticulously in the same way to a measurement of about two feet wide by one foot deep and one inch thick (for sheets). The blankets were similarly folded, two encasing the sheets in a sandwich like some sort of Liquorice Allsort, while the third, folded longitudinally to a width of two feet, would be wrapped round the other bedding so that the ends of the wrapping blanket met under the package at the head of the bed. One's mug and KFS were then laid out on top of the blanket roll.

Bearing in mind that this always had to be done very quickly because time was at a premium in the morning before 6 o'clock, the corporate expertise accumulated in no more than a few days was remarkable. We could see nothing wrong with our efforts in this regard. The Corporal, however, would bounce in for his inspection as we 'stood by our beds' and, apparently quite arbitrarily, would take his cane to two or three of the bed rolls and violently tear it all apart and throw the pieces on the floor.

'Airman! I take this as a personal insult!' he would scream. 'I'll be back in two minutes and I want to see these bed rolls perfect ... inch-f****** perfect … an' if they're not, the whole bloody lot of you are on an extra bull-night tonight!' He'd stump out in high dudgeon and we'd all hasten to help the poor sods whose work had been thus defiled and which had been perfectly all right in the first place.

From the forbidding tales of poor recruits *in extremis* told by the Corporal mentioned earlier, it was clear that there were times, even for survivors, when the pressure could be borne no more and the recruits' aggression became both overweening and channelled into a corporate assault on one or another particular Drill Corporal or Sergeant. We heard that at least two were set upon at night in a dark part of the camp, not necessarily at Kirkham, and badly beaten up. It was alleged that one was tarred and feathered (literally) and barely survived. Although we never heard, and it was certainly not us, it was likely that none of the perpetrators 'squealed'.

Some of the worst provocation came after the periodic 'Full kit inspection' when not only a Corporal and Sergeant but sometimes also a junior Pilot Officer would attend at the hut to examine every single bit of an airman's kit, every item of which had to be laid out in particular positions and styles. Everything had to be clean laundered, washed and darned, i.e. singlets, underpants, shirts, handkerchiefs, socks and even ties. Haversacks, ammunition pouches, webbing harness and buckles polished, blanco-ed, impeccably laid out with pieces of cardboard inside to stiffen them into shape and displayed. Even our greatcoats and 'best blues' (formal walking-out uniform) had to be hung on hangers on the coat hooks behind our beds, every brass button sparkling like a diamond and fastened, the sleeves folded behind the back and tucked into the half-belt there. The slightest imperfection would bring down a wholly disproportionate tirade from the Sergeant or Corporal with all manner of threats of 'jankers' and other nameless punishments if a remedy were not immediately forthcoming. No wonder some of the more feckless young lads succumbed.

The Professors were, however, made of tougher stuff. Our own group name for ourselves was, for a number of reasons, including the subjects of Daz and Ped's cartoons, 'The Goons', though none of us really wanted to breach the copyright of our radio heroes. We quickly developed a strong sense of corporate identity which was nourished by the general principle that we'd wear the bastards down before they did us.

There were also among us a number of very witty as well as very resilient characters and many an occasion when murder might have been done was diverted by laughter. How we achieved the wearing-down process may well be protected by the Official Secrets Act, but it did involve such ploys as ensuring that when the Corporal arrived back in his little room at the end of the hut after a relaxed and beery evening in the NAAFI, he would find that his bed had been completely dismantled. Nothing was stolen (an offence), every part of the bed was present and (nearly) in position. To meet the Corporal's deeply engrained need for tidiness and order, every single piece of wire, of several hundred, which formed the diamond pattern bed spring had been separated from its neighbour, the frame itself had been meticulously unbolted, the ends set apart, and the bedding folded with a complexity which only an expert topologist could have unravelled, and the whole laid out in neat rows on the floor. Nobody knew how this could have happened.

At awkward times, the Corporal's phone would ring to summon him to an important meeting with the Station Adjutant, or to supply a urine sample in the morning to the Station Medical Officer. A dread disease had apparently broken out amongst some of the recruits and it was feared that some of the staff might have contracted it. He never discovered which of us it was who discovered his PBX number, nor who was the born mimic with the Adjutant's voice. Clearly, his seniors got round to thinking he ought to have done so. Half way through the twelve-week course, pressure told and we suddenly found we had a new corporal – Corporal Smith.

He was a more genial soul, none too bright, though brighter than his predecessor, but not malicious, so we gave him an easier time and even won the 'Banner' for him. The 'Banner', with all the logic of HM Services, was, of course, not a banner at all but an old World War One wooden propeller with a brass plaque on it which was awarded to the best Flight on the Station. The privileged Flight could hang this modestly aesthetic object on the wall of the hut while learning to live with the mixture of jealousy (hard to believe, but true, and a measure of how far the harsh techniques could actually force some of the Service values on us), scorn and abuse showered on us by the other Flights. We had been given the worst hut, the hardest time by the DIs and our share of ribald

and scurrilous comment by all the other Flights – but the 'F******
Professors had stuffed them all in the end!

One of the features of recruit training camp was that from time
to time, another Flight would arbitrarily decide to wreck the hut of
another (especially that of Banner winners) and to lay out as many of that
hut's inhabitants as possible before the staff and the Military Police could
intervene. We therefore lived in a state of perpetual watchfulness at any
time when the Corporal was not in his little room at the end of the hut.
His proximity to a phone made the whole operation just too fraught with
the hazards of military discipline for it to be feasible. However, the
advantage did lie with the defenders since the attackers had to infiltrate
their men into the near proximity of the target without seeming to be
involved in a raid. Moreover, we could lock the door, given time, and it
took a pretty hefty shove to burst the lock or hinges.

Prior to this experience, I had never thought of myself as being
at all pugilistic, and certainly not as having any prowess in hand-to-hand
combat. The last punch-up I had engaged in had been in Primary 6 when
Jimmy Wood had bled my nose for me (thus honourably ending the
fight) at the foot of Bellevue Road in a fight over a marble game. We
have been good friends ever since. However, it appears that I had
become naturally quite strong and the diet and routine of a Service
recruit does conduce to fitness and bulk. Thus it was, that at any threat to
Flight 58A, our hero, having been seen successfully to have flung out
(literally) several marauders from a previous episode, was called, at the
first signs of trouble, to man, with Tom Campbell, another mild
mannered giant, the door, and hopefully, to prove yet again that attack is
the strongest defence. 'Get your retaliation in first!' he would adjure me.
We might have been described as competitive rather than aggressive but
it was amazing how our little home was eventually left strictly alone by
other Flights and we could settle back into the normal evening routine of
coarse badinage, letter writing (for food parcels!), blanco-ing and
obscenity.

Other off-duty time was normally spent over a pie and beans
and a mug of tea in the NAAFI with two or three of the others from our
hut. There was little mixing with other Flights. In our more benign
moments, we might share something of our varied pasts, and, more
rarely, something of our hopes for the future – excluding our perennial

wish that one of the guard dogs might happen to chew the balls off the Drill Instructor. When we had really been put through the mill on the square or on the battle course that day, the tea would be sipped to the accompaniment of a detailed peroration on the pusillanimous but persistent sadism of the pock-marked, moustachioed, but immaculately turned out tormentors who had the power and opportunity to make us dance to their every whim – usually in double time.

It has to be said, nevertheless, that, whether or not there was some special selection of pathological obsessionals into the staff of recruit training camps, the turnout of these DIs was unbelievably smart and precise. We all believed that they must have been issued with some sort of wonder-uniforms with permanent razor-like creases in trousers and sleeves, a smooth and unblemished surface to their battle dress and shellac over the permanent blinding brightness of their polished brasses. At least they had to blanco their webbing with the rest of us because we saw it run on wet days before they got their capes on.

'You lot think we got special gear don't you, you 'orrible little men. You think we don't have to do our own bull like you 'ave', they would intone with something between an aggressive snarl and an irritating smug but totally false smile. 'But we don't. We got exactly the same f****** issue as you 'as – but we bloody well got to work on it just like you 'as to. We ain't perfect – oh no, but we're gettin' there. We sets the standards 'ere. Just consider yousselves bloody lucky you ain't at Bridgnorth (another recruit training camp). There's a DI Corporal there who's so f****** smart 'e can only take drill on dull days. Recruits in front of 'im on a sunny day goes blind when 'is cap badge flashes in their eyes an' there's some of 'is Flight 'as to go to Sickbay with cuts on their 'ands cos 'e 'appened to walk too close to them with 'is trouser creases!' We grinned dutifully, not entirely certain he was lying.

Corporal Smith, in a moment of intimacy when we had congregated in the hut round the stove for some old Oxford Group-type conversation one cold night just before Christmas, had clearly decided there was pressure on him to confess. The chat about Heidegger on religious philosophy, sex, Eysenck on the dimensions of personality, sex, Ryle or Hoyle on physics, sex, Lloyd Wright on architecture and finally, sex, was stifled in favour of Masonic-like disclosures of the secrets of DIs' turnout. Hesitantly ('I don't really like to talk about this sort of thing

– except with close relatives or my priest') he began to unbuckle his puttees. Anxieties that he might undress to show us his impeccably blanco-ed skin or his brasso-ed nipples were quietened when it transpired that he was simply going to demonstrate how he carefully folded the bottoms of his trousers before gripping them with the puttees, and, better still, how he achieved the immaculate and regular overhang of cloth over the tops of the puttees by placing an eight-inch diameter 'necklace' of string, weighted along its length with lead shot at intervals of an inch or so to hold down the overhang of trouser above the puttees.

A subsequent revelation was that the knife-like creases were sustained, not just by careful ironing, but by careful ironing of a mere quarter-inch width of an adhesive material called Wondaweb along the length of the crease, this, after scrubbing out any excess of woolly strands from the worsted with a wire brush. I doubt if any of us would have gone to such lengths had we been in the RAF for a century rather than a mere two years – but then, we weren't DIs. The mystery variants of toothbrushes and special cloths he kept for polishing his brasses were not revealed – perhaps he'd gone too far already. The secrets of the coven were not to be dispensed too freely. But he did demonstrate a good way of getting four brass tunic buttons into our 'button-sticks' for polishing and holding them so that Brasso didn't get on to our uniforms. Button-sticks were simply thin brass plates about 7" by 2" with an eighth of an inch slot open at one end of the plate to allow the buttons to be slid over the plate for polishing. These too had been part of our official kit issue along with two boot polishing brushes, one of which I still retain to this day with 2536746 still indented along its length.

That evening was the exception to normal in that we were not being driven daft by extra duties of a punitive nature and could indulge in something close to normal conversation. Many of the tensions and pressures of our frustration would find release in a general lowering of the standards of decency and good taste that might normally be expected of 'Potential Officer Material'. The language of the hut was fearsomely profane and coprophiliac. There was a general level of coarseness and obscenity which became so habitual as to be almost unnoticed. The gratuitous addition of adjectives and participles beginning with 'f' was general. It had all been suddenly brought home to me a week or so before by the sound of a normally mild-mannered classics scholar from Wales suddenly promising to 'smash in the f****** face of that c*** Corral if he once more bawls "Stand still!" in my ear.' Such an expostulation was merely greeted with nods of tacit agreement as we spat and rubbed at the shining toecaps of our ammunition boots.

These were expected to outshine the mirror of the Mount Palomar telescope and there was a whole mythology about the secrets of success. It was constantly averred that a mix of spittle, Cherry Blossom, the heat from a candle and rubbing with a knife handle could achieve the best results. Perhaps my salivary 'ph' was all wrong. Perhaps my knife handle was not of the pure ivory of the aristocrat. Perhaps the candle was poor quality NAAFI issue, regurgitated by starving Eskimos. Whatever the cause, the boots of 746 Clark never really blinded anyone on a sunny day, least of all, the Corporal!

Alternative pleasures of an evening or weekend were to be found in the camp cinema. Unfortunately, the few WAAFs available on a recruit training station were mostly already ear – and sometimes otherwise – marked by the Regular staff. The rest were not sought after for all too obvious reasons. Even Danny Daniels, our resident authority on women, and full of wise saws such as 'You don't look at the mantelpiece when you're poking the fire!' considered them total 'dogs'. Outside company of either sex could not be brought into the camp. In consequence, there was a perpetual cinematic diet of *San Demetrio: London, Dawn Patrol* or *The Road to Mandalay* … Casablanca … or anywhere. These streaky black and white dramas were frequently enhanced by the noisy snores of those for whom the weekly excitements of British Movietone News were insufficient to counter the soporific effects of the flickering darkness on bodies thoroughly knackered by the day's exertions, or by the equally uninhibited breaking of wind engendered by the NAAFI beans. Both were best left in the cinema rather than left to grace the midnight hours in the hut where they could never win friends even if they did influence people. One of the less reprehensible verses about such phenomena to fill out the poetic repertoire of our merry band was:

> *'A rift is but a puff of wind*
> *That comes up from the heart,*
> *But when it takes the downward path*
> *It constitutes a fart.*

A fart is but a puff of wind
That gives the belly ease.
It aerates the blankets
And suffocates the fleas.'

The Muse sat seldom by our shoulders during these harsh days in the billet, with the possible exception of the few cases who would aspire to versify – or even wax poetic – in their letters to their girl friends. The risk that any of these verses might stray into the public domain was guarded against with a powerful combination of guile, surreptitiousness and occasionally ferocity which would have made Ghengis Khan seem genial and mild mannered.

Some of the high points of life with Flight 58A were achieved thanks to the efforts of two Welshmen, Ped (short for Pedro, a modification of Peter!) Morris and Daz (I never did find out what that was short for, if anything) Barbour. Till then, I had thought of Welshmen as dark and gloomy pessimists from the Celtic fringe, given to endless choral singing as they grimly swung their Davy lamps, trudging home from the pit. The only pit with which Daz and Ped were at all familiar would have been an orchestral one from which their music soared; or from a garbage pit, only from where, we concluded, could have emanated their constant stream of quips and jokes. Ped and Daz had apparently known each other at Art College before being called up into the RAF and they had a nicely rehearsed line in jazz and swing music for four hands at the NAAFI piano. The latter, having had serious amounts of beer lubricate it at various times, perhaps did them less than justice, but the rest of us were not averse to supplying a catholic variety of ditties from the nightly libretto of the hut. A favourite, oft-repeated by National Servicemen down the years, allowed of appropriate substitutions, and described the Station one happened to be on at the time:

'They say that old Kirkham's a wonderful place
*But the organisation's a f****** disgrace –*
There's Sergeants and Corporals and Flight Sergeants too
*With their hands in their pockets and f****** all to do.*

They stand on the square and they bawl and they shout.
*They shout about things they know f****** all about.*

And for all the effect, they might as well be
A-shovelling shit on the Isle of Capri!'

But these were the least of the Welshmen's talents. Both were interested in pursuing their post Art Diploma lives as illustrators and/or cartoonists and were seldom seen without pencils and crayons when the rest of us were finding time to write home or sew on buttons or just have a quiet fag. Although smoking then did not have the anti-health and anti-social connotations it now holds, most of us were non-smokers but there were still some in the billet who cosseted their addiction. The billet walls were soon the repository of several witty and biting cartoons of various Station worthies – including the Corporal, the Station Warrant Officer and the Station Commander – a sufficiently remote figure to be dealt with somewhat less harshly than the local worthies. Our artists also did us proud by illustrating various military and so-called safety and fire procedures using gross or ludicrous caricatures of ourselves to demonstrate what a total 'Goon' would do in the circumstances in question – to be contrasted with what 'Ginger' (the ideal airman) would do when well trained and indoctrinated. At that time a rather cocky and ebullient 'Ginger' figured in Air Ministry recruitment posters all over the country, smilingly perched over the rubric 'Ginger's Back!' This was aimed at encouraging those of us serving only our Natonal Service two years to return and sign on for a further stint. Ginger and his ill-judged return consequently became the unwitting subject of our varied imprecations.

Several of Daz and Ped's artistic efforts found their way to the Adjutant's office and thence to Air Ministry printing works for general promulgation, so effective were they. Our hut complement was meanwhile gradually becoming known not so much as the F****** Professors as the 'Goons'. This secret society terminology was much prized by ourselves since it was taken to reflect, not so much the idiocies of our mythical mad airmen of the cartoons, as the zany, surreal and hugely admired radio humour of Spike Milligan, Harry Secombe and Peter Sellars. Daz also doubled as the hut hairdresser, living down to his name, until one miserable morning parade inspection when one of our number displayed traces of unorthodoxy in the 'short back and sides' beloved of all Drill Sergeants. He was asked in the usual 120 decibel stage whisper,

'Who cut yer 'air, laddie?'

'Barber, Sergeant'.

'Which barber, for God's sake?

'Daz Barbour, Sergeant!'

There was a pause for effect before the storm broke. Both tonsure and tonsorialist were to report at the Guardroom after the day's work for more bin scraping or the like. The Station hairdresser did fractionally better financially thereafter.

The ten weeks at recruit training were calculated to instil into us a variety of Service skills, some relatively warlike, such as learning to bawl and shout as we bayoneted the enemy and to twist the bayonet properly as we pulled it out of the 'body', usually a sack of sand and straw hanging from a rack. We learned what were the 'Immediate Actions Nos 1 and 2' in the event of a Bren gun jamming; or how to disable an attacker assaulting you with a knife by deflecting the lunge and briskly kicking him in the balls and shin as viciously as possible. Mind you, some of our number (not in our Flight, of course) had been practising such skills nightly in the back streets of Glasgow or Birmingham for years before being called up. We also learned, first with dummies, to throw hand grenades – easily, next to firing a Sten gun, the most dangerous activity on the ranges we ever participated in. There would always be some butter-fingered idiot who would manage to drop the live grenade after pulling out the firing pin.

'What do you do when an Irishman throws a pin at you, laddie?'

'I don't know, Corporal.'

'You run like f***, 'cos he's still got the grenade in 'is mouth!'

Such merry quips were food and drink to the staff on the firing ranges. They must have dreaded the first arrivals of a new Flight, bristling with their shiny new Lee Enfield .303s, Sten and Bren guns, grenades and Colt revolvers. For once, we could see the need for absolute discipline and the establishment of good firearm habits. The irritating habit in any recruit of turning toward the speaker, often the Sergeant, when spoken to, and unconsciously thus directing a loaded Sten gun at his stomach, was not seen to endear one to the hierarchy. Words, loaded with asterisks, would be exchanged.

Other skills were more domestic but totally unusable in civilian life. To this day I have never blanco-ed anything since being demobbed, nor have I felt the need to repeat the Royal Navy or Army equivalent ranks to an Air Vice Marshall or Wing Commander. A few skills were of direct value in subsequent years. Not the least of these was a realistic sense of what stresses one could tolerate with at least near-equanimity, a capacity to eat, if not to enjoy, almost anything without complaint, and unpurchasable experience in making independent evaluations of one's fellow men and, as a result, often forming valuable friendships within a spirit of camaraderie unknown at any other time. I often thought back to my first year at university when, as a callow youth, like many of the AC2s in other Flights, I had blundered naïvely into unsuitable associations and wasted days, even weeks, with people whose friendship I would not normally have sought or enjoyed simply because I had not developed any skill at making the necessary observations and judgments.

The days at Kirkham were long and hard. One favourite ploy of the Drill Instructors was to arrange various activities in quick succession which all required a different form of dress. Not that black tie and tails came into it much. The more usual thing was for us to have to parade in front of the hut for early morning inspection in plain battle dress only. We would then be dismissed and have to turn out immaculate in full webbing battle order with tin hat, rucksack, ammunition pouches, rifle bayonet and puttees. There then followed an hour or so of unremitting toil on the square, wheeling, marching, standing STILL, shouldering, lowering and porting arms, opening the breech, closing the breech, standing STILL, giving the wholehearted impression of listening intently while the Drill Sergeant briefly outlined your dubious ancestry to the gathered assembly from one inch behind your ear, standing STILL, quick, quick and slow marching – but never a tango – and at last, the blessed command in a hoarse but piercing falsetto, 'Dissss-misssss!' No sooner did that occur, however, than came the command to return to the billet, perhaps half a mile away, strip into PT shorts, vest and Plimsolls and turn up at the gym in five minutes – 'and the last man there's for jankers!'

Here, a much healthier brand of sadist awaited us. PTIs (Physical Training Instructors) affected a working garb of tracksuit bottoms and white roll-neck jerseys. When the going got really tough they would then peel off the outer shell to reveal rippling muscles, hairy chests and a perpetual smell of wintergreen from the self massage they so narcissistically indulged in as they built muscles before the gymnasium mirrors. Their faces were very clean, and their minds very dirty. They loved to humiliate the less mesomorphic recruits, especially those wheezing from overindulgence in mother nicotine or those whose abdominal adipose tissue flowed over their belts like snowy cornices on a mountain ridge.

Press-ups were the favourite penance. Sins of the wall-bars or the coir matting were measured in numbers of extra press-ups. Any reluctance to comply or any sign of physical incapacity led immediately to that individual's selection to go three rounds with one of the instructors in the boxing ring. Since one of them had been an international cruiserweight, the contest was usually less than equal – with easily foreseen results. Fortunately, some of my pals and myself had not long since been running, boxing or rowing for our various universities so these physical forfeits offered us little threat. On one notable occasion, another chap and myself who had both run long distance for our respective university national teams took much pleasure in totally knackering one of the more cocky PTIs in the course of a six mile run in which he was blatantly torturing some of the less fit eighteen-year-olds from another Flight training with us. One of the great advantages enjoyed by 'The Professors' was that all of us (because of the deferment of our service to allow us to take our first degrees) were about three or four years older than most recruits called up at eighteen.

Hot and sweaty from these exertions, we were given no respite. A further string of commands and we, yet again, would gallop back to the billet (no time for a shower!) where we would change into denims – a rough, cotton-type of battle dress for dirty work, webbing and rifles, and we would parade, yet again, outside the hut, confident in the knowledge that the wretched Corporal had taken the opportunity to grab a cup of tea from the NAAFI van which circulated round the camp at various times, while we changed. Then came a march up to the MT (Motor Transport) Unit where we piled into three-ton lorries for the transfer to the range, some miles away. The range was a place for water colourists – wide raw sienna skies washed by Payne's grey veils of rain and hail, never quite blown dry by the raw salt winds whistling in from the west over the salt flats of Morecambe Bay and the Irish Sea.

It was not a place for anyone with numb fingers, tear-filled eyes from the blast of the wind and the unremitting shiver from the combination of cold and apprehension about the scathing commentary of a brand new batch of Sergeants and Corporals whose whims and weaknesses we had not fathomed. These were Arms Instructors, some from the RAF Regiment, who would teach us to shoot to kill whether we were standing up, crouching or lying down. 'Rounds' were handed out (they were never called bullets) carefully counted and pressed into magazines in the approved fashion. Even with a university degree, some of us managed to get them in back to front. This appeared to raise the temperature (and blood pressure) of the bosses without warming us in the least. Coarse and peasant analogies were drawn between inserting rounds into a magazine and a variety of other bodily and sexual functions, only a few of which many of us were familiar with.

'Right, then, you lot; gather round!' This was a new and rather gentler address than we'd been used to. But that was the 'Soft Man'. The 'Hard Man' was lurking in the background (also a Sergeant) and like most of the instructors, sported on his sleeve the crossed rifles badge of the qualified marksman. There were several tales circulating about some of these chaps, most of which became quickly discredited but a few of which were equally promptly endorsed. Among the wildest were stories of how one could cut his initials in a target with a Bren gun at 300 yards and another could put three bullets from a sniper's Lee-Enfield rifle through each floret of the ace of clubs at 100 yards. However, some of these chaps were Bisley experts and were so much at one with their weapons that we could only jealously assume that they were really impotent and that the rifles were phallic substitutes.

Enter the 'Hard Man'. 'Can you all 'ear me?' he bawled at nobody in particular. 'Because I ain't goin' to spend the whole bloody mornin' repeatin' myself!' He had let his voice fall slightly with the last sentence.

'You!' he snapped, pointing a rock steady digit at poor Gerry Humphries, the only resident Barrister among us FPs, who had been idly wiping the drizzle from his large and rather thick glasses. 'What did I just say?'

Gerry, with all the languid charm with which he would no doubt, in a year or two's time, engage a Court, replaced his glasses and replied, 'You invited us to respond if we could not hear you. We did not, so you can assume either that we all did hear you or that we are all stone deaf, which is less likely. Also you added a rider to the effect that you would be disinclined to repeat yourself.'

'Shut up, smart-arse, and pay attention!' quoth the Sergeant, redundantly, and perhaps a shade more limply than he might have wished.

We were then put through a rapid but technically accurate description of the .303 Lee-Enfield Service rifle, the first weapon in which we were to be instructed, lethal at up to a mile but probably accurate in combat conditions only up to about three hundred yards. There was particular emphasis put on the use of the safety catch. All of us were, I think, glad of that.

Probably because it was by now raining steadily, we were then instructed to get down in the prone position with our legs suitably splayed, the butt of the rifle tucked into our shoulders, and our eyes squinting along the sights on the barrel. The sights were then set to the probable range of the targets by turning a milled screw on the backsight, and in lots of ten, we were each given corresponding man-sized wooden targets to aim at, and hopefully to hit, 100 yards away. At the appropriate commands, off came the safety catches, there was a general rattling as the bolts were worked to cock the rifles, and, 'In your own time, single shots, Fire!'

The best that the instructors could hope for would be that, for each man, at least most of the five shot magazine bullets (sorry, 'rounds') might hit the targets somewhere above the midriff. The reality was a sight not inclined to encourage the confidence of the lieges in the capacity of their Servicemen to defend this sceptred isle. Although a few early shots rang out and puffs of mud and sand from the banking behind the targets proclaimed near misses, the rest of us 'marksmen' were vainly trying to control the wavering muzzles of our weapons as their 9lb weight gradually tired our unaccustomed muscles and the wind and rain conspired progressively to cloud our vision and corrupt our motivation.

'I said "Single shots, Fire!" you dozy bastards, not go on f****** holiday', intoned the Sergeant, the 'Hard Man', kicking idly at the foot of the nearest laggard at the trigger. Spurred into despairing action, the rest of us loosed off a volley in the right general direction, only to suppress our own curses as we discovered what a kick the recoil of a .303 could give. Bruises soon accumulated on clavicles and cheekbones as we adjusted bodies and weapons to more suitable positions, only to be chastised for our little departures from orthodoxy.

Back in the deep trench behind the targets, the target markers waved signal flags to indicate no hits. We loaded again, utterly convinced that we had deliberately been issued with weapons which had been tampered with or had bent barrels or broken sights. Apprehensive of the recoil, we nevertheless set about our task again and this time some of us actually perforated our targets. Of course, we could not be sure that we had 'wounded' the target we were supposed to be aiming at rather than the next one along the row, but took the view that if we all fired at about the same time, the instructors would not be able to tell. Three more shots each and our magazines were empty. Tight-lipped and pale with frustration, the instructors really tried to be patient with us and went round kicking and prodding us into 'the correct attitude' as a further five rounds were issued.

'Christ Almighty, I've never seen anything like it. You'd all be bloody dead as dodos if you shot like that in combat! Don't look for the bloody trigger – feel for it! If it 'ad 'air on it you'd find it quick enough! Give me that rifle, laddie.' So saying, the 'Soft Man' spread himself in the 'correct attitude' alongside the airman next to me, released the safety catch and promptly drilled five neat holes in a small circle round the black disc on the central torso of the target. So much for the 'bent barrels'!

'Listen again, you 'orrible little pansy boys. You cuddle that weapon. You caress it like it was a woman – firm, not too slack, not too tight. You sque-e-e-ez-e the trigger. You do not pull it. You breathe in, then, gently release your breath as you hold the sights on target. As your lungs empty then squ-e-e-e-z-e! Right then, let's see if you're capable of learning ANYTHING'. He passed Tom Campbell, the airman temporarily deprived of his rifle, another magazine.

We wiped the tears from our eyes, the product not of emotion but of the steady downpour, and this time there were signs of modest success. I remember getting four of the five shots on target but at the cost of a growing swelling over my right cheekbone where the lower knuckle of my thumb was driven into it by the recoil as I 'cuddled' the stock. Half an hour and a couple of magazines later, we were beginning to get just a trace competitive, even cocky about our newfound prowess. That was, however, just the signal for our instructors to do it standing up, so to speak. Turned slightly sideways, with no friendly Mother Earth on which to rest our left elbows and body, we found the rifle even more unwilling to settle comfortably on that distant black disc. We soon had the cockiness knocked out of us and had to concentrate all over again.

The low opinion held by our instructors of the marksmanship of the average recruit was evident in the deep and solid brick and earthwork trench and barricade, piled with sand, which protected the target checkers and haulers. These targets of wood and card in the shape of, happily, soldiers rather than airmen, seemed of Charles Atlas dimensions at fifty yards. Until firing commenced (in the Services, things always 'commenced' rather than 'began') one wondered how they could be missed. At 300 yards, however, you had to rub your eyes even to see the blooming things through the sights of your wavering weapon, no less try to hit them in the vital area between waist and shoulders – and preferably in the middle. With cheekbone bruises swelling up as the session wore on, it became even more difficult. Nevertheless, we were fortunate to get a couple of fine days for the 300-yard range and in due course, most of us became adequately proficient, at least against a static 'enemy'. Those who did not may have been re-allocated to become cooks, padres or medical orderlies.

The Bren gun, by comparison with the Lee Enfield, was a delight to fire. The recoil was gas absorbed into re-cocking the weapon and it simply slid and quivered gently as the gunner pumped bullet after bullet into the few square inches of the selected target. In fact, so accurately could one fire a Bren gun, that it was deemed a rather poor machine gun. To wreak most havoc, the latter should really spray bullets around a bit more and not drive them nose to tail through the same hole. Fired 'single-shot' it was as accurate as a rifle and with the same range.

Now the Sten gun, a close combat weapon essentially for street fighting, was a different kettle of fish entirely. It was a cheap and nasty weapon, perhaps ideal for the situations it might be used in, but such that, once cocked, it would loose off its whole magazine of about thirty bullets if you gave it a dirty look, no less actually pulled the trigger. It had also the endearing habit of pulling to one side as you actually fired it in bursts. It was one of the minor miracles of National Service that so few recruits, or even hardened warriors, were killed or wounded by that nearly autonomous piece of weaponry. However, it had been adopted by most of the armed Services because it used ammunition of 9mm calibre widely used by our then potential enemies. Captured loot could, therefore, be used by our side.

Plate 4: *Picture Post* **in November 1954 showed Sten gun practice in the Army. In the RAF we were never afforded an officer to demonstrate to us. But then, we never made it to the** *Picture Post!* (Hutton- Getty)

One of our mornings 'home on the range' where no 'deer and (no) antelope play' was much enlivened by one of our number dropping his cocked Sten at his feet. From that relatively uncontrolled position, the gun thereupon loosed off some twenty or more rounds of live 9mm ammunition in a way that generated the most amazing physical reflexes among the assembly. Since one burst had already been fired from it before the drop, the gun quickly expended its magazine around at least a 200° arc as it bounced in surprise at its own recoil – and ours! One pair of trousers (Service denim, airmen, for the use of) was holed without the leg within being penetrated, and several other pairs were later changed in a way that suggested that their owners had discovered that adrenalin is brown and runs down your trouser leg. For a moment (variously judged as between four and six nanoseconds) the Sergeant instructor was speechless. Immediately thereafter, we were treated to a spectacularly florid exposition of all known profanities, apparently in several languages, and a few hitherto unknown descriptions of ourselves, since we all reaped the benefit of our poor comrade's indiscretion. For some reason, he never again appeared on the range. Nervous readers will be glad to hear that that was the end of one of the three or four life-threatening experiences the RAF flung at me.

No sooner had we demonstrated adequate proficiency with our weapons than we were introduced to the elements of Ground Combat Training and the Battle Course. Some of us were inclined to wonder why, and in what circumstances, members of the Royal Air Force might be expected to engage in close hand-to-hand combat or to have to bayonet to death some hostile assailant. However, it appears that all, regardless of what arm of the Services one served in, had to be instructed in these rather nasty arts. It all began in the gym.

The PTIs took great delight in explaining that, when it came to 'the real thing', we would not be cosseted by having nice soft mats on the floor to break our fall, our attackers would not be pulling their punches or giving us time to think out the next hold or counter blow. 'So, you 'orrible little men, you will pay attention and you will learn well and you will learn fast. Next time you will not be in a nice warm gym in your clean shorts and singlets. You will be in full battle order and you will be out in the rain and the mud.' Then the wintergreen and muscle men would select one or two of the more slightly built specimens to demonstrate the basics of self-defence and counter-attack. They took positive delight in throwing these poor ingenues around the mats before they had picked up enough know-how to defend themselves and they smirked their way through their demonstrations of a variety of holds and stratagems with another instructor. None of us took this very seriously – at least not until the instructors later began to select out those they thought to be fractionally less committed to breaking each other's bones for more serious little bouts of 'airman versus instructor'. After a few big bruises, a bleeding nose or two and the odd twisted muscle, we began to take it all more to heart. In the interests of self-preservation, we paid a bit more attention until the final moment of triumph when we might elicit a stifled curse from the instructor as we upended him, perhaps a trace over-vigorously. That didn't happen often.

A week later it all happened again, but out of doors on a grassy area near the parade ground. We were indeed in 'denims and webbing' (sounds like Marshall and Snelgrove) boots and puttees and this time we had rifles and bayonets. First, the moves and countermoves so bruisingly learnt the week before were rehearsed and special little tricks only applicable if one were to be wearing ammunition boots were added to these. For example, if your adversary in a close grapple tries to kick you on the shin-bone, the move is apparently simply to lift your own foot above his boot, keeping your own toes firmly in the direction of the approaching leg of the assailant. He then impacts his own shin-bone on your steel edged toecap before his slides harmlessly under your foot. Well, that was the theory. We certainly did improve our agility but we'll never know whether we had the killer touch.

The most ludicrous of all our ground combat training activities was one about which most of us would have felt acutely embarrassed had we been spied at it by normal people outside. It was the 'how to use the bayonet' one in which we charged fifty yards or so shouting and bawling nothing in particular until we plunged our bayonets into straw and sand-filled sacks slung from gantries by lengths of rope. A variant was the bayoneting of other 'recumbent' sacks on the ground, being careful to penetrate the 'body' with at least four inches of blade before twisting it as it was withdrawn, both to do as much damage to the poor victim as possible and to prevent the bayonet being trapped between the ribs. Quite how we were to effect transfer of all these skills from straw-filled sacks to a mobile, tough and aggressive enemy who would, no doubt, be shooting at us all the while, was never, to my mind, fully, or even partially, explained.

The screaming and shouting as we charged was mandatory. Any whimper not sufficiently dervish or maniacal was immediately castigated and subsequent failures put one at risk of 'jankers'. Presumably the function of this was both to 'terrify' the enemy and to deaden our own judgment or feelings as we pursued our deadly trade. In the post-atomic era, there was something primitive and macabre as well as supremely irrelevant about our frenzied charges. As I pounded toward my hessian target, images from Erich Maria Remarque's *All Quiet on the Western*

Front flashed through my consciousness. A couple of verses from Wilfred Owen's *Spring Offensive* were triggered by the sixty pounding feet around me, the bayoneted rifles and the shouting. Lancashire evaporated and the mud and horror of Ypres and the Somme took its place.

> *'So, soon they topped the hill, and raced together*
> *Over an open stretch of herb and heather*
> *Exposed. And instantly the whole sky burned*
> *With fury against them; earth set sudden cups*
> *In thousands for their blood; and the green slope*
> *Chasmed and steepened sheer to infinite space.*
>
> *Of them who running on that last high place*
> *Leapt to swift unseen bullets, or went up*
> *On the hot blast and fury of hell's upsurge,*
> *Or plunged and fell away past this world's verge,*
> *Some say God caught them even before they fell.'*

We corrupted those images by our futile antics. Our feeble shouts were false. The reality was bizarre and the screaming injunctions of our mentors were insufficient to reduce our shame and embarrassment at this futile, outmoded and demeaning exercise. Even the less aware and critical amongst us ended that afternoon oddly subdued and yet conscious of the undertones of the activity we had had thrust upon us. As usual, the tension was released by one of us as he cleaned his bayonet and thrust it into its scabbard again. 'What a bloody fiasco that was!' Tacitly, we all agreed.

The battle course, various forms of which we were to meet at later stages of our careers, was threatening to some. For those of us who had been fortunate to keep up our general fitness and athleticism from varsity days, however, it demanded no more than a cool nerve, a bit of aggressive 'devil' and good balance. Battle courses varied in their severity. In some cases, including our first one, they could be something like a kind of open-air gymnasium which had to be negotiated at speed whilst encumbered by guns and gear not particularly well designed to facilitate rapid or balanced progress.

They usually started with a gallop toward, and then under, a layer of tarpaulin pegged to the ground, followed by another gallop toward a set of poles a few inches in width which were set horizontally at various heights from the ground and reached by running up shallow ramps of the same material. Next might come a layer of barbed wire entanglement held about eighteen inches above the ground by steel posts and under which we had to crawl for ten or fifteen yards. Getting through suspended old lorry tyres was not a problem in PT kit. It was hell in battledress and equipment! Obstacles varied from camp to camp but few were devoid of some sort of water hazard – usually one which had to be swung over, Tarzan-like, on the end of ropes gained from a platform ten feet above the pond or ditch. Nothing pleased our bosses more than a lost grip on this little venture. Inevitably, a soaking in foul muddy water ensued and that did not make the climbing of a set of widely spaced horizontal bars or a brick wall, perhaps ten to twelve feet high, to come later any easier for having liberal amounts of water splashed all over the available areas on which one might get a grip. The wall was not negotiable unless one cooperated with two pals. The first backed against the wall with his two hands cupped in front of him as a foothold for number two, who then could be heaved to the top of the wall. Up there, he then helped and hauled the other two up behind him. Sweating with effort, we dropped over the other side into more soggy mud.

All this of course went on accompanied by violent urgings and shouting from our instructors, usually coupled with pithy descriptions of what 'a lot of poncy wankers' we were when our errors of judgment or strength led to failures, falls, or, at the least, coarse and noisy philosophising on our part. At the end of all that exertion we were expected to have kept our rifles clean enough for firing and our bodies free enough of the quivering and shuddering consequent on our efforts to allow us to take aim at a series of targets not too far distant. We were expected to plant at least a majority of the five bullets in a magazine within a prescribed area of these. In the cold and sleet of early winter, none of that was too easy, but we did at least burn off a substantial number of the calories accumulated from the diet of much white bread and greasy food in the cookhouse, and evening beer, pies and beans from the NAAFI.

Thus did our twelve weeks of recruit training drag on. The constant high carbohydrate diet, supplemented as reported above by other 'luxuries' and the occasional weekend 'thrash' in the high life of

Blackpool's Winter Garden, resulted in a very sturdy lad, nearly a stone heavier, and no doubt a trace tougher mentally and physically than when he joined up.

It is widely appreciated in clinical psychological circles that matters to do with the presentation, consumption and evaluation of food are frequently indissolubly bound up with other emotional crises or preoccupations and attitudes. This is especially so in institutions such as prisons, ships at sea, large factories and military establishments. Two processes militated against any major food-associated rebellions in recruit training camps. Firstly, we were all so hungry after our strenuous and long days of training that we only wanted to wolf down whatever was put in front of us. Only the most squeamish, or the independently rich, could pick and choose what they ate and depend on the NAAFI to supplement their diet. We even drank up cup after cup of the tea from the urns. And that was in spite of the long-standing rumour (apparently universal among His Majesty's Forces) that the powers that be enforced the lacing of the tea with bromide in order to suppress what was thought to be our overweening sexual powers. Those in whom sheer fatigue had reduced their sex drive significantly were inclined to believe the worst. Most of us, however, noticed little or no difference – although the distinction between sexual powers and sexual aspirations and fantasies could become rather blurred at times.

The second deterrent to mutiny was the routine formal visit to all the tables by an NCO – or occasionally even the Catering Officer – when we would be fixed with a steely eye, and the query, 'Any complaints?' fired at us. There was a rumour that any recruit who voiced a complaint would suddenly disappear and probably finish up in the soup (literally!) so, needless to say, I cannot remember ever hearing one at my table. By that, of course, I mean hearing one articulated in that context. Plenty vociferous and pungent commentaries were passed on the quality and quantity of food presented from one day to another – but not in the presence of anyone likely to do anything about it. Coarse little cries would from time to time emanate from a table, like, 'Who called the cook a c**t? only to be followed immediately from the next table by a querulous, 'Who called that c**t a cook?' Apocryphal tales abounded:

Sergeant: 'Any complaints?'
Airman: 'Sergeant! There's a mouse in my soup!'

Sergeant: 'Well, shut up about it, laddie – or they'll all be wanting one!'

All of us had become accustomed to the routine process of washing up our KFS (remember? – knife, fork and spoon) in an unsavoury-looking trough outside the cookhouse as we left that building. Theoretically, this vessel contained a constant flow of boiling water through which we were to drag our cutlery, thus cleaning and sterilising it, and hot enough to dry it as we marched back to the billet. In fact, though it steamed impressively, like an Icelandic geyser, with the rain, and sometimes the snowflakes, falling steadily into it, the resemblance to anything of such Nordic purity was little more than superficial. Management's aspirations to perfect hygiene tended to evaporate in the face of the permanent scum of dissolved fat, fragments of vegetable, tea leaves and fag ends which each of us in turn swished around to ensure an equitable distribution of bacteria to all.

Curiously, in spite of all our tribulations, there were some high points and laughs in the billet. We, the Goons, had by now developed a very high corporate morale amongst ourselves. We had repeatedly repelled night invaders from other Flights (at some cost to themselves!) so we now enjoyed a reputation that deterred more recently admitted Flights from troubling us. We had actually 'won the Banner' for the sake of the more genial Corporal Smith and he, in his turn, now spent much less of his free time in his sacrosanct little room at the end of the hut, and more in our hut, nattering round the (gleaming) stove and picking up little bits of knowledge, if not wisdom, from the F****** Professors. It turned out that he too had spent some time at Art School and he was delighted to foster the cartoon work of our own comic geniuses Daz and Ped.

Even the Station Commander and Adjutant came down to the hut one day to examine the producers of these professionally funny, beautifully drawn coloured cartoons with the apposite RAF remarks on them. We all basked, not least Corporal Smith, in their reflected glory. Ped and Daz not only turned out their marvellous A1 sized cartoons in full colour (to which several of us who 'fancied our barras' as script writers added captions) but they regularly entertained the NAAFI with swingy renditions on what must at one time have been a half-decent piano.

All of us were more proficient at the routines of 'bull nights' and personal turnout, we had apparently succeeded at all the brutish skills required of us and we were near to being told the results of the various batteries of psychological tests which had been administered to us at various sessions during our early weeks in camp.

One of the less pleasant activities of recruit training was the obligation, at some time, to mount overnight Guard Duty. This involved parading at the Station Guardroom, in full battledress and armed with our rifles, where we were shown a hut in which bed frames and 'biscuits' only would be available for us to rest on during our two hours on and four hours off duty throughout the evening and night. Technically, the Officer of the Day would be Guard Commander and there was also an appropriate NCO i/c to dispose us around the various security positions around the Station.

There was a formal 'Fall-in' of the Guard by the Guard Commander, often by the Station flagpole, when formal responsibility for the security of the Station was handed over by the departing Guard, and thereafter the pairs who were on first stint would march to their areas, while those off for the first period would make tea in the guardroom. Because there had been some IRA intrusions and thefts of weapons from certain Units at the time we were there, we were issued with firm rules of challenge and appropriate action and were issued with one magazine of rounds each – to be handed in afterwards. From then on we did our best to stay warm and vertical by little marches to and fro at our position, slinging rather than shouldering our rifles, but always on the watch more for the sneaky advent of the Guard Commander or NCO who would be checking us out than for thieves, spies or intruders of even more malevolent intent. Our challenges to the occasional passing airman or especially to the Guard NCO were loud and formal – just to prove that we were not asleep! The main enemy was the cold. I have an abiding memory of the brass butt plate of my shouldered rifle firmly freezing to my bare hand as I watched the magically bright stars and planets sparkling in the gaps between the buildings we were guarding. We often wondered whether we would have been able to react fast enough had there been any emergency, so frozen were our limbs. The hands of my watch seemed to have frozen too. 0200 hours, when I could repair to the Guardroom for some tea and a lie down (fully clad) seemed to have been fifteen minutes away for hours. Fortunately, provided one avoided punishment duties, Guard duty came round very infrequently.

The other unpleasant event of these weeks (to be repeated several times during subsequent training) was our training to cope with gas. After the usual homily from the Corporal about the necessity to check and re-check the fitting of our issue gas masks, and about finding our way about in reduced visibility, we would be ushered through a gas chamber filled with tear gas, first with our masks on, and then without our masks. Out we stumbled, reddened eyes and noses streaming while we struggled to breathe normally again in the open air and the Corporals had us jogging around to clear our heads. Fortunately, I was always able to cope easily enough with the experience and the effects of the gas wore off quickly. There were some, however, who were more adversely affected and there were a few whose claustrophobia made the whole thing something close to terror. For them, not just the gas, but the confines of the gas chamber and its swirling 'fog' were severely threatening.

Back in the billet, however, when all these unpleasantnesses had been survived and we had begun to harden to the daily routines and persecutions of the DIs, our casual off-duty conversations with each other, especially with those in adjacent beds, were usually interesting and we all picked up information and impressions from each other about different lifestyles and different jobs. From Tony Cawthorpe, I learned a good deal about geography and from Bert Clayton, I heard about his noble part in designing a new public lavatory for Nottingham. He did aspire to better things and talked wistfully of Frank Lloyd Wright, le Corbusier and Eero Saarinen. Gerry Humphries was frequently sounded to see if there was anything in the National Service Act of 1948 which we could dredge up to get our instructors in trouble or evade the nastier aspects of our training, and Davies, Willis or Adams, our classicists, were always good for a Latin or Greek aphorism.

Naturally, much was expected from their resident psychologist, a great deal that I could not supply, as I tried in vain to explain that I had a first degree only and my post-graduate professional skills training still awaited me. However, they did discover that I had dabbled in hypnosis even as an undergraduate and there were clamant demands for me to effect magical things with the NCOs we least appreciated. Disclaimers that the cooperation of the subject was required were paid little attention to and some of our group claimed that they had been hypnotised in theatres by professional hypnotists without their cooperation. My scepticism led to the discovery that one of us had undergone just such an experience and he turned out to be a very good hypnotic subject.

Inevitably, one evening, young 746 Svengali had to demonstrate to the hut how deeply our friend Mr X could be put in a trance. There was no problem with that and I gained a transient prestige. Unfortunately, Mr X had found the process (as do many hypnotisees) quite pleasurable and I was asked to do it again another evening. We had been talking about the phenomena of post-hypnotic suggestion and how a hypnotised subject could be primed to respond to a certain defined signal after he had come out of the trance and would be unable to prevent himself responding to it, given that it did not conflict with his basic personality and habits of behaviour. Accordingly, when poor Mr X was 'well away', I asked the lads what he should be asked to do when a pre-arranged signal was given. The signal was to be the familiar shout, 'Stand by your beds!' usually uttered by the Corporal or Drill Sergeant on his entering the hut. The response on X's part was to stay where he was and say 'Piss off!' We were all ready to enact this little charade (Tom Campbell was to be the Sergeant) when, to our horror, the hut door burst open and the Drill Sergeant, complete with pace stick, bawled 'Stand by your beds!'

We leapt to obey. Mr X, still lounging on his bed, dozily raised an eyebrow and declaimed, 'Piss off!'

There was a deathly pause.

'What did you say, airman?' This was not in the script so poor X simply lay there befuddled and uncomprehending. I felt it incumbent on me to speak up and explain.

'Permission to speak, Sergeant?' I quavered.

'Who's speaking to you, laddie? Shut up!' and, in the same breath, to our Mr X, 'On your feet Airman, or you'll be in the Guardhouse so quick your feet won't never touch the ground again!'

At this point the corporate will of the group reasserted itself and several voices addressed the Sergeant. I'm sure one even was heard to say, incongruously, and rather feebly, 'Please, Sergeant … ' He did take stock at this point. It was, after all, about 9 p.m. and he would not normally visit a hut in our off-duty hours. (It turned out that he was only visiting to see the latest Goon cartoons).

746 Clark then tried to explain what had happened and the others nodded sagely. The trouble was that we were known to be a dodgy lot of Mickey-takers anyway and this little episode bore all the hallmarks of another of our ploys aimed at NCOs. Drill Sergeants nearly always carried with them an undercurrent of paranoia in any case (at least *vis à vis* recruits) so there were some minutes of hasty explanation before we could persuade him of the true nature of the episode.

'All right, then, X, you're dismissed. So are the rest of you!' I relaxed and headed for my bed-space, '– except you, Clark! You will report to me at the Sergeants' Mess tomorrow evening where you will demonstrate some of this bloody mumbo jumbo in what I think you would call (and this with a smirk) a controlled situation!'

My heart fell. I knew my skills were limited and that our poor Mr X was a very suggestible subject. If none of the Sergeants' Mess members was equally suggestible, not only I, but the whole hut was in the shit. 'Jankers' loomed for the lot of us – and just when things had been going pretty well for us. They would have no problem with describing taking the piss out of a Drill Sergeant as 'conduct prejudicial to good order and discipline in the Service.'

The next day was one of unremitting anxiety. I went about the usual duties and exercises automatically, constantly turning over in my mind what awful consequences had derived from something which, reviewed in later life, makes my hair curl. Not only had I exceeded my 'expertise' but I had also compromised the future careers of every one of the Goons, the F****** Ps. If we were put on charges, that would remain on our records forever. POMs we might be today, but would we be tomorrow? However, my habit has always been to keep as cool as possible and to marshal my thoughts quite quickly in problem solving situations. I decided that the only hope of success lay in my enhancing the group suggestibility once I was in the situation and in delaying the demonstration long enough for the Sergeants and Warrant Officers (who shared the Mess) to down a few pints and thus blunt their critical faculties. I thought up a few authentic (and some less than authentic) tests of suggestibility which I would try out on them in order to select the best possible candidate. This would have the effect of adding a bit of 'magic' to the proceedings and giving me a chance to make an impromptu assessment of the most likely candidate for my demonstration.

The final test was when everybody, including our Drill Sergeant, was sitting round in an attentive half-circle and I asked them to clasp their hands on top of their heads. Pausing for dramatic effect, I then suggested that some of them would, when I gave the word, find it almost impossible to remove their hands. Earlier I had noticed some signs of high suggestibility in a certain Warrant Officer, so, fixing him with my beady eye, I gave the word.

It was hard not to show my relief when his hands remained firmly clasped on his pate even after his ribald mates noticed this, noisily. It gave me a chance further to enhance the atmosphere by demanding complete silence while the subject (whose permission I sought rather over-officiously) was put into a trance. He drifted off most satisfactorily. We agreed, after the subject was quietly 'sleeping' in his chair, that the signal words would be 'Rule Britannia!' and the behavioural response would be for the WO to drop his pants. The subject was primed in his hypnotic state, wakened up, and a minute later one of the Sergeants exclaimed 'Rule Britannia!' Looking around rather sheepishly, my subject turned into a corner of the Mess and began to lower his pants. I felt it decent to intervene at that point and relieve him of his embarrassment. The Drill Sergeant came up to me.

'You're a lucky little bastard that I decided to give you a chance. Now I don't want a f****** word of this to get out from these four walls, d'ye hear, Airman?' But in spite of this firm admonition, he still had the decency to buy me a pint! My report to the Goons was simply to the effect that my venture had been successful. I was cheered and took the chance to remind them that they too owed me a pint! I saw the WO about the camp several times before we were posted elsewhere but he seemed reluctant to meet my eye.

It was an amazing fact that, by the time for 'Passing Out' from recruit training, not only had we developed an unnatural desire to be the smartest, best-drilled Flight on the Parade, the 'Banner' carriers, teeming with marksmen, athletes and natural killers, but all of us had avoided any sort of illness beyond the dreaded 'virus alcoholis' of early Sunday mornings. One not insignificant reason for this was that reporting on

'Sick Parade' was a matter of such tedium and complication that one's own funeral would have been easier to arrange.

It was well understood that Drill Sergeants and Corporals felt entitled to draw upon the 'expertise' of any of their charges who happened to have skills appropriate to the task – and sometimes not so appropriate. Little AC2 Balls who had entertained us in various ways on the parade ground, was in fact a skilled motor mechanic and it was inevitable therefore that much of his 'free time' would be spent draped over the bonnet of the Corporal's clapped-out Morris Minor. Gerry Humphries in our hut, who happened to be a barrister in 'real life', was frequently drawn aside by some anxiety stricken Sergeant, when he was more intent on grabbing some sausage and egg in the NAAFI, to advise on how to beat the debt collectors from 'the Clubbie' book or to advise on how much might have to be paid out when some exasperated wife claimed the divorce she so richly deserved.

Thus it was that a strange Corporal from some other Flight appeared like a genie from a lamp in our hut one evening to quell, by his presence alone, the usual innocent blanco-ing and boot polishing conversation about football, sex, Corporals, sex, 48-hour passes and, of course, sex. While we 'stood by our beds' as we had to when any such superior being entered our hut, this bullet-headed, sharply creased, but ever so slightly hesitant paragon of parade ground virtue stalked from bed to bed peering at the little buff cards above the bunks until he found one with an entry under 'Civilian occupation' which he couldn't quite read. 746 Clark was duly interrogated.

'Zis yer bed, Airman?'

'Yes, Corporal.'

'You're a fyskol … a physochol … you're the nearest f****** thing we've got to a doctor in this hut?'

'If you say so, Corporal'.

I waited for him to show me his operation scar.

'Follow me!'

A short and wordless quick march led to the little room which was his worldly home at the end of another Flight's hut. As he carefully closed the door behind me, I shut from my consciousness fleeting, unformed but perceptible fears about being assaulted by a sado-masochistic homosexual. Although a certain RAF Station had something of a name for such activities, RAF Kirkham was not, so far as local lore had it, one of these. Was I suspected of being the one responsible for totally dismantling our own former Corporal's bed (every wire from every spring) one night while he enjoyed the fleshpots of Blackpool? Was awful retribution at hand? Was he 'doing a job' for the WO I had hypnotised? But there was no acolyte there to do his bidding and with my new-found skills in hand-to-hand combat, I thought I might just manage him. But no! In what he no doubt thought was a gesture of deep humanity, he removed his cap and flung it on the bed.

'You know anyfing abaht pills, Airman?'

'A little. What sort of pills?'

'The kind yer can get to make a woman sick an' that to get 'er to 'ave a period ye knaow. I got this girl friend an' she says she's up the stick. My wife'll f****** murder me if she finds out. Corporal Smith says some of you F****** Professors would know wot to do.'

A trace of ambivalence about the implied flattery must have flickered over my features because I was quickly told that this was 'no f****** laughin' matter' and that I'd better keep my mouth shut about this conversation. However, I had to advise him to see the Station MO as my concerns were not pharmacological but with what went on between the ears rather than between the legs, and in both respects I was unaware of anything to interest me in him. Somewhat deflated both by my apparent lack of the requisite knowledge and by my lack of motivation, but unaware of the barb in my last comment, he summarily dismissed me.

A week later, it appeared that my signal unhelpfulness to that particular Corporal had not got around the Mess – perhaps for the most obvious of reasons. Another hefty bruiser of the same rank and trade appeared one evening to ask in his accustomed stentorian tones if any one of us among the 'FPs' was anything like a vet. Danny Daniels did look something like a vet, or at least like one of a vet's patients, but was in fact a schoolteacher, so he did not qualify. Again my polysyllabic profession stood trial and I was marched off, smirking to my mates at this new show of power, to yet another hut where, this time, a moribund fox terrier lay gasping its last in front of the Corporal's stove.

'That's my best pal, Airman, – worth more to me than the whole f****** lot of you wankers put together. I want you to sort him out – double time!'

Free association and dream analysis, all the rage at the Tavistock Clinic at this time, did not seem to offer too much help in situations like this. However, I did dredge my memories of physiology and common sense medicine and came up with the brainwave that the Corporal should grind down a couple of aspirins in warm milk and a tablespoonful of brandy and feed this to the poor hot-nosed wee brute. If it didn't help the dog, then it might allow it to die in peace and comfort.

It would be an exaggeration to suggest that the whole complement of our hut hung anxiously about the telephone waiting for the dread news of the hound's death, but there was at least a measure of relief on my part when the word came round later the next day that the dog had much improved and seemed likely to live. The Corporal was said to be 'chuffed'. He spoke to me a day or two later with something close to a smile. I pretended omnipotence but in fact wrote off my 'success' to spontaneous remission or an auto-immune reaction – the dog's recovery, I mean, not the Corporal's smile!

So it was that twelve tough weeks drew to an end. A short time before the final Parade in front of the Station Commander and his acolytes, we had reported to the Adjutant's office. There stood the Station Warrant Officer, a kind of Angel Gabriel whose main function was to endorse in ringing tones all the opprobrium heaped upon us by the Drill Sergeant and Corporals as well as to protect the 'Hoffisors' from anything likely to disturb their gins and tonic. He, along with, for once, one of these self-same 'Hoffisors' went through the process of allocating us all to our futures in the RAF. Many of the 'FPs', not unnaturally, were allocated to officer training as cadets destined to serve out their two years in the Education Branch. Others found themselves heading for the same OCTU (Officer Cadet Training Unit) as prospective Engineering or Accounts Officers.

Some of us with the right test results and A1G1 fitness records, even after the rigours of recruit training, were allocated to GD (General Duties, or the Branch involving flying duties). Our technical/flying training would be added to our officer training in a further protraction of the time during which we would not actually be useful for anything in the RAF. However, we were given little white plastic discs to affix behind our cap badges as soon as we arrived at our new posting. At one fell swoop we had moved from being addressed as 'Airman!' to 'Mr!' Only time would inform us of the hugely varied inflections it was possible to apply to that time-honoured mode of address. There were those who declared that this state of limbo between being an 'Airman' and a 'Sir' was a true Purgatory. There were times when we were inclined to concur.

A forty-eight-hour pass marked the transition from recruit training. After the formalities on the parade ground on our last day at RAF Kirkham, we used our Rail Warrants to visit home and/or girl friends just after Christmas in that cold winter of 1951/52.

For many of the 600 who had entered Padgate with us a couple of months before, the Passing Out Parade (nothing to do with fainting – though some did!) represented their *summa cum laude* in the RAF. In consequence, some of those with more local roots had invited their parents and friends to watch the proceedings and listen as the band blew raindrops and some of the notes of *The Dambusters' March* from their instruments. For their sakes at least, we all tried to make the parade the success our Drill Corporals and Sergeants had prayed for. The 'FPs' were, literally, shining examples, to say nothing of the immaculate blanco and sparkling toecaps, as they marched and counter-marched with rifles at a perfectly uniform slope, hair all perfect 'short back and sides' and every man jack of us quite capable, at last, of STANDING STILL when required.

To us, however, it represented the first splitting up of a band of men who had quickly formed quite close bonds of friendship and mutual support in the face of adversity. Make no mistake, these weeks were tough and testing for all of us – even the strongest, both mentally and physically. By then we were no longer surprised at how many poor young lads had succumbed to the pressures forced upon them and had opted out in the most irreversible way possible. Happily, none of us had done so. We had all survived our rites of passage, and as a number of us were still to be posted together for radar, fighter control and flying training, we awaited notice of our new postings with more equanimity.

Plate 5: Passing Out Parade of a Flight of recruits at RAF Wilmslow in May 1952, six months after the writer's at RAF Kirkham (D McNeill)

CHAPTER 4

Cadets

RAF Middle Wallop nestled between two pubs and ancient Danebury Hill in deepest Wiltshire. It was a grass airfield of Battle of Britain vintage and still, on my arrival, buzzed with the radial piston engines of a miscellany of Anson, Harvard and Oxford training aircraft. There was even, one day, a visiting Tiger Moth. The air was rank with the soon to become familiar, and to some, not unpleasant, smell of burnt aviation fuel. It contrasted oddly with the sweeter, gentler odours of honeysuckle blossom and climbing roses which filled the villages later in the year. Nevertheless, it gave its own kind of romance to our new tasks.

Oddly, the perimeter track was concrete paved but only the sodium vapour marker landing lights, which were movable to accommodate the prevailing wind, gave any indication as to where the runway of the day might be. A quick look at the windsock gave a clue and made sure you took off and landed into wind! When it blew from the northwest, several of us had an uncomfortably close view of the said Danebury Hill on the approach. In the latter days of our being at Middle Wallop, both our flying habits and our pursuit of the WAAFs were interfered with by some Army chaps who had started to use the airfield for learning to fly helicopters and light artillery spotter aircraft, Austers or Cessnas, I think. Little did I think then that my young brother Tom, who did his National Service in the Royal Artillery, would finish up there doing exactly that.

Rail warrants had been issued to us when we were told of our postings at Kirkham. Our move had therefore been accomplished by train, via Crewe, London and Andover. There we detrained to hunt for a bus in that bustling market town, so different from the bare greyness of Kirkham and the treeless wastes of the ranges by Morecambe Bay. Even in dead of winter, there was a geniality about the air. The sun was shining and a mile from the town we were skirting dense, if leafless, copses and admiring the clarity of quick running chalk streams, later in the year to be full of brown trout and watercress. Thatched cottages, characteristic, to a Scot, of archetypical rural England, were scattered about the few villages we passed through. The air was cool but without the dank bite of a Lancashire winter. There was plenty of room on the bus for our kit bags and other gear and we listened now to completely different accents from the locals.

Initially we had thought that someone was having us on when we read our destination on the travel warrants. Middle Wallop sounded like some mythical location for a Goon Show or the film set for some light-hearted rural romp produced by Ealing Studios.

There would be a pub swarming with 'local characters' – 'Ahrr, 'e be a bit soft in the 'ead, but we listens to 'im just the same!' There would be a noisy squire with a rotund beer belly endlessly organising the weekend cricket match. There would be a few heavily cardiganed, well-made but strident ladies of uncertain age pedalling by in their wellies on high, rusty bicycles to visit the vicar. Meanwhile, the odd Jersey cow would be quietly chewing the cud as it cunningly deposited soggy, greenish-brown, round skid-pans for the fielders on the village green come Saturday. There might even be one or, preferably, a dozen or so, pouting and nubile fair maidens lingering provocatively of an evening in the ivy-strewn lanes round the pub. We were not so far from the truth in some respects, but Middle Wallop was real enough, set in the rolling wolds of Wiltshire between the Upper and Nether Wallops. The locals of both sexes, however, young and old, were old hands at sussing out the RAF lads and successfully avoided our worst excesses – most of the time.

The switch from raw recruits to a sort of intermediate stage was not marked by anything very tangible. For the next few months we would shuttle from Middle Wallop to Spitalgate and Cranwell, gradually acquiring all the new skills King and Country required of us. Here, there was a slightly more confident and worldly-wise air about us as we reported at the Guardroom at the gate of our new Station just as there was a more relaxed and human approach to us from the other side of the desk from the Regular who directed us to our quarters. We walked, smartly, in twos or threes rather than marched under the unremitting aegis of any two-striped martinet. We saw more officers than we ever had up to now – and had to get used to flashing up a smart salute (promptly returned) when they hove in sight. Several of them were about our own age and there was the odd 'brown job' or 'pongo' (an Army man). Together with the sight and sound of the aircraft on the ground and in the air, it all created a sense of our being in a far more business-like and properly RAF setting. Most of us were well pleased with that.

Plate 6: The 'F**** Professors' soon after arrival at RAF Middle Wallop, 1952. The author is on the extreme left of the middle row, apparently sound asleep** (author)

We were greatly taken with the modern (for that time) H-blocks with two storeys which accommodated us, the personal lockers with locks and keys, the central heating (no great black cast-iron monster of a stove to black lead). The 'H' blocks were so-called because of their plan view when looked at from the air. They were entered by double swing doors midway along the verticals of the 'H', the cross-piece of the 'H' being ablutions, laundry rooms, stores and so on for cleaning materials, while the four limbs of the 'H' were the actual living accommodation. Certainly, we still had to bull up the linoleum on the billet floor and we still skated around on blanket 'pads', but there was more bed space and twenty to a billet. The 'bed-space' was, for anyone in the Armed Services, one's sacrosanct domain. This small area containing one's bed, wardrobe and locker and about three feet of floor on one side of the bed was yours. Nobody set foot on it but by invitation. Even the Corporals and Sergeants would keep to the middle of the floor when addressing you within the billet, with the exception of kit inspections.

Upstairs, which my pals and I occupied, was a simple replication of downstairs. It was all a lot more salubrious than Kirkham and there were even plugs in the sinks! We had wardrobes for our greatcoats and best blues rather than just a hook behind the bed and there was nearly always hot water. Bull nights still occurred, but were seldom more than once a week and we went about our business on these more jovially. The joviality usually took the form of our re-enacting, badly, elements from our most recent favourite sketches from the *Goon Show* or our attempts at choral singing – swirling descants from classics like *Eskimo Nell* or *The Ball o' Kirriemuir*. Impromptu new verses, appropriately scatological and full of sexual metaphor, were occasionally created on the spot, with barely noticeable errors in the scansion. Bull nights, however, had now become necessities for a clean and ordered life rather than punitive occasions.

Best of all, when we looked out of the windows, some of the passers-by were actually WAAFs! Their quality and reputations varied greatly, so we were to learn, but at least a regular glimpse of the feminine form and a chance to fraternise, in perhaps a less than brotherly way, with some of them in the NAAFI or the village pubs of an evening made a welcome change from the monk-like existence of Recruit Training Camp. Like many monks, all we finished up with were a few dirty habits. We would speculate, in what would now be seen as a very politically incorrect and entirely male chauvinist way, as to whether the WAAFs who wore slacks had good legs or not, and how it could be that some of them could make even the uninspired working uniform look quite sexy, whilst others, walking out in even their 'best blues', could fail so miserably to create the same impression. Endless discussion as to whether it was a matter of 'body' or 'mind' failed to lead us to any definitive conclusion. It seldom occurred to us that the self-same WAAFs probably ran the rule over some of us in exactly the same way.

The other novelty of being in a trade or skills' training camp as distinct from being simply on 'square-bashing' was that we got out and about at weekends and came into line for the occasional forty-eight-hour pass when we could get home if we wished and were near enough, or perhaps go up to London and spend a night at the Union Jack Club. The latter was a godsend to lads from the more northern extremities of the UK who could not actually get to Stornoway or Thurso, or Banff for that matter, and back within forty-eight hours. The Club was open to all non-commissioned ranks of the Services and offered the usual amenities and a comfortable room for a very reasonable charge.

George Forty, in his book, *Called Up*, has told how, in the first fifty years since it was founded by King Edward VII in 1907, the Club, near Waterloo, catered for nine million guests. I seem to remember that in 1951/2 it cost about 5/- (25p) for a room for the night and breakfast. It was open to all the Services and home-based troops could stay for up to fourteen nights. Troops from abroad could stay for twice as long. One memorable feature was a complete roll of all holders of the VC in the Memorial corridor.

When we did get out of camp and into the village at weekends, rather than go further afield, one of the most frequented of the pubs in the Wallops was owned and run by the former Norwegian Olympic skating champion, Sonja Henie, and her husband. Even then, we still thought she was a glamorous and charming woman and tried to behave ourselves a bit better than usual. That was none too difficult as we had so little cash and a few half pints of bitter was all we could aspire to on any one occasion.

The only times we got ourselves a shade over-lubricated were when we took the bus into Andover some Saturday nights and there the general conviviality (with or without WAAFs) was facilitated by a sturdy potion described as scrumpy. It tasted fine enough although it had the look of an early morning Sickbay sample full of casts and protein. After a couple of jars we reckoned it was only bits of apple. The locals, however, attempted to persuade us that all manner of strange additions (mostly small dead animals) were habitually introduced to the brew at some stage well before it had properly matured for drinking. We were never in the area when the cider apples were being picked, but we did, from time to time, cast a paranoid eye or two over the orchards as we passed in the bus or the RAF three-ton Bedford trucks we were sometimes ferried about in. It was not impossible that, amid the leafy detritus and dead grasses under the trees that we could see, the odd carcase of mouse or rat might also go to the presses with the fruit. Though sceptical, we fostered the mythology, especially when introducing some newcomers to the Station and, in due course, the pubs. Strange, weird and wonderful effects, mainly on potency or on the drink's capacity to effect very fancy effects on the inebriate, were ascribed to the beverage with or without its organic supplements. We all swore to look out for each other at the end of the night, to ensure we all got on the last bus, and, not least, to avoid the unwelcome attentions of the White-caps, or 'Snoops' as they were sometimes called.

The tough physical life we had led at recruit training camp now gave way to a more regular and, in many ways, more civilised routine. We actually had a timetable for a week set out with a detailed programme of lectures, demonstrations, practical sessions, flying time, physical education, ground combat training and even the odd 'study hour' for 'revision'. The attitude of our bosses of all ranks was now quite different. We were there to learn, to waste neither our time nor theirs, and while some of the instructors remained pretty peremptory and cool, most were clearly keen for us to grasp what they were on about and were ready to answer reasonable questions with equally reasonable patience. Lecturers of varying seniority and intellectual impressiveness explained, for example, the mysteries of radiation lobes in metric and centimetric radar arrays, hydraulic and other control systems in various aircraft, general aerodynamics and the principles of flight, meteorology, navigation, radio communications and a curious subject called airmanship.

Much of this was replicated at a somewhat higher standard at RAF Spitalgate and Cranwell a month or two later, but for the moment, our structured days of study and learning new skills were a welcome change from the hectic and often pointless physical activity of Kirkham. Not that there wasn't something of the latter at Middle Wallop either! On the regular Wednesday afternoon sports' hours (except when the weather was good for flying) we were still committed to regular training for athletics, cross-country or football (in my own case) and some of the rest of us played rugger, after a fashion. That applied to those of us who had had sporting habits at university or elsewhere and still saw some merit in maintaining our fitness at a high level. Most, however, found ways of skiving off. One classic technique, exercised by some, if I may put it that way, was to claim an interest in 'circuit training' in the gym, toddle off there with a pair of plimsolls and a packet of fags and then maintain an easy-going circuit of the changing rooms, the bogs and an occasional recce of the gym itself to see that there were enough enthusiastic 'others' sweating away to ensure that specific faces would not be missed.

As time went on through the spring of 1952, it became apparent to one or two of us (having suffered at the shin-hacking and body-checking that purported to be soccer matches) that prowess of any sort in some sports could become the best way of all of skiving. Skiving was the fine art of evading regular, and often noxious duties by engaging in some sort of ploy which made it seem that one was heavily involved in something vital to the Station's activities but which could not be easily checked up on by anybody in authority. It was a skill at which many National Servicemen became expert. Some authorities maintained that, in its purest form, it involved nothing more complex than walking about briskly, going nowhere in particular and coming from nowhere in particular, with an important-looking piece of paper in one's hand.

As we patched up our bleeding shins in the showers after the game, we heard then that several of the teams we had been playing with (and against) were footballers, who, prior to being called up, had been playing, either as schoolboy signings or as full professionals, for Football League teams in several of the main English and Scottish Divisions. They had very quickly been identified by the staff as having great value to the Station's prestige on the sports' field and had already been marked down for inter-Station (and in due course, inter-Group and inter-Command) competition. Once thus identified, they were excused, they told us, all manner of tedious RAF duties in the interests of keeping up their training for the weekend match against RAF Cottesmore, Upavon, North Weald, or whatever. That news quickly confirmed my intention, and that of a couple of others, to take our athletics training a bit more seriously. We became careful to ensure that the PTI Officer noticed us both in the gym and on the track.

To my retrospective regret, I failed to take the opportunity to learn to play squash at Middle Wallop. There were a couple of courts on the Station and we were told that the Wing Commander (Flying) was very keen on us all playing at least once a week and that he was reputed to examine the court booking book to establish which of his 'young men' was taking the hint to get in his good books. Unfortunately, the Regular Officers on the Station seemed to have all the best times booked and we got fed up trailing all the way to the courts to find no times when we were off duty and the courts available, so I never learned the game till I returned to work in Scotland in the late 1960s. What we did do, however, was to hedge our bets by signing up our bookings in our own names but letting some others of our pals, who weren't particularly bothered whether they played or not, on to the court to pat about a ball or two instead!

In spite of all that, perhaps the hardest physical activity we were engaged in while at Middle Wallop took place just after we had returned from what was, I think, our first forty-eight-hour pass. There had been an unusually heavy snowfall, at least for that part of the world, and all the roads around and through the Wiltshire wolds were filled with drifted snow. Buses and trains had come to a standstill and we were picked up from Andover in a mixture of three-ton Bedfords and half-tracks from the RAF Regiment. No sooner had we expressed our gratitude to them for fetching us so thoughtfully than the Duty Officer had us paraded in denims on the square.

'Right, you lot, you will all be suitably refreshed from your weekend in the bosoms ... of your families' (said with a lift of the eyebrow) 'so you will now abandon your usual quest after knowledge and skill and do something really useful for a change!' He paused for effect as we heard some strange rattlings from the back of one of the trucks. 'You all think these white flashes behind your cap badges indicate that you are Cadets, don't you?' he asked rhetorically. Another calculated pause. 'No. You're wrong again. They mean that you are on snow clearing duty. You are going to earn the undying gratitude of the people of Wiltshire by systematically removing all the snow from the road from here to Andover – if necessary; and the Flight Sergeant and I are going to ensure that you will do it properly. Over to you, Flight!'

The Flight Sergeant was not messing about. In two minutes flat, one of the three-tonners had rumbled up with the source of the mysterious rattling noises aboard. It turned out to be a loose pile of several score of broad bladed shovels from stores. We selected one apiece. We noted gloomily that they were heavy even with nothing in them. Now that we were suitably armed, the Flight Sergeant piled us back on to the vehicles and we were out through the main gates again in a flash and heading, not for The George or any of the other local hostelries but for the most deeply filled byways of beautiful (white) Wiltshire.

The sparkling Christmas-card scene was then defiled by the rude and heathen soldiery who were left in no doubt by those in charge that they would be swinging their shovels at the snow drifts 'all bloody day until the road is black again from here to Andover!' Neither the squash-players, the footballers, nor the runners were exercising the right muscle groups at all. The Sergeants stretched their vocal chords and we ricked our backs heaving at snow that, as the day went on, got heavier and heavier as it began to melt in the low sun. Given the chance to take in all the charms of tree branches swinging heavy with diamond studded snow fleeces, the blue-white convolutions of wind-blown cornices over the hedgerows and the shimmering confetti as pines discarded, under gentle persuasion of the breeze, the snowflake decorations from their needles, more poetic souls than us would have lapsed into Wordsworthian reverie.

The reality was that, starting the seemingly impossible task with shivers of cold, we soon fluctuated between becoming sweaty and hot from our exertions and freezing again when we stopped for a cup of tea and a 'wad' (sandwich) which was dispensed every two hours or so from one of the trucks. We inclined to dark mutterings about the staff who would normally have been instructing us in warm hangars and classrooms. They were probably idly scrutinising the tabloids in their respective Messes over innumerable cups of coffee and thanking their lucky stars that the weather precluded any flying (the snow was too deep to let any aircraft take off) and that all the trainees were doing the work of the Wiltshire County Council. More snow fell that night, but not enough to undo all of our labours, and by the morning of the next day we had done enough to let the official Roads Department snow ploughs take over. No doubt the CO got a warm letter of thanks from some senior bum-polisher at Council HQ. If he did, its contents remained unknown to us.

The unexpected snow-clearing apart, a great deal of our normal time was taken up learning about ground and airborne radar, VHF communication, and aircraft performance in different flying conditions, at different altitudes and at different speeds. To that end, we would spend many hours in GCI (Ground Controlled Interception) cabins watching the persistently rotating ghostly greenish-yellow radii of the Plan Position Indicator tubes (PPIs) in darkness while the little greenish-yellow sausages about three-quarters of a centimetre long traced by the scanner represented aircraft going about their lawful business in the sky. Crackly VHF radio messages were exchanged by pilots and controllers. We students had some difficulty in deciphering accurately the exact contents of these communications then, although it was a skill we were to develop quickly. But at least the spells in the control cabin were a practical learning experience and the whole atmosphere was filled with a satisfyingly 'operational' ambience.

Hours and hours had had to be borne, prior to that, laboriously listening to our (possibly equally bored) lecturers and writing detailed notes and diagrams about the principles of radar (an acronym of 'radio detection and ranging'). Coming from the north of Scotland, I was well aware of the early work on radar by Robert Watson Watt from Brechin, later to be knighted in 1942, and a near contemporary of my father.

Watson Watt was a graduate of St Andrews University who had subsequently taught at University College, Dundee. Other than that, he had largely worked in a variety of government positions from the period of World War One until 1952. His first work was as a meteorologist. In that context he became interested in constructing devices for locating thunderstorms. In fact, the general public were much less aware of his work in developing a cathode-ray direction finder for studying atmospheric phenomena than it was later to become of his development of radar. It was only when working at the National Physical Laboratory as Head of its radio department that he turned to work on the radio location of objects in the atmosphere. As early as four years before World War Two broke out, he had succeeded in locating aircraft seventy or seventy-five miles away by directing radio waves at them and then measuring the time it took for the reflected wave to return to his receivers alongside the transmitters. He died in Inverness at the ripe old age of 81 in 1973.

Although Watson Watt has probably rightly been seen as the inventor of radar proper, the origins of his work probably derive from the experiments of Heinrich Hertz, the German physicist who proved that radio waves not only existed as characteristic forms of radiated energy but demonstrated that they behaved just like light waves, especially in their capacity to be reflected, just as images (light) can be reflected from a mirror. This particular analogy was much beloved by our tutors.

'Don't all of you think that we were the only side to have some notion of what radio detection of aircraft might be all about!' would intone our instructors.

'During the early 1930s, not only ourselves and the USA but also France, Germany and the Soviets were carrying out the first experiments in developing radar for military purposes. The main differences between our approaches and theirs were in motivation and pragmatism. So far as the first of these was concerned, the government encouraged the research from 1935 to 1938 because it was convinced that war was on the way very shortly. As for the second, Robert Watson Watt was enough of a pragmatist to realise that the apparatus which he had developed may not have been a fully perfected system, but that it was something that worked and was currently available. He saw no merit in striving for an ideal solution which might arrive a couple of years too late.'

This sort of quality lecturing was far beyond anything we had enjoyed at RAF Kirkham. It actually made us listen reasonably carefully to what we were being taught and gave context to the more technical details that followed. Our notebooks filled with little diagrams of the patterns of radiation (lobes, as they were called by our instructors) of the various types of radar at the time.

A little less than a year before war actually broke out, Britain had set up what was described (for no clear reason that any of us could ever discover) as the Chain Home radar system. This consisted of sets of huge, and very obvious, aerial arrays set up on tall and relatively heavily built pylons at various points along the most vulnerable coasts. The signals they transmitted/received were at about 30MHz, in the short wave, high frequency band – quite low frequencies for radar when compared to later developments or even when compared with some of the German and Soviet radars of the time which were around 75MHz (in the VHF band). It was ironic that the Germans had actually developed slightly further with their radar than any other country early in the war but they stopped all development of this late in 1940 because they thought that the war would soon be over. They had actually installed some radar on the ground and in at least one of their pocket battleships by 1936, but events did not turn out as expected and by the time the Germans had realised their mistake, it was too late to catch up.

Nearly all the successful radars that were developed early in World War One were not only ground based, rather than carried on aircraft or ships, but they all operated in the VHF band below about 200 megacycles.

'What, gentlemen, is the biggest problem with radar that operates at such frequencies?' The Flight Lieutenant Engineer cast his eyes round the class, hopefully searching our faces for some small glimmer of understanding. We gulped and cast surreptitious glances at our hastily scrawled notes. I tried to remember some of the stuff I had gleaned as a schoolboy at a time when making one's own small radio receivers was all the rage. Since nobody was essaying any answer, I had a go.

'VHF frequencies have only broad beam widths?' – this with a quiver of uncertainty and a rising inflection.

'Aha, so we're not all totally asleep, are we?' quoth the instructor. 'That is true, Clark. But there is more, is there not?'

Nobody was that awake.

Plate 7: This old cigarette card illustration shows the early sound detection apparatus in action about the beginning of the war. There was hope that it might be used in conjunction with searchlights to pinpoint the position of enemy aircraft but was of low reliability and depended very much on the individual skill of the operator.

'Remember, narrow beam widths are likely to give you greater accuracy, better resolution and will minimise ground echoes. Secondly,' and he flourished his notes before us, 'the VHF portion of the electromagnetic spectrum does not permit the bandwidths required for the short pulses that allow greater accuracy in assessing the determination of distance. The beam width of a fixed size antenna is inversely proportional to the radar frequency. I shall ask you all this tomorrow and by then you WILL know it, or I'll want to know the reason why!'

We were in due course to move from an understanding of what might have been called metric radar to centimetric radar (which was airborne as well as ground based) and which, because it used UHF (ultra high frequencies) was very narrow beamed and accurate and allowed us to look at 'spots' rather than 'sausages' on our radar screens or PPIs (Plan Position Indicators).

The two main operational night fighter jets of the 1951–2 era were the Vampire NF10, a single-engined, twin tail-boomed De Havilland model and the Gloster Meteor NF11, a twin-engined, more orthodox-looking variant of the Meteor 8 day fighter version. Unlike the single crewed day fighters, however, these aircraft carried two of a crew, pilot and navigator/radar operator, side-by-side in the former and tandem in the latter. Both carried then the AI Mark 10 airborne radar sets which were centimetric though relatively short ranged. It was the duty of the fighter controllers in the GCI on the ground to vector these aircraft close enough to the enemy for their airborne radar to take over for the closing mile or two.

Fighter control techniques really emerged as a means of tactical fighter management in the year or so immediately preceding World War Two. It had originally depended on information about enemy aircraft movements being collated from a number of relatively unreliable sources such as directional sound detectors and the ears and eyes of the members of the Royal Observer Corps. This is in no way to imply that the latter were in any way guilty of dereliction of duty. On the contrary, the men, women and youths, originally volunteers and only later incorporated as a formal arm of the Services cognate with the ARP and Fire Services, who manned their posts in all weathers day and night for the whole of the war, were intensely enthusiastic. They would endlessly revise their aircraft recognition skills, just as the writer and his pals had done as boys during the war, quizzing each other with printed silhouettes and solid models of German, Italian and Japanese aircraft. The chances of any of the last two appearing in British airspace were about the same as of winning the National Lottery, but they were not deterred. They would check their binoculars and the simple pelorus they used to get height and azimuth angles on any aircraft they could see, and laboriously record even friendly aircraft that passed overhead.

The problem was that human hearing is not good at locating direction accurately, especially in poor weather conditions such as in rain or gales. The average British climate too, with frequent partial or complete overcast, meant that clear visual sightings and identification of aircraft at almost any height were relatively rare. Nevertheless, when conditions were good enough, the ROC reports received by the Fighter Control Units and Sector Commanders were often more accurate than were the relatively primitive radar reports. Because Observer Corps posts were scattered every few miles across country, they could at least triangulate with their peloruses – or should it be pelori? – and get angles of elevation which would give accurate heights on raiding aircraft. The difficulty was that those evaluating the reports had to judge whether the Observers had triangulated on the same aircraft!

Radar then was quite inaccurate in every aspect except that of getting distance right. Estimates of height and relative angle to the radar receivers were much less dependable. Air combat is of course three dimensional and the pilots of the 1940s could be seriously frustrated by being vectored on to a plot, only to find that the enemy aircraft were 5,000 feet, or worse still, 15,000 feet above them. Sound detectors were not much better than the unaided human ear since at times there might have been almost as many friendly aircraft as enemy aircraft in the given air space at the same time. The distractions of anti-aircraft and machine gun fire and sometimes exploding bombs, did not make the listeners' task any easier.

It was no small wonder then, that most scientific effort went into improving radar and soon the listening apparatus was discarded as a technique for locating enemy raids. Originally, however, there were significant difficulties encountered in the process of making radar signals available to both pilots in the air and to the controllers on the ground who were in radio contact with the aircraft. Firstly, the early radars were so sited that they could detect enemy planes approaching from the other side of the southern North Sea or the English Channel. Once the enemy was over Britain, the plot was lost until more radar stations were opened later in the war to look at the interior. Because the early radars were also essentially non-directional, it could be difficult to know whether signals were generated by aircraft, so to speak, in front of, or behind the radar arrays. A third difficulty was that communication between the radar stations, the ROC posts and the Fighter Control Officers was by telephone. Even with direct lines requiring no dialling, any messages took some minutes. They then had to be collated and assessed before a meaningful picture of the overall combat situation could be conveyed to the pilots in the air.

The first attempts to coordinate such information took place just prior to 1940 as well as during and after the Battle of Britain. Fighter Command was headquartered at Bentley Priory in Stanmore, Middlesex, where Lord Dowding was then in overall charge. There, policy and strategic matters involving the overall course of the air war preoccupied staff officers. For tactical purposes, authority was then passed down to Groups of several squadrons each, based at a variety of airfields within a defined geographical area. Within each Group, control of air activities was invested in a number of Sectors. Each Sector Controller, usually of up to Air Commodore rank, held the devolved day-to-day responsibility for maintaining their Sector aircraft and crews in readiness and coordinating control of these aircraft both on the ground and in the air. Sector Controllers, in turn, handed on the business of 'hands on' control of his fighters to the Duty Controllers at GCIs in their various 'holes in the ground', often several miles away from the Sector HQ. That was not necessarily always so but was often determined by having to site GCIs where the adjacent topography suited effective radar trans-mission/reception.

The coordination of the Sector's operational effort was effected in what was called the Filter Room. In that room, sometimes well underground, and earlier, simply a reinforced building above ground, the Sector Controllers would look down from a balcony on to a large plotting table marked out as a map of the relevant area with a superimposed grid, described as georef, which was replicated on the pilots' maps. The Georef system allowed positions to be defined by two letters and a series of numbers very much in the way that walkers and climbers now use Ordnance Survey maps to define their position using a six numeral reference of 'Eastings and Northings'.

On that table, RAF and, mostly, WAAF plotters would move small, differently coloured plaques representing both enemy raids of varying strength and the position of friendly fighters attempting to intercept. The plotters, commanded by a Filter Officer, would be accepting from their headsets information from both radar stations and the Royal Observer Corps outposts on the last known position of enemy aircraft. They would then, in the light of those messages, move their plaques on the table with long rods in the hope that the Controllers would gain some inkling of the current (or at least, recent) positions and thus the intentions of the raiding aircraft. It was well recognised, however, that there was likely, at best, to be a four minute delay between the information being generated and its finding its way on to the table, four minutes in which all the aircraft represented might have travelled some twenty to thirty miles. The plaques did carry some estimated height information but that was very uncertain in accuracy until several years after the war when height measuring (centimetric) radars were gradually perfected.

Plate 8: Operations' Room with plotters at the plotting table and controllers in the gallery above (Roy C Nesbit)

All this, relatively recent history to us then, was imparted in the course of our instruction at Middle Wallop, a one-time Sector Fighter Station during the 1940 Battle of Britain. We were probably using the self -same Filter table and Ops Room from which much of the Battle of

Britain had been fought just over ten years before. Rumour had it, because of the high level of partial unserviceability and breakdown, that we were aiso using much of the same radar and radio equipment! That last detail might have been apocryphal but the heavy involvement of Middle Wallop during WW2 is well documented elsewhere.

In Norman Gelb's book, *Scramble: a Narrative History of the Battle of Britain*, he quotes Wing Commander David Roberts, Sector Commander at Middle Wallop at the time:

'There was a fair bit of damage when Middle Wallop was hit. A stick of bombs came right across the hangar area. Two chaps were killed when shutting the doors of one of the hangars. One bomb hit an air raid shelter and killed a workman there. Two or three aircraft were hit on the ground and lost. Thank God, the Ops Room wasn't hit. It was only a wooden hut. I stayed there. I was controlling at the time and I had everything in the air. More raids were coming in and they had to be met. When the bombs came down near us, we all went flat on the floor. The WAAFs were under the table. My Flight Sergeant, the senior NCO in charge of the Ops Room said, 'This is where we're all on the same level, Sir!' (p 207)

Although Gelb's book was not yet written at the time we were at Middle Wallop, the very high activity level and historical significance of the Station had high impact value for us both in the Filter Room and in the GCI itself. Several of our instructors were ex-wartime flyers and some had been decorated. Additionally, our chief instructor was Squadron Leader 'Tealeaf' Holmes, a successful and respected Fighter Controller from wartime operations. A somewhat dry and sardonic man, he was so-called because of his addiction to a 'cuppa' when things were getting a bit hot and pressured in the GCI Unit. There was also something of a suggestion that when he lost a plot on his PPI, for technical or other reasons, he would look at the tea leaves in the bottom of his cup and by reading them he would magically fathom (usually with remarkable success, when the missing plot came up again) where in the sky the target and/or the controlled aircraft might then be.

For us normal mortals, until we were trained otherwise, the sudden loss of the plot was a major disaster and gave rise to huge anxieties and jittery messages to the pilot. Tealeaf and a number of other Controllers made it their business to introduce us to the techniques of

Fighter Control both at its ground level and in the air by having us fly later on practice interceptions under ground control (PIs). No teacups allowed.

Some of the difficulties experienced by controllers and aircrew alike during the war were still apparent to us new trainees when our time came to settle in to our hours of fighter control practice in the GCI cabins. One in particular caused problems when several aircraft were simultaneously in the air and being controlled from the same GCI. That was related to the fact that when pilots took off from their airfield, they would switch from the local (Tower) airfield control radio frequency to what was called Sector control frequency. Although other frequencies were available to pilots for inter-aircraft communication and for other purposes, the Sector control frequency would sometimes be used for getting navigational fixes as well as for control purposes. VHF radio is such that if one pilot is transmitting on the frequency, no one else can also transmit and be heard simultaneously and no-one else can hear the transmissions of any other person such as a controller. An auditory 'mess' of bleeps, whistles and garbled speech ensues. Hence the disciplines of good VHF radio habits were immediately instilled into us and the hazards of not observing these rituals would become immediately very real to us, in practice, both on the ground and in the air. It also meant that pilots and controllers had to fit in their messages to each other between the conversations of all the other pilots and controllers using the same frequency. Pilot to pilot conversations could of course take place on another channel, though they were not expected to be using these much, if at all, whilst under GCI control.

Looking back from the later experience of operational stations and GCIs in particular, it is apparent that we were let into the skills and secrets of fighter control activities in a very gentle manner. The number of aircraft involved, the relatively slow speed of these and the simple exercises we were expected to understand and carry out were ten times easier than the realities of life with an operational night fighter squadron and active GCI. A couple of plotter's PPIs and two more for the controllers were all that was necessary to furnish the control cabin at Middle Wallop. A pair of Airspeed Oxfords tooling around at about 110 knots at 8,000 feet with the 'target' aircraft holding a comfortably predictable and level flight track might not have been thought to present too many problems to young, keen and healthy cadets such as ourselves. That was what we thought!

Tealeaf or one of his Flight Lieutenant controllers would patiently explain to a couple of us at a time the significance of the repositioning of the half-inch long, slightly curved green blips on the PPI each time the radial green arm representing the scanning aerial rotated round the circular PPI – like a 20" cathode ray tube. With cool, accurate and impeccably intoned R/T patter he would call up the pilots on the VHF and set up the first interception. The GCI would have had a code name, as would all the aircraft in the Flights or squadrons concerned. It would have gone something like this. (Tealeaf speaking, coded call-signs are fictional.)

'Snowbird 17, Snowbird 17, this is Groundsel, this is Groundsel – do you read? Over.' He released his 'Transmit' key.

'Groundsel, Groundsel, Snowbird 17 reading you strength 5. Over.' This response could have been heard in the controller's earphones but for training and other purposes it was broadcast on a loudspeaker in the cabin – a loudspeaker which also broadcast any other VHF messages on the same channel, perhaps from aircraft with nothing to do with our little venture.

'Snowbird 17, Groundsel, vector 126°, make angels 9.5 Over.'

'Groundsel, Snowbird 17 – Roger, vector 126, angels 9.5 Out.'

Then, in a minute or so, old Tealeaf would suddenly come all alert and crouch more determinedly over the PPI. The VHF crackled incessantly with his and other messages and we watched wide-eyed as the blips representing target and hunter aircraft were, by skilful adjustments of height, course and speed, instructed by the controller, brought from transverse courses perhaps fifteen miles apart, to coincide as one blip with both aircraft on the same course and at the same height. At this point the pilot, now in visual contact with his target aircraft, would call:

'Groundsel, Snowbird 17, enemy in sight, Tally-ho!' and the old maestro would push his chair back with a trace of arrogance and intone to us greenhorns.

'Right. Who's first? Get into that seat and see if you can do the next one without killing some of your pals up there and making an ass of yourself in public!'

The worldly-wise Senior Aircraftmen height-reader and plotters in the cabin smirked knowingly. They'd seen this all before with previous courses. On our part, the sudden rush to the PPI with its bank of switches and knobs including the radio switch in front of it would have come nowhere near to beating Marie Antoinette had she been asked voluntarily to turn up at the scaffold in a tumbrel. For one thing, two of our number were up there in the Oxfords at the other end of the radio and we had to live with them in the billet a few hours later. If we made a dog's breakfast of it, not only would it become all too apparent from their viewpoint in the air, but they would be much more scathing in their comments on our performance than was even old Tealeaf. Tealeaf promptly eradicated our natural modesty.

'Mister Clark, I hear you're a bit of a smart-arse in class. Plant your bum on that seat at Console 1. You've got 17 (pronounced 'one-seven') as target aircraft this time. He's ten miles west of Salisbury and tracking 055. Snowbird 18 is on the control frequency. He's at angels 11 and tracking 190, south of Romsey. He's all yours.' He, and the other three temporarily relieved cadets made way, a trifle over-willingly, I thought, for the new controller.

Suddenly I was aware of two things. First, I had not been to the bog for hours, and second, Snowbird 18 was just disappearing off the southern edge of the PPI on its present calibration. It would all just be too much if I lost him before the game had even started.

'Snowbird One-eight, Snowbird One-eight, this is Groundsel. Turn on to 010.'

Before the pilot had even time to answer, Tealeaf was on to me.

'Clark, Clark, how the hell do you know that the poor bastard has even heard you. Establish two-way communication first!'

So I start again.

'Snowbird 18, Snowbird 18. This is Groundsel. This is Groundsel. Do you read me? Over.' That was what we'd been taught in the classroom.

'Groundsel, Snowbird 18. Reading you strength 5. Over.'

'Snowbird 18, Groundsel. Vector 010. What is your present height? Over.'

'Groundsel, Snowbird 18. Port turn to vector 010. Angels 9. Out.' (Angels 9 meant he was at 9,000 feet.)

In initial establishment of radio contact all call-signs were repeated. After some messages they would be shortened to 'Groundsel' said once only and the aircraft would simply use the digits without the call-sign, i.e. '18' rather than 'Snowbird 18'. With the higher speeds involved with the aircraft we would be using operationally later in our careers (if we ever got through all these earlier stages) there simply would not be time for too much talk. Vectors, or courses to steer, were always given in degrees magnetic, corrected to take account of the compass variation assessed for the area in which flying was taking place, which at that time, in most of the UK, was about 10° west. This allowed the pilot to steer by his compass directly. Thus, flying true north would be vectoring 010° magnetic rather than 360°. Incidentally, for those not familiar with RT jargon, the use of the word 'Over' at the end of a message means a response from the receiver is required. The use of the word 'Out' means a response is not required and closes that particular little conversation.

Gradually, as I watched the other 'target' blip as the rotating aerial scanned the 360° of sky every few seconds, I established its track and got an approximate height from the airman or WAAF plotter on my left. Speed had to be estimated from the displacement of successive blips on every scan rotation and these displacements depended on the particular calibration of the tube at the time. A radius of the tube might represent anything from 100 miles to 10 miles or so. The controller was meant to establish his own calibration, by the use of appropriate switches, and estimate accordingly. The centre of the tube (PPI) represented the geographical position of the GCI and was usually blurred by 'ground echoes' from features in the near vicinity of the aerial. Ideally, one tried to arrange that the interception took place with the blips representing the target and interceptor aircraft somewhere halfway between the centre and the outer circumference of the tube. At least that was the story in training. Later, on an operational base, it was amazing how difficult that could be when one was trying to vector a 'gunned-up' night fighter on to some Russian 'Bear' bomber trying to nudge itself into our airspace north of Shetland. However, at Middle Wallop, they tried to break us in gently.

The ideal interception at that time was for the attacking aircraft to approach the 'enemy' ahead of, but at right angles to it, thus allowing for a 90° final turn calculated to bring the attacker on to the immediate tail of the target and either slightly higher or level with it. In daylight, the controller would hope also to attack from 'up sun' (to blind the target crew) and at night, when there was a moon, from 'down moon' (so as not to get the attacking aircraft silhouetted against the moon). Ideally, in daylight, if the attacking aircraft were approaching his quarry from the left side of the enemy's track, the attacker could be somewhat ahead of the target, and might expect to have the target appear first just in front of his starboard beam – at about 2 o'clock. That has nothing to do with the time of day. Relative positions of a target in relation to the observing pilot were described as if one were in the middle of a horizontal clock face. Thus, 12 o'clock would be directly ahead, 6 o'clock would be directly behind, 3 o'clock would be broad on the starboard beam and 9 o'clock would be on the port beam.

Looking back from our performance in operational conditions a year later, it became apparent how simplified were the conditions in which this elementary skill level was fostered. The training aircraft were slow, targets held their course, there were no electronic counter measures exercised by the targets, the airwaves were not cluttered with many other aircraft on the same frequency, on the whole the radars and VHF radios did not break down at vital moments and all the controllers and aircrews' thinking and planning could be spaced over perhaps two or three minutes rather than over a third of that, even just seconds.

Back at the controller's console in Middle Wallop, I went through the rituals of establishing contact with my pilot in 18 and turned him on to an initial course that, allowing for drift at his particular altitude, would direct him toward the theoretical point at which the target and attacking aircraft would converge if the target held its present course and my sequential vectors, height and speed instructions to 18 were accurately gauged and transmitted at exactly the right times.

It would be tedious to describe the difficulties one could get into in what would seem to an outsider to be basically a simple task. Suffice it to say that my, and even the brightest of my colleagues' efforts, initially resulted in some very fed up pilots and tracks on the PPI which had all the smoothness and easy curvature of a jigsaw cutter with Huntingdon's chorea. To our discomfiture, our R/T conversations were all recorded and the plots of both aircraft were similarly traced as spidery and wavering lines on the chart by the plotters for later scrutiny on paper. Sometimes we would forget that drift would vary at different heights with varying wind speeds and direction and yet advise our pilots to climb or dive from time to time without our checking by a glance at the Met board where daily wind speeds and directions were recorded at 5,000 foot and sometimes smaller intervals. Partly, this was because the control room was always completely dark but for the eerie glow of the tubes and small indicator lights on the various switches on the consoles. Mostly, however, it was due simply to our not being, at that stage, ready to assimilate all the data we required to do the job properly in the very short time we had to do so. Information overload was always one of the biggest challenges to both Fighter and Air Traffic controllers.

Often we would make our course corrections too small and too late to be effective or would ask the pilots to carry out some manoeuvre which, if they tried to comply, would have either ripped the wings off or burned out the engines. Most of our first efforts finished up as vain tail-chases by the attacking aircraft, well behind and often to one side of the target, and well out of gunfire range (we had no missiles in those days). No exultant 'Tally-ho!' greeted our final turn in. Tealeaf would sigh despairingly and threaten to get on the phone to Disneyland. 'Pluto or the Seven bloody Dwarves would do it better than you lot!' He had a number of variations on that theme.

Only our own experience in the air while our colleagues in the GCI committed these very same errors could facilitate our quick learning of what it was reasonable to ask a pilot to do in a particular aircraft, each type with its own particular performance characteristics. That was why, week about, we flew and were controlled and criticised the controllers, or controlled and criticised the flyers. Needless to say, most of us did eventually get our various skills sorted out although one or two suffered 'an early bath', as the footballers say, and were returned ignominiously to some more menial task as an AC2 pay clerk or plotter on another Station. *'Per ardua ad astra'* became for them *'sic transit gloria'*.

Unexpectedly, I was struck by the way smells have remained with me so long after these days at Middle Wallop. In the GCI cabins there was a peculiar mix of odours. Artificially ventilated, the controllers' cabins were, in spite of the fans, filled with a mix of the slightly exciting smell of overheating radios and radar consoles and the much less fascinating whiffs of a staler aroma from the damp oxters of anxious controllers and from various other bodily recesses of the plotters and technicians, bored by periods of inactivity interspersed with hectic action and overheated in their working battledress. Decent Chief Controllers usually allowed shirtsleeve order in the cabins.

The parachute shed had another smell again, of canvas chute covers and of the silk canopies which we drew from the shelves there and which we hoped we'd never have to use. We watched the slick WAAF parachute packers carefully but quickly and skilfully laying out, folding and packing the chutes, checking the cords and the pilot chute that sprung open and dragged the main canopy from its case. Depending on the aircraft we were flying, we might draw a chest pack (clipped on to the front of our Sutton harness if required but normally left in a rack in the side of the aircraft near to hand) or the more conventional 'bum hung' pack which, with an inflatable dinghy, we sat on as a cushion. Later, of course, when we were on an operational station, the aircraft, with the exception of the NF 10, which you were expected to invert and fall out of, carried ejector seats in which the chute and dinghy were integral. Even in the latter, however, some crews elected to wear a small dagger on their harness with which to stab an accidentally inflating dinghy in the cockpit. Night fighter cockpits afford very little spare space and there was always a slight chance that a sleeve or anything else might accidentally catch on the inflation cylinder when no emergency was present. If that happened, one might find the dinghy exploding into life between one's legs and trying to push forward the control column, perhaps lethally, unless it could be stabbed and thus deflated in time.

The characteristic smells of an active airfield, and the hangars especially, live on in the memories of nearly all who have experienced them. The air itself carried a residue of burnt aviation fuel and exhaust gases. The hangars were redolent of a compound of fabric dope (in those days), paint, oils of various consistencies, the sharp tang of recent welding, hydraulic fluids and hot metal. The aircraft cockpits carried something of these odours until they wheeled out as far as the end of the perimeter track. Then they themselves had their own smell – a kind of electrical/bakelite/camouflage paint mix, almost indefinable but quite characteristic. Of course, all these were put paid to as soon as our oxygen masks with their inbuilt intercom and radio microphones were on, for then only the rubbery overtones of these predominated.

The best part of fifty years on, it is difficult to remember at which point exactly in our training various subjects were taught us. Principles of flight, aircraft systems, meteorology, military history, air combat tactics, military law and current affairs (not the ones with girl friends) and so on jostle in the memory for precedence.

Of all of these, perhaps meteorology is the one that has been of most use and relevance in subsequent years. Adiabatic lapse rates, the significance of dew-point, characteristics of weather systems and the behaviour of weather fronts, interpretation of cloud patterns – all the subject of much hectic note-taking in 1952 – have stayed with me as a lasting interest, even when viewed from ground level. It says much for the competence of our lecturers that they could generate such interest and awareness in a relatively brief course. Perhaps the immediacy of the course's contents helped. To ground based souls, the indications of impending rain or snow might matter. Farmers and seamen might need to be more sophisticated about wind speeds or fog and factors such as frost and humidity, but only at ground level. In the air, however, wind shear becomes important and the awareness of how wind direction and strength could vary at different altitudes influences not only courses to steer but endurance and speed.

There were times in our lectures on the principles of flight when my mind would wander to the very first time I had ventured into the air near home in the North of Scotland in 1934 or thereabouts. The lecturer droned on ' … There are four key forces acting on an aircraft in straight and level flight: 'lift', an upward force; 'drag' a retarding force which is antagonistic to lift and accentuates the friction of the aircraft moving through the air; 'weight', the effect of gravity on the aircraft; and 'thrust', a forward acting force contributed by the engine. Lift depends on the aerofoil section and angle of attack, … '

It was a far cry from a muddy field near Macduff where Sir Alan Cobham's flying circus would occasionally put on a show. My parents argued about whether it was safe enough for both my wee brother and one or another of our parents to fly in the same plane simultaneously and whether the ten shillings per person (a lot of money in 1934!) was a reasonable expenditure on what, I have no doubt they thought, was a risky venture – but of high educational value! It was finally decided that my father and I should at least go first. We picked our way through the cow-pats to where this bi-plane with two engines was rocking gently in the summer breeze. I was later to discover that it was some version of the De Havilland Dragon Rapide, the structure of the fuselage being, it seemed to me then, all too flimsily made of fabric stretched over a slim metal frame.

The memory of my father strapping himself and me into our canvas and metal seats and being careful not to perforate the flapping canvas fuselage alongside us is still sharp. There was a faint incongruity in the sight of him still wearing his black Homburg hat and heavy long black overcoat, compared to the dashing pilot in his leather jacket and helmet. One or two other adventurous citizens sat in front of us but I was lucky to have a window seat and watched, intrigued, as we taxied down wind, turned and, with every joint, spar and strut rattling and creaking, we revved up, bumped and jarred our way down the field until, magically, everything suddenly became so much smoother, though not much less noisy, as we were airborne, and Dad told me we had already flown hundreds of times further than the Wright brothers in the moments of their first success little more than twenty or thirty years before.

We climbed over Macduff only to swoop down over Banff, my familiar hometown, and the Links where the normal Sunday crowds of that day were distracted from their paddling on the seashore to crane their necks at the sight of this aeroplane dodging and weaving overhead. A port turn over the distillery and the village of Whitehills and by then it was obvious that our ten bobs were running out for we soon headed back in a slow climb over the Hill o' Doune, then on to a down-wind leg, an easy turn on to finals and back to earth with more of the rattling, bumping and swaying as before. The engines were cut and my father started breathing again. I doubt if I saw it as quite such an adventure as did my father but it was still an experience of great significance to me and, in retrospect, well worth the ten bob!

My first flight in a twin-engined aircraft since then was consequently in one of the Middle Wallop Airspeed Oxfords. They had, unlike the De Havilland Dragon's in-line water/glycol cooled engines, twin radial, air-cooled engines of, for their era, fairly modest performance. The airframe was, however, very much sturdier, being of aluminium monocoque construction. Nothing flapped that shouldn't have when we took off. There was a slight sense of insecurity at first if you, as trainee, were in the right-hand cockpit seat since just to the right of the rudder bar, you could look straight down at the ground through a large Perspex 'bomb-aimer's/photographic' window in the floor. The instrument panel was, however, fairly straightforward with the usual six 'key instruments' of airspeed indicator, artificial horizon, altimeter on the top row and below that, the turn and slip indicator, directional gyro and rate of climb/descent indicator. The engine and radio dials and switches were simple, and trim wheel, throttles, flaps, undercarriage and mixture control levers fell easily to hand. Because both propellers rotated in the same direction, there was a tendency for the aircraft to yaw to the left. Many single-engine trained pilots used to grumble when converting to twins that there was just twice as much waiting to go wrong, but were in the end pleased enough to cope with the problems of asymmetric flying when they had an engine fail over mountains or sea.

Plate 9 Dragon Rapide similar to the one in which the author first flew (Forbes Law)

In any event, a key part of our training was this business of learning about control by ground radar and the experience of watching the effects in the air of good versus bad GCI control. For a couple of hours at a time, we would take off in pairs and climb laboriously to, say, 8,000 feet and head for a spot in the local airspace where the controllers' radar could 'see' us easily. Then we'd punch the button for the radio frequency chosen and call the GCI.

'Groundsel, Groundsel, this is Snowbird 22. Do you read? Over.'

'Snowbird 22. Groundsel. Reading you strength 4. Over.'

'Groundsel, Snowbird 22. Reading you strength 5, orbiting over (giving a Georef position) at angels 8. Request vector. Over.'

The clarity and strength of the radio signal was rated from 1 to 5 and 'angels' was simply the shorthand code for height in thousands of feet. Most practice PIs on a training unit, as distinct from when they were carried out on an operational unit, were done under VFR (Visual Flying Rules) and in daylight when one could look out and see what was going on. Massive increases in cloud in the course of the flight could lead to cancellation of the exercise since, with trainee controllers and perhaps bored or inexperienced pilots, the risk of collision in cloud was too great. The radar of the time was inexact and the apparent convergence of two plots on a PPI, because the plots were relatively large, could mean either that the aircraft were 500 yards apart or on top of each other. Even boring through hefty chunks of stratocumulus on a late afternoon could have you periodically craning necks and watching your wingtips for the approach of anything more solid than fly-shit when you knew the controller was in the later stages of an interception. With normal flight plans for 'cross-country' flying, low visibility in cloud mattered much less since planned height separations were at least 500 feet, dependent on the compass quadrant within which the direction of one's flight was taking place. Under immediate GCI control, however, these separations did not apply.

The merits of the exercise were that crews could actually observe the competence or (more commonly, early in the course) the incompetence of the controllers. This could be seen in terms of the space between the target and attacking aircraft after the vectors for the final turn-in had been given. The crews of the target aircraft were under orders to hold their course as given at the outset and the pilots of the 'attacking' aircraft were similarly under orders to keep scrupulously to the vectors given by the controllers, even though they might see that they were not going to work out. If you liked a controller and thought he 'had the makings', it might be possible for the 'target' aircraft to bend the odd vector by a few degrees without the ground radar picking it up too obviously so as to be able to give the 'attacker' a 'Tally-ho!' at the right time.

There were many occasions when a controller would mistime his instructions for the final turn in on to the target aircraft by just a few seconds and from the target aircraft flyer's point of view, what happened was that the 'attacking' aircraft would suddenly appear perhaps three or four hundred yards on the starboard or port beam flying parallel and possibly a couple of hundred feet above or below the 'target'. This was not satisfactory for if one translated this performance into the reality of vectoring in a night fighter on to a target, the beam width of its airborne radar would not be wide enough to pick out the target when both aircraft were flying parallel with each other. In cloud and pitch darkness, no target 'Contact' would be made with this sort of inaccuracy on the turn-in. In the contemporary scene, at the time of writing, this does not matter since modern airborne missiles will deal more than adequately with such a situation. In the 1950s, however, the knock down had to be achieved with only machine guns or cannon which required the attacking aircraft to get relatively near to the target and to close on it at an angle such that its airborne radar would pick it up satisfactorily and keep it 'locked on'.

The theory of good fighter control technique was that the controller, by detailed and accurate scrutiny of his PPI, would predict the impending course of the 'enemy' aircraft and attempt to give the intercepting pilot, then perhaps about fifteen miles away, a series of 'vectors' or compass courses which would bring him in from abeam and somewhat ahead of the target, flying nearly at right angles to the target's course until the final vectors would effect a 90° turn just at the right time and point in space for the attacking aircraft to come up behind the target at the end of the final turn. At that point, day fighters would have a visual contact and night fighters would be able to pick up the target on their airborne radar and proceed from there. On our operational units later on, we would learn other more exciting and varied interception techniques, but this was good enough for beginners. Since the assessment of the necessary vectors necessitated the second-to-second consideration of the two aircrafts' relative position in three dimensional space from an often erratic and none too accurate radar 'blip', it was not so easy as it might sound to the layman. Awareness of wind speeds and direction at different heights (to correct vectors for drift) as well as the flight limitations of the aircraft being used had to be taken into account by the controller in deciding his instructions to the pilot. Controller error might result in simply 'losing' an aircraft (geographically) or worse, putting the aircraft at serious risk of collision, especially at night or in total cloud.

Apart from the usual frustrations when the controllers would, sometimes in desperation because they knew they were already going to miss the interception, ask the aircrew to perform feats of aerobatics or demand levels of aircraft performance that the 'kites', as we called them, were utterly unable to cope with, these hours and hours of PIs were on the whole not unpleasant. The exchange of roles whereby we were more or less flying one day and controlling the next led to mutual appreciation of the difficulties and was also conducive to fast and well-reinforced learning of all the appropriate skills.

Moreover, it was by now moving into springtime in those southern extremities and the sparkling clarity of the air after a cold front, allied to a touch of new greenery in the land, made life on the ground, but especially in the air, pleasantly exhilarating. Our classroom work was now clearly geared to our improving skills. We had got to know several of the Regulars who serviced our aircraft in the hangars, the wireless operators who manned the D/F stations round about and we even took words of a generally friendly nature with such unlikely specimens as the SWO (Station Warrant Officer) and the catering staff. '*O tempora, o mores*!' Compared to square-bashing, this new life had much to commend it. We began to read books other than King's Regulations, Pilot's Notes and Radar Manuals. We spat, farted and swore less, didn't mind saying 'Sir' to officers nearly so much and caught the bus to Andover regularly on Saturdays for a few pints of scrumpy in the pubs.

Even in an Oxford, the transition from a lumbering and bumpy taxi over the grass of Middle Wallop to a noisy but smooth lift-off was thrilling. The slow climb into wispy stratus, relics of the morning mist, and, a couple of thousand feet higher, past white fluffy lumps of fair weather cumulus, gave a chance to practise one's map reading. A port turn, still climbing, over Danebury Hill and on towards Winchester one day, straight on toward Salisbury and the flashing red light at the top of its cathedral's elegant spire on another, would be our routine. With a few bumps, we would watch our shadow dodge over the swelling white bellies of the scattered cloud before ground detail was gradually lost and only the meanders of the river Test, a railway line or main highway like the A 303 could be reliably identified. Then the radio checks would be complete, we would have lumbered up to working height and were back in business … 'Groundsel, Groundsel, this is Snowbird 22 … '

Our elders and betters at that stage in our careers were generally kind to us in that they were disinclined to have us venture into the air if the weather was seriously problematic. Our worst moments usually came when a sudden deterioration in conditions late in our endurance might force us to fly at unexpectedly higher altitudes above ten-tenths cloud at a stage when both fuel and oxygen were getting low. Normally, most PIs at that stage in our training were done at around 8,000 to 10,000 feet when we could do without oxygen and were under VFR (Visual Flying Rules). We would recognise different controllers coming on the air from time to time, each with his characteristic VHF manner and style – some hesitant and timorous, some confident and brisk, some laid back and low key. There were eventual successes and failures from among these and we would do our best to fly the vectors they gave us. Sometimes we would hear either one of the qualified controllers or even old Tealeaf himself take over as some poor cadet got himself in a fankle having given a wrong height or a vector 10° in the wrong direction. On the whole, however, these sorties were uneventful and less boring than we sometimes claimed when back in the billet.

One notable occasion which subsequently left me with a few bad dreams (they're called 'post-traumatic stress flashbacks' now) occurred when. toward the end of one rather difficult session of PIs, the two of us crewing an Oxford became aware of a subtle but steady change in the cloud patterns. On the previous PI on which we had been the 'attack' aircraft, it had become all too apparent that as the vectors changed more rapidly in the course of our turn-in, so also had the broken cumulus that we had hardly noticed all afternoon begun to mount ever higher in great, billowing lumps. Below us, they had been sparkling white cotton wool in the sunlight. Now, however, we were beginning to bang and bump through a number of higher tops which suddenly lost their charm as the erstwhile white 'cotton wool' now swathed us in impenetrable grey – and knocked us about a bit into the bargain.

We advised Ground Control that we were now outside VFR (Visual Flying Rules) conditions and requested permission to climb above the 'clag'. Anxious to get as many PIs done as had been planned, they put us up another 1,000 feet. A quarter of an hour later we were having to climb again to keep in the clear. Worse still, there were now appearing all too few clear gaps through which we might descend in VFR (Visual Flying Rules) conditions.

Plate 10: An Airspeed Oxford of the type used at Middle Wallop (*Aeroplane*)

On the next PI, we were the 'target' aircraft, flying a fixed course given us by the Chief Controller. The boredom of doing so was relieved by our checking over the instruments and radio frequency boxes. It was then that we noticed that, having connected up our oxygen at 10,000 feet as required by safety, the gauges showed us to be already very low on that necessary commodity. Because it had not been thought that we would be above about 8,000 feet on that particular sortie, no less well above it as we were now, the ground crews had not loaded spare oxygen bottles and we were simply running on what was left from the previous day. That in itself did not worry us much because we were aware that we were probably on the last PI anyway and would be diving for base shortly.

We were now more in cloud than out of it at about 11,500 feet and it dawned on us that not only had we seen no sign of the 'attacker' but also that there had seemed to be a strange paucity of VHF 'traffic' on the radio. Our intercoms were working OK but nothing was heard from the ground. We keyed in a few, and then all, the other working frequencies and found the same gloomy silence. We called 'Groundsel'. Nothing. We called the Fixer frequency to get our position. Nothing. We called the sector frequency and the Tower. Still nothing. Then we noticed an acrid haze of smoke coming from the radio box behind us. The whole 'works' had overheated and burned out, so we had no radio, no way of telling the ground that we had none and we had only a sketchy notion of where we were over the ground. Worse still, not only was there no sign of the friendly bright yellow fuselage of the other Oxford, we were now flying on instruments (IFR) because the cloud had really bubbled up and we had the wipers going.

My pilot/instructor that day was an ex-wartime Pole whose name I had frequently seen written on the crew room blackboard and on his logbook but which, to this day, I still cannot spell properly. The notion that he might have been a Highlander was fostered by the fact that the first few letters were 'Mac' but the middle syllables were devoid of vowels and seemed to consist only of the harder consonants and finished with … czik. It was easier just to call him Jan.

'Kadett Clark', he addressed me rather gutturally as he juggled the controls against the now quite severe turbulence, 'do you see if zer ees flames in f****** TX/RX?' (as he was wont to call the radio unit). I had to slacken my Sutton harness in order to turn round far enough to check and gave my face a firm blow on the back of his seat as a particularly vicious up-draught hit the aircraft just as I did so.

'Jesus, Jan, hold the bloody thing steady for a minute! … No, there's just a little smoke. No flames. Nothing obviously burning, but I'm sure it's as dead as a dodo.'

I turned back just as we broke through to a lighter chunk of cumulus and some friendly sunlight. Jan had taken us up to angels 13.5 by now, hoping that in the clearer air we might see the other Oxford or let him see us. The sky above remained brilliant blue and white as the cloud formed busy lumps, active as yeast, vying with each other to climb over us and gobble us up in their rumbling and restless digestive systems.

Not an aircraft was to be seen, however. We also noted (without remarking about it to each other) that some of the tops away to the north were very high indeed and beginning to show signs of the torn-away anvil shape of the dreaded cumulonimbus – the thunderclouds that no pilot will willingly compete with.

Jan leaned forward to give one of the fuel gauges a brisk tap with his finger, trusting that the needle would suddenly lose the sluggish inertia that seemed to be keeping it against the 'Empty' stop. It juddered up a millimetre or so. Meanwhile I was, slightly desperately, scavenging my memories of my most recent lectures on airmanship for the rules of procedure in a situation like this. Spurred by an efficiency born of necessity, I came up with the textbook answer. We were, in the event of total radio failure and having been under ground control up to that point, to fly five-mile square legs until another aircraft could be vectored on to us by the GCI. That aircraft would then lead us down in close formation to base. The result of our flying square legs would be to trace a small yellow/green square on the PPI on the ground which would identify our position and allow our 'rescue' plane to fly on to us. Theoretically, the ground plotters or one of the controllers should quickly spot the little square of all too rapidly fading yellow produced by our orbiting. We were, unfortunately, all too aware that, in practice, the rapid decay time of the trace on the tube of the clapped-out old radar sets in the GCI might result in nobody picking up our distress signal and we just hoped that one of the Instructors was at the console.

It turned out later that we had indeed been just within the range of the ground radar (which we feared we might not have been) but that our 'square' had been more of a parallelogram. That was because we had no idea of the current wind speed or direction at that height and consequently could not correct for drift and fly appropriate courses to represent a perfect square over the ground. It took us nearly ten minutes flying to complete the five-mile square and in that time there were two further anxiety-provoking developments. By the last leg, we were again bumping around in total cloud and both our oxygen bottles and one petrol tank were almost empty. It did not therefore encourage us to hang around at that height any longer. No aircraft vectored on to us without its own airborne radar (and none at Middle Wallop at that time had such a facility) would have had a snowball's chance in hell of finding us and indeed might have collided with us.

So we commenced a shallow dive, turning on to a southerly course, both to save fuel and to head towards what we both thought might be the coast. In an attempt to assess our geographical position, I had tried unsuccessfully to remember all the courses we had flown that afternoon, both as target and as attack aircraft, but it was a vain quest. Dead reckoning in these circumstances, without written notes, was like being blindfolded, spun in a rotating chair a few times in the middle of a field and then being told to walk directly to the gate, still blindfolded. However, previous experience of these PI sessions in which we were more or less always within the relatively limited radar coverage of the Middle Wallop GCI led us to guess that we were probably somewhere to the west or southwest of Salisbury when we were marking our 'square'. Several times before the cloud increased, we had seen the elegant needle of Salisbury Cathedral spire on our starboard side. Given that we'd done several PIs and nearly an hour's flying later, we could estimate our ground position as being perhaps near Shaftesbury. That being so, a compass course of 170° or thereabouts should bring us over the coast in about fifteen to twenty minutes' flying time where a let-down through cloud would be a bit safer, given that the QNH and QFE (barometric pressure settings on the altimeter for sea level and the airport level respectively) had not altered much since we took off. So long as we made it to over the sea then the ground altitudes did not matter.

Now at 5,000 feet, wipers barely coping with the rain streaming over the windscreen and neither of us able to see anything ahead or even able to see the wingtips, we were being fairly viciously banged about by the turbulence. The port engine revs began to drop and the engine itself to splutter and miss rather disconcertingly. Mac … was now sweating a bit under his helmet and oxygen mask with the effort of trying to keep the aircraft on course and the right way up.

'I zink ve might haf to go up a bit again and bale out if ve don't break cloud by 500 feet. Too many f****** hills on Dartmoor and in Dorset to hit. Gif me a hand with this f****** aeroplane. I'm tired of f****** Oxfords', he added feelingly. I had actually learned the Polish equivalent to the 'f-word' but for some reason known only to himself, Jan never seemed to use it.

The Oxford had, of course, dual controls and I had already, almost instinctively, had my feet on the rudder bar and my hands on the yoke, but now I was adding a bit of strength to counter the sudden lifts, yaws and drops of the turbulence. With the engine behaving as it was, I left the throttles and trim to Jan. We were now at 2,000 feet and had gained a bit of airspeed in spite of little power in the port engine. Then it dawned on me that baling out was not going to be straightforward even if we contemplated it now. Our chutes were the chest type which clipped on to the front of our harness and they were, at that moment, stowed in a rack on the side of the fuselage some feet behind us. One of us was going to have to unclip, leave his seat and clip on the chute as well as passing another chute to whoever was flying the plane. Wearing one of those in the cockpit and working the controls was virtually impossible so it would be a case of leaving them off until just before abandoning the aircraft by the emergency hatch.

We had at that time done only a minimum of parachute drills on the ground and I was far from enthusiastic at the prospect of launching myself into a wet and murky void. Jan, who had mastered a whole range of English expletives for just such an occasion, indicated to me that he was of the same mind.

'OK. Ve take her down – all the f****** way till ve break cloud. You vill call me airspeed and altitude all time. I look out of f****** window till I see somesing.' He throttled back a little more and I felt the stick move forward.

'Right!' I croaked, dry-mouthed, as he leaned forward toward the windscreen.'115-4.5 … 4 … 116-3.8 … 120-3.3 … ' and so on as we continued downwards through the rain and cloud. The turbulence was less now but we could still see nothing and I anxiously checked the clock to gauge the distance travelled since we began the let-down. Surely we must be near the sea now.

Unconsciously, Jan was easing back the rate of descent. Both of us were now sweating as we passed through 1,000 feet. There was high ground on Dartmoor more than 700 feet above that height and although we both knew that it was highly unlikely that we had wandered as far west, we also were uncomfortably aware as we came below 900 feet that there were several areas of high ground about that level just north of Dorchester and we could well be near those.

'Jesus, come on, let's see you', came over the intercom. I hoped Jan, who was probably a Catholic, was referring to the ground and not speaking too literally.

'120 knots, 550 (I was now calling the heights in feet, not thousands of feet) ... 118 knots, 500 ... 115, 400 ... '

Could there be just a trace of dark grey beneath the cloud now? Was it? Was it?

'116 knots, 350' and quite suddenly, at 300 feet, we broke cloud and saw, to our huge relief, through the streaming canopy, small waves breaking on a dark grey sea. We had just crossed the south coast. Jan levelled off, turned east on to 090° and we slumped back in our seats. It was like a reprieve. But only then could we fix our position visually from scrutiny of the coastline and only then did we see that the other fuel gauge was now reading nearly 'Empty' as well and we only had a few minutes flying time left.

We had apparently, from a hasty map read, crossed the coast about five miles west of the Needles which were rapidly taking clearer form as we approached only a couple of hundred feet above the waves. Soon we turned up over the Beaulieu River, skirted the east side of Southampton, and with both engines coughing and hesitating, and both fuel gauges reading empty, we watched with a strange kind of detachment, a sea of anxious faces turned up against the rain, amongst the many umbrellas dotting the streets with spots of colour, to watch us stagger over Romsey. The watchers clearly had as little faith as we then had that we'd make it to the nearest large field. However, as we cleared the town, we could see the B3084 immediately below us and knew that if we could stay airborne for another five minutes, we might even make the airfield. Failing that, we reckoned we could put down in one of several large fields between there and base if need be.

Any minute, we expected to hear a last cough from one of the engines. There was no way we could have continued asymmetric flight on one fuel-starved engine when we were nearly at stalling speed as it was. But every minute took us nearer the familiar hump of Danebury Hill and, just beyond it, the flat grassy heaven of Middle Wallop's blessed field. Unable to climb over the 470 feet of Danebury, we came round the east side of it. I opened the window and fired a red Very light since we could not communicate with the Tower. Fortunately, the weather was now such that there was nothing in the circuit and Jan planted the Oxford down, with the stall warning ringing in our ears, on the very periphery of the grass field in what was, in the circumstances, a very respectable landing. We had had so little airspeed on the approach that we had hardly dared to drop the landing gear because of the extra drag it would induce but were fortunate that the wind had come up strongly from the west since we had taken off and that helped our indicated airspeed a bit. We taxied part of the way toward the hangars until both engines stopped, of their own accord, about 400 metres out. We were soaking wet and the canopy was not yet open. It was sweat. Our hands were shaky and we did not trust ourselves to stand up properly if we climbed out. So we just sat until a tractor came out to tow us in.

'Jesus vept!' exclaimed Jan, unoriginally, but to the point, as the props stopped and he rather unnecessarily closed the throttle.

'And not much f****** wonder!' I replied, in time honoured fashion, unclipping my harness and withdrawing the intercom plug.

The rest of the cadets and crews gathered round from the GCI cabin and the hangars to greet our return with a variety of ill-chosen remarks about our navigation and airmanship.

'We missed our bloody tea because of you guys!' complained Bert Clayton who'd been flying in the other Oxford of our pair. 'Why can't you get in at the same time as the rest of us?'

It transpired that our 'square' had been spotted, but just as old Tealeaf was calling up another plane to vector on to us, the plotters reported that we had dived and they lost the plot. That was when we had decided to go down and chance it. They knew that our radio had gone because they had been calling us in vain for some time before we even noticed that we'd had no signals. It was thought that because we had gone down below the radar level, we'd 'gone in', and Air-Sea Rescue had been notified. Hence the measure of nervous enthusiasm and complaints of missing tea when we turned up 'with nothing on the clock and nothing in the tank'. We needed a shower before reporting on the episode to the WingCo (Flying) and getting our tea but were somewhat gratified at the concern on our behalf shown by our mates. They didn't give up their tea lightly.

The remaining weeks of our course at Middle Wallop were much less eventful and both our fighter control duties in the GCI and our flying experience showed significant improvement – to the grudging approval of our instructors. The whole period at Middle Wallop had been like living in a different world from RAF Kirkham. We had generally been treated with fairness and only enough firmness to ensure that we grasped the importance of the duties we undertook. We respected our instructors because they genuinely did things better and knew more about the job than we did – and it showed! A few didn't reach the required standard and they just slipped away at the end to some other, probably less interesting work. Most of us from the original F****** Professors, however, did and we looked forward to our next stage in becoming Officers and Gentlemen at OCTU during the coming weeks.

At Middle Wallop we had been spared a lot of the unnecessary kit parades, firing on the ranges and cookhouse fatigues that had been such a drag at Kirkham. We had had regular sport, weekends off-duty in London or Andover and were actually rather proud of our new skills. Whether by accident or design, our officers had treated us as intelligent humans and in our turn, perhaps unconsciously modelling ourselves on them with a view to our prospective futures as fresh young Pilot Officers, we had begun to watch how they went about both their technical and flying duties. We also had begun to observe the more subtle processes of man-management in a Service which has always been rather proud of its capacity to work with a special blend of good Service discipline and relaxed informality when appropriate. This represented a huge change in both our perceptions of, and attitudes to, Service life as compared with how we had felt and acted at Kirkham.

CHAPTER 5

'OQ' MYSTERIES

Our Officer Cadet training was to be at RAF Spitalgate, near Grantham, with some activities at nearby RAF Cranwell. We still operated in Training Command. Fighter Command would only receive the benefit of our more mature expertise if and when we 'passed out' and received our Commissions. By this time, the spring of 1952 was well under way in the south of England, though letters from home in north Scotland indicated that up there they still languished under snow and ice. Given railway warrants to whisk us from Andover to Grantham via London, we shouldered our kit bags with a certain jauntiness as we headed north. The usual three-ton Bedford trucks rattled and bumped us up the hill from the railway station at Grantham to RAF Spitalgate, and dumped us unceremoniously at the Guardroom. Our smiles and jaunty bonhomie were to be short-lived.

What turned out to be the SWO (Station Warrant Officer) and a huge Drill Sergeant strode toward us in a forbiddingly business-like way. The latter addressed us from the minor plinth of the Guardhouse pavement edge. Unwittingly, or, more probably otherwise, he thus gained another five or six inches over his already massive six-foot frame. Effortlessly dominating the group, he paused, eyed us all dyspeptically, and began.

'Welcome to RAF Spitalgate Officer Cadet Training Unit, gentlemen. You will be Course No 44. Notice please that I described you, foolishly, I know, as 'gentlemen'. This may come strangely to your ears after your earlier experiences in this fine Service but it is what we here hope to make of you, yes, Officers and Gentlemen, in the course of the next few months. I cannot call you 'sir' because you are not yet Officers and Gentlemen – and indeed, by the look of you, some of you never will be, in spite of our best efforts. You will not be called 'airmen'. You are officer cadets and will be addressed as 'Mr'. You will continue to address me as Flight Sergeant and all commissioned officers as 'sir'. Have you got that? I will not, I trust, require to repeat what I have just said. Am I right?'

'Yes, Flight Sergeant!', we chorused as we inwardly thought, 'Christ, this is just going to be bloody square-bashing for sophisticates all over again'.

He called over a friendly looking Corporal who happened to be passing. 'Corporal, this unlikely looking shower is the new Course 44. Be so kind as to direct them to their billets.' Turning again to us as we shuffled rather aimlessly in front of him, he started again. The Corporal, no doubt inwardly cursing his luck that he should have happened to be there at just the wrong time, stood deferentially to one side of the assembly, aligned neither with the masters nor the slaves, as he waited for the Flight Sergeant to finish.

'Now, you lot, inside this poor body and brain (for I have never been an officer) there are two Flight Sergeants. One is the kindly, tolerant and smiling-faced Fairy Godmother you see before you, fair and gentle as the day is long. I have welcomed you genially in spite of the fact that none of you has even had the decency to get properly lined up. You're camped on that bloody roadway like a set of ignorant gypsies.' We shuffled embarrassedly into something a bit more orderly.

'The other Flight Sergeant in me has the capacity to turn your life here into a living hell. Cross me, show the slightest lack of application, give anyone, yes, ANYONE, the impression that you're treating RAF Spitalgate like a holiday camp and your arse will be out of that gate so fast you'll have to reset your watch when you land! You have two hours to get some food and sort yourselves out in your billets. Thereafter you will muster on the parade ground, working blues only, no rifles or webbing, where I and certain other members of the staff, officers and NCOs, will advise you on the most painless ways to survive the rigours and hardships of your Training Course. Dismissssss!'

We checked our watches and followed the Corporal.

The afternoon of our first day was half spent when we eventually straggled out on to the parade ground to face like men the new rigours we anticipated. The Flight Sergeant, plus a Squadron Leader, I think, appeared with the usual magic suddenness from some nearby fastness. We were entirely unused to facing up to such seniority and unconsciously straightened ourselves up in the columns of three in which we had assembled even before 'Flight' barked, 'Course, Attennnnn ... shun!' and almost immediately afterwards, 'Course, Standat ... Eesss!'

The fact that we had been already standing at ease (in the formal sense, with legs comfortably apart and hands clasped behind our backs) when they turned up was ignored. The two supererogatory commands were the perennial ritual indulged in by the bosses to remind us that we were but puppets whose strings were firmly in the grip of our masters. We would forget that at our peril!

Plate 11: A Warrant Officer Drill Instructor, complete with pace stick, sorts out a batch of cadets (© Crown Copyright/MOD)

Additionally, many of our officers, like those at Middle Wallop, had been decorated, sometimes multiply, for courage in the face of the enemy and other substantial achievements during the war only seven or eight years previously. We tended not to make too much of that in any overt way but all of us were well aware of it. In practical terms, the biggest difference it made to our days was that much communication was spoken rather than shouted. Even so, when our drill and ground combat instructors did try to emulate the gentle menace of our quieter-spoken officers, their efforts largely failed. They would have a minor success with the first sentence – a slow and deliberate growl, like that of a wounded lion in the scrub – but that would inevitably be followed by a rising crescendo of vituperation as their inevitable frustrations showed.

There was a general theme pursued in those early days by our instructors in the 'brawn' rather than the 'brain' departments, i.e. drill, military activities like ground combat, escape and evasion, general fitness and endurance and weapons handling. It was to the effect that we were to become officers. Not only would we be able to do everything that the book said we had to do, we would also learn to do everything better than those we would eventually command. It was a taxing goal to pursue but it was pursued seriously and realistically and we were expected to more than meet the challenge. It may be hard for those who have little or no experience of the military scene to grasp that the word 'command' is an integral part of it. As 'erks' (aircraftmen, 2nd class) we learned to jump to every command without question and immediately. As officers we had to learn that we would exercise that command which all ranks below us would jump to, not forgetting of course that even when we were Pilot Officers, there were as many ranks above us as there were below us in the overall hierarchy

In the 'brains' departments, our mentors were generally officers who would guide us through the key relevant features of military history, principles of (air) warfare, strategy and tactics and the intricacies of military law and Queen's Regulations. The latter had suddenly changed to that from King's Regulations one day while we were still at Middle Wallop. The billet radio had suddenly announced the return of Princess Elizabeth to London from Kenya on her father's death and her accession as Queen. It was enough to give us pause in the activities of the moment, but, unlike those thousands of earnest souls who seem to have total recall for what they were doing at the moment of such events as the announcement of J F Kennedy's death, I, and probably those with me at the time, have completely forgotten the details of these activities. The style of these officers who instructed us now was very much more like that of university lecturers, something that we were all more used to. They not only credited us with the capacity to work and assimilate information at a reasonable pace but also allowed themselves the luxury of some dry humour and a worldly-wise, throwaway style which appealed to many of us.

Perhaps one of the less appealing features of the course was the still unknown process whereby we were to be transformed, not only into 'officers', but also into 'gentlemen'. In spite of the fact that it had been the returning troops from all the Services after World War Two who had contributed largely to voting in, by a substantial majority, a Labour government in 1945, the Services generally maintain in practice and attitudes, a rather conservative general ethos while outwardly eschewing any political stance as such. Most senior officers I met were, so far as I could assess, more right than left politically and equally clearly confirmed royalists. They had their own notions of what being an officer and a gentleman was about and stories used to be bandied about which had originated at the start of the 1939 war.

At that time, many officers and senior NCOs had become RAF officers, drafted in from the pre-war Auxiliary Air Force and RAFVR. Auxiliary Air Force members at that time were often university graduates and staff who had learned to fly at university or in private clubs, or were aristocrats with plenty of money, a relaxed way of life and sometimes even their own planes. Members of the RAFVR who tended to have joined from the middle classes, were more work-a-day types in general, grabbing their flying from where they could and less inclined to form close knit groups or even cliques. As a consequence, it was said that those joining the RAF from the Auxiliaries were gentlemen trying to become officers, that the RAFVR chaps were officers trying to become gentlemen and that the Regulars were neither officers nor gentlemen but were trying to become both. Where National Service types like us would be put in that particular hierarchy was, so far as we could tell, left unsaid.

On that first day at OCTU, however, the Station Commander and his most senior acolytes greeted us cordially enough but within minutes of the first introductions, it was entirely clear that this was going to be no pushover. First, we were going to be taxed physically to the limits. Second, there was enough classroom work and demand on our rates of assimilation and capacity for retention at an intellectual level to keep our heads down in study where before we had been 'blanco-ing' and blethering. Third, and most disconcerting of all, we were going to be under constant scrutiny, on duty and off, on the base and even in the town, by a whole regiment of spies ('observers' was the actual word used). Any officer involved with our course could 'observe' us at any time and we had to remember that on the Grantham High Street or at the local swimming pool which several of us frequented in off-duty hours, we might not recognise the dapper gentleman in navy blue blazer and dark flannels peering at our reflections in Gieves's window as Squadron Leader X. Still less would we know that the scrawny and hairless wonder we saw doing a carefree backstroke at the pool on a Saturday afternoon might be Flight Lieutenant Y.

The point of all that 'observation' was to discover whether we were lucky enough to possess the appropriate accumulation of 'OQs' (Officer-like Qualities). At no time were we given any detailed description of these. We tried often enough. One afternoon, towards the end of a lecture which had ranged from the *obiter dicta* of Von Clausewitz to the rejection of the principle of fighters attacking in 'vic' formations, I even challenged Squadron Leader H, a distinguished and interesting lecturer on war history, strategy and tactics, myself. He paused, then ... 'Do any of you know Keats?'

A very dapper and rather brash young Regular Sergeant F, recommended to try for a Commission by his Commanding Officer for qualities which, though high on leadership, did not run to an advanced level of literary awareness, was right in there.

'Yessir. If you rub in some DDT powder you can get rid of 'em in double quick time!'

'Thank you, Sergeant. I was actually thinking of something between the ears, not between the legs. Perhaps I might remind you of the famous line from 'Ode to a Grecian Urn', – and Sergeant, this has nothing to do with where you obviously keep your hair dye, 'Beauty is Truth, Truth Beauty – That is all ye know on earth, and all ye need to know'. Keats did not attempt to define Beauty but he knew it when he saw it. OQs are just the same. We know them when we see them.'

There was an unsatisfied restlessness in the classroom. One of our number, I think it was Graham Davies, an erudite little Welsh Classicist, who perked up. 'But Sir, am I not right in thinking that it was Ovid in 'The Art of Love' who said, (and I translate) 'Judgment of Beauty can err, what with the wine and the dark.' His quotation was deliciously double barbed since we had heard already that the officers had enjoyed a rather well lubricated Mess Night Dinner the night before.

'Well now, Mister Davies, I think we'll close this class just now and let you and your brother Cadets consider overnight whether this little foray into the classics has either earned you or lost you some of those mysterious OQs!'

There was a great rattle of chairs as we came to attention for his departure from the classroom and, when he had left, a sudden outburst of indignant chatter to the effect that '... that bugger still hasn't told us a damned thing about what they think they're looking for in OQs!' Others thought Graham had really scored with his quote and were vicariously pleased at his quickness and his learning. Some, however, feared he'd dropped himself in the 'clag' for being a bit cheeky. Sergeant F had disappeared.

We all knew on our first day at OCTU that any one of us would fail if we failed on any one of the tripartite elements of the Course – the intellectual, the physical or in this matter of 'OQs'. You could be a veritable Schwartzenegger on the battle course, never eat peas with a knife or never be seen outdoors without gloves when in 'best blues', but if you thought or wrote in stumbling monosyllables, and spelt them wrongly at that, then you were OUT. If you were an intellectual giant in the classroom, and a tireless athlete in the field but your genes or whatever had failed to endow you with the magical 'OQs', you were OUT as well. We therefore sought the answer to the OQ problem as knights of old sought the Holy Grail – and it was equally elusive, always just a reach away.

It was in fact quite interesting to watch how different cadets interpreted what OQs might encompass, or how they might present themselves to demonstrate how they burgeoned with these mysterious qualities. Some regressed to their square-bashing days and became strangely punctilious about their trouser creases, their blanco and their boot shine. Others were seen to cultivate an over-obvious bonhomie and an excess of easy familiarity with their colleagues – especially when an officer was looking – in spite of the fact that they had been reticent to the point of being taken for Trappists heretofore. Strangely, and in spite of the fact that we could observe certain of our officers to demonstrate these very characteristics every day, nobody seemed to consider that a style of quiet introversion and personal containment correlated with officer-like qualities. But we never really knew what the powers that be were after.

Many of us were convinced that elements of emotional balance, self-assurance, demonstrably good judgment and personal consistency in our habitual reactions, both to stress and to success, were what OQs were about. One's general good physical bearing and related self-confidence and mental alertness in a variety of settings seemed also to have been looked upon with favour. By the end of the course, we were, of course, able to validate these calculated guesses against our experience of those who fell by the wayside and were RTU'd prematurely. Usually it seemed to the rest of us (the successful ones) that the ones returned to their units before the end of the course might well have failed to reach the necessary standards on two of the three broad qualifying areas. Needless to say, none of us was at all keen on the dreary prospect of failing the course and spending the rest of our two years as AC2s again in some lonely, one-horse Maintenance Unit in the backwoods of the Welsh borders, in leaky wooden huts in a gale-ridden, remote and barely active radar post near Cape Wrath or on the flat beaches of Norfolk. We knew such places existed. We had often enough and at several prior stages of our RAF careers, been threatened with them.

Course 44 consisted of a mix of National Service cadets, almost all between about nineteen and twenty-two, and others, with a much wider spread of ages, from the Regular ranks. Whether that was a factor or whether there was also simply the growth of new and slightly unexpected interpersonal rivalries and feelings of competitiveness growing from our determination not to fail the Course now that we were on it, there seemed, in these early days at OCTU, to have been a slight undermining of the strong sense of solidarity we had previously enjoyed. Especially amongst the 'FPs' from Kirkham and Middle Wallop, that solidarity had seen us through many assaults on our personal integrity, our stress tolerance and even our sanity. We therefore came quickly, if tacitly, to the corporate conclusion that this undermining process must not be allowed to continue.

As early as the end of the first week, the 'FPs' determined that, whether or not we could decode what behaviours were OQ laden or not, we would try to support each other as much as possible. We would not become 'swots' of Queen's Regulations or the history of air warfare. We would not write essays on the problems of airborne radar and the history of air warfare such that military publishing house editors the length and breadth of the land would be leaping desperately on to trains to Grantham to sign us up for their next book contracts. We would get through all the route marches, the battle courses, the weapons' tests and so on but would do nothing which might make some of our number who might have certain difficulties on some of these activities be shown up as less competent by comparison. We all agreed to do enough – but stubbornly vowed not (wittingly) to excel.

With a few exceptions, we all stuck to these principles throughout the course. Perhaps, had our instructors been privy to this philosophic position we had taken up, they might well have considered that we all lacked the necessary OQs! However, with only one or two exceptions, we all followed these principles and remained solid comrades in arms. There were two or three of us who had, as it turned out, genuine defects of ability at either the mental or physical levels. We could do nothing to save them – although it was only at the very end of the course that they suddenly disappeared.

There was also, much more reprehensibly, one notable 'creep' (who had shown certain rather selfish characteristics even in his square-bashing days) who did not share our ethos. He swotted. We even found out later that he was said to have smuggled a copy of Queen's Regulations into the lavatory to swot up the more abstruse points of military law, unseen by his peers. Had we found that he was hefting that considerable tome there only to use its usefully sized pages for a purpose more appropriate to the location, he might have been forgiven. But he was not. The word went round that he was found out by one of our number who noticed that this single-minded aspirant had been an unconscionable time in the 'bog' and, fearing that he had become ill, the observing cadet looked over the partition from the next cubicle to see the culprit, trousers round his ankles, intently poring over the merry and quip-laden paragraphs on the duties of officers at Courts Martial – or something! The rest of us were promptly apprised of the truth by our 'spy' who had slunk back to us unseen by the paragon of virtue.

The latter was also seen to use every stratagem to make himself known to the 'observing officers'. He would ask apparently intelligent but, we thought, completely unnecessary questions after nearly every lecture. He would linger in the classrooms to have the lecturer 'clarify some interesting point' for him personally, if the lecturer, unlike most, did not vacate the room at a high rate of knots after the lecture. In the case of one of the hot-footed latter, this particular cadet would arrange to sit at the end of the row of desks nearest the exit, and being more rotund than the rest of us, would heave himself to his feet right in the path of the fleeing officer. The reader will not find it hard to guess who, amid all the competition, came high in final marks at the end of the course. The rest of us were grieved about it, not because none of the rest of us had done as well, but because, while pretending to adopt the group ethos of easy-going proper completion of the course without too much effort, this customer had covertly been 'pot hunting'. But his victory was at the price of being thoroughly rejected as a person for much of the rest of his Service career by many of us who knew how he had achieved it.

Perhaps because I had a flair for writing exam papers, was strong and physically sturdy in the combat exercises and had run on the athletics field for the Station, the Group, and eventually Command while a cadet, I was Course runner-up – but at least I had followed the unwritten code and achieved a modest level of pass just a smidgen ahead of the others! By the time of our Passing Out parade at the end of the course, we had all become aware that the continuity of comradeship we had so far enjoyed in the RAF was about to come to an end. That growing awareness had itself contributed to each of us quietly and almost imperceptibly forming in our own minds what sort of an officer each of us would become.

As in the case of all role modelling processes, each of us would find only one or two of the various qualities our mentors showed to be such that we would either consciously or unconsciously incorporate them into ourselves. Back at university I had been enormously influenced by Rex Knight, the then Professor of Psychology at Aberdeen. He was charismatic at a time when only those who could read Χαρισμα knew the word and I was well aware that my own personal philosophy, my later lecturing style and even my hand-written signature were a straight take-over from him. We had, in my own view, at least, a couple of lecturers who bore characteristics of approach, competence and style which were to influence me far beyond OCTU. One was the Squadron Leader H mentioned before who could always be interesting, totally composed and well in command of his subject. The other was a much younger man – not much older than ourselves – with a name that sounded either French or Channel Islands in origin, who was an Education Branch Flying Officer with a languid, very witty, 'Cambridge' style who could imbue our lectures on Government, Politics and Current Events with quality and humour which hugely enhanced the syllabus content.

Strangely perhaps, we did not seem to get quite so close to the officers who dealt with us on the rather more practical and work-a-day subjects like ground combat tactics, weapons, man-management, aircraft control surfaces, engines and hydraulics, radio communications, radar and so on. These subjects were just that bit more prosaic and simply had to be learned up. There was little or no room for discussion or evaluation on our part. What, after all, is there to debate in the learning of what rank in the Army or Royal Navy is equivalent to Wing Commander in the RAF? Or what is the correct way to escape in emergency from a Vampire 10?

Perhaps the element in our early OCTU instruction which took many of us by surprise was the series of lectures on dress, in and out of the Mess, and on correct social etiquette when we would be junior officers posted to a Station. To a Scot heavily indoctrinated with largely class-free and wholly democratic views on how people should be judged and behave, all this talk of presenting cards to the wife of the Station Commander on our first social visit after being posted to a Station seemed rather rarefied, even effete. We were to carry, if not necessarily wear, leather gloves when in uniform, summer and winter. In the Mess, even when off duty, officers were required to present themselves in collar and tie, wearing something like blazer and flannels, lounge suit or smart sports jacket etc. All this may have come easily to the English Public School fraternity accustomed to doing obeisance to the Squire or Headmaster, but seemed just a bit too irrationally prescriptive for us Scots to live comfortably with. Of course, we complied. After all, we never knew when we might need to throw down a challenging glove before the officer who might insult our girl friends! Moreover, little white visiting cards, in impeccable good taste, with the title 'Pilot Officer' preceding our names, did appeal a bit to our essential narcissism – even if it was dangerously anticipatory at that stage when we weren't even officers at all.

Prior to OCTU, we had inclined to the view that gloves were worn for their functional rather than their symbolic properties, when it was cold enough, and that people, regardless of rank or job would be judged worthy of respect on the basis of their performance at whatever level it might be exercised. The notion that a Group Captain was inherently a better man than an AC2 by dint of rank alone was quite alien to me. 'The rank is but the guinea's stamp, The Man's the gowd for a' that!' (Burns)

In fact, there were times when as 'Mr Vice' (the most junior, not the most sexually predatory, officer in an Officers' Mess) at all the pomp and ceremony of a CO's Dining-In Night, I found myself turning over in my mind the second verse of that great poem:

'What though on hamely fare we dine,
Wear hoddin grey, and a' that;
Gie fools their silks and knaves their wine,
A Man's a Man for a' that:
For a' that, and a' that,
Their tinsel show, and a' that;
The honest man, tho' e'er sae poor,
Is king o' men for a' that!'

I then passed the port to the left, as I had been instructed.

These occasional lectures on etiquette for officers, as well as our formal 'practice' Dining-In Nights with the Regular Staff Officers, were our training in proper behaviour – how we would be expected to comport ourselves when we were eventually junior officers on our own Station. They were, in a strange way, somewhat out of tune in the context of so much else that we did and were taught.

In the RAF generally, and especially after the rigours of 'square-bashing', it became clear that there was a general ethos which obtained in man-management and in relationships between officers, NCOs and other ranks. That ethos was clearly perceptible and bore all the hallmarks of enlightenment, fairness and relaxed efficiency. I kept for many years after I had left the Service a small credit-card sized blue card which I had been given either just before or just after I became an officer. It bore one or two valuable precepts which I had been expected to follow as an officer and man-manager. They all stood the test of time in many other contexts but the first of these was in bold type and said, 'In any human problem or dispute FIRST, FIND OUT ALL THE FACTS!' Even if it was a bit facile in its suggestion that 'finding all the facts' could always be promptly achieved, it was nevertheless a valuable and effective guide then and in myriad human situations I have subsequently encountered.

Other, more specific, kinds of man-management were inculcated in us as well. Up until now, and indeed a good deal of the time we were still cadets at Spitalgate, the parade ground and regular drills were still a significant aspect of our lives – except that we were expected to be true paragons of excellence compared to the 'sloppy, ne'er do well shower' we had been elsewhere. The new feature was that we had to learn to be the Drill Commander as well as the subjects of these commands. Accustomed to respond to all the screamed and exaggerated neologisms which passed for marching orders with tight-lipped silence, we were now liable to be hauled out from the relative anonymity of the squad by the Drill Sergeant and set in front of it like sacrificial virgins. Then it was our chance to see whether we had the awareness, the timing and the command of these strange utterances, to say nothing of the lung power and vocal cord elasticity, which would have twenty-five or thirty cadets move as one.

'Squa-a-a-a-d ... ab – out ... ton!' (There was no 'snap' about the word 'turn' if we persisted in our Highland burred 'r's'). If we shouted something like 'turrren', the end of the word on which the squad acted, fell a pace and a half after it should have and a merry shambles ensued. 'Preee-zent yams!' and 'Ohdah yams!' joined our working vocabulary along with the heavily overused 'As you were!' The last command flew in the face of philosophical accuracy. If we were right about change and our existence in time, we could never be truly 'as we were' but the writer of the Drill Manual was not apt to refer to Bentham, Hume, Kant, Voltaire or even to the logical positivists. And Stephen Hawking was not known, even to us, at that time. So far as a drill squad was concerned, 'As you were!' (uttered with more of a sigh as the day progressed) was the simple command which set up the whole fiasco for the umpteenth time after we had fully rehearsed every possible variation of a cock-up of what we were assured, in no uncertain manner, should have been 'a bloody toffee-dawdle for the residents of a looney bin'. Like philosophy, political correctness was unknown to our bosses on the parade ground. We were constantly reminded about how our bumbling incompetence as Drill Commanders sat ill against our allegedly high IQs and academic qualifications.

'Leaders of me ... leaders of men! ... You lot couldn't lead my granny's pussycat to a saucer of milk,' we would be advised. 'Come along now, gentlemen, just for once – to please me – bloody well get your fingers out and get it right for once! As you were!' And eventually, of course, we did.

Other secrets of the coven to which we were introduced included how to run a kit inspection or a Court of Inquiry, what the basics of bar and Mess-accounting, management and storage of firearms were, what was involved in being the Duty or Orderly Officer of the day, and so on. Having been on the other end, so to speak, of kit inspections already, we were well aware of what the officer and NCOs were usually on the lookout for. We did, however, pick up a few more wrinkles that might ensure that we could, if we chose, become amongst the most hated officers on the Camp to which we would, if successful at OCTU, in due course be posted. We were advised that, if we really wanted to find some dust in a billet, we should run a quick finger along the end bar of the bed-frame nearest the stove, or along the top of the trim plate over the lintel of the outside door. We should check out every now and again that, what purported to be a pair of socks rolled together, was just that and not one sock with a paper ball in it and rolled over itself to look like a pair, and so on and so on. In fact we were amazed that we had survived all our kit inspections as 'erks' without once being put in 'jankers'.

RAF Spitalgate had its bright side too, though. Spring was 'y'cumin in' and beneath the blue southern skies flecked with fair weather cumulus, we found the hard physical demands made on us were a bit easier to take. We also had an occasional visitation from nearby Cranwell of some chaps in Harvards who had come over to do 'circuits and bumps' with us so we had some fresh faces to lunch with in the Mess. I had also met a new pal, Tommy F, who had joined us from another unit but who had also decided, with me, that a keen interest in athletics was very worthwhile. It was believed to earn OQs and it gave great opportunities for a skive!

Tommy was a 440 yard high hurdler – one of the most taxing of all the sprint races. I was more of a distance man myself, coping occasionally with the mile, but preferring the three or six mile races.

Nevertheless, we were temperamentally suited to each other and interspersed our speed and distance training routines to fit in with each other's schedule. The most important feature of that arrangement was to ensure that we carried out the tough bits in good view of any officers who might care to pass by the training track and to be equally certain that our relaxation sessions were usually discretely indulged in where we could be equally sure of sunshine on a fine day and the absence of interested inquirers into the technical aspects of our regimes.

Wednesday (sports) afternoons were often quite idyllic. Hot, sweaty, but pleased with our most recent training times and comfortably tired after exertion as only really fit athletes can be, we would lie back on the airfield grass and watch the fluffy cumulus cotton wool buds gently traverse the sky. We hardly ever talked about 'work' on those occasions – only about our chances of doing well enough in the next athletics match against North Weald or Wittering or whatever. We knew the Groupie (Station Commander) would be chuffed if we sorted out the other Stations in Group and we might get a chance to run at Command level. Tommy was really aiming at running for his country in the next Commonwealth Games so he was the more assiduous of the two of us but he did drag me along in his wake in a useful way. (I was told he eventually did run in the Commonwealth games and may have won a medal.) Both of us did eventually run successfully both for the Station., Group and eventually, Command. There are two or three ancient medals mouldering in a drawer at home to prove it. My grandson, eyeing them cynically one day, found some difficulty in stretching his reasonably elastic imagination to encompass the possibility that 'Gramps' might once have moved his now not insubstantial and senescent frame at anything more than the pace of an arthritic tortoise.

Although we thought of it as a bit of a skive, the athletics training we did served us well in the long run – if I might put it that way. All the ground combat training we were now engaged in involved us in harder marches, higher standards of marksmanship (with the addition of the use of the Colt 45 revolver which was standard side arm for officers) and a variety of very tough battle courses. Unlike our experience of these things in square-bashing, we now had to learn to command a platoon in combat tactics as well as simply to do what we were told when required.

Quite early in our stay at Spitalgate, we had heard whispers of the final 'qualifying' two-day and night battle course at a country area called Saltby Heath. There, we would be assessed by being covertly observed while we engaged in a realistic battle situation in which we would take turns, depending on our orders, to command our platoon, either in a defensive or an offensive operation. We would exist on such rations as a hastily erected field kitchen could provide and if we were to sleep at all over the fifty or so hours of the exercise, it would be in a shallow ditch, rolled in a gas cape, if our pals in the platoon were willing to keep watch for an hour or so. They never were. So aware were we that 'observers' might happen upon us at any time, that none of us wanted to blot our copybook at that late stage.

Prior to that, however, we were put through some tough unarmed combat routines by instructors who, for all we knew, might have been Black Belts in umpteen forms of esoteric oriental martial arts. They did try to impart the rudiments to us as best they could, but their long practised and over-learned skills meant that the most important part of the training for us was 'learning how to fall properly'. They took huge delight in ensuring that we fell frequently and from increasing heights. Perhaps most disappointing of all was the instruction we had in effecting a series of literally 'killer' blows and twists. They were demonstrated in slow motion and in detail but we were never allowed to practise them for real – least of all against the more sadistic of our mentors whose early demise we came to yearn for more and more as the instructive battering went on.

One of the minor tragedies of National Service for several of us was that we became quickly and totally disillusioned about the accuracy of that historic weapon of the Wild West, the Colt 45. Ian Fleming had already assured us that '007', although he was known to use a Colt .38 Police Positive as well as the more traditional Colt .45 in his early days, preferred to settle for a Beretta .25 or a Walther PPK 7.65 mm automatic in a shoulder holster. All that, in spite of the fact that the silencer of the former once got caught in his holster and nearly cost him his life. Not being '007' in anything other than our fantasies, we were compelled to use the 'revolver, Colt .45, officers, for the use of,' and without benefit of a silencer.

For years as a boy, I had admired the casual nonchalance of Wyatt Earp, Hopalong Cassidy, Billy the Kid and so on as they casually shot dollar coins out of the air without so much as a passing glance. Baddies fell like ninepins as they palmed the hammer of the Colt and aimed from the hip at the same time. The drooping fag would be shot out of the snarling mouth of the gambling cheat. Fair-haired, Nordic-looking small boys of the far West would gasp in wonderment as the handsome stranger taught them to defend their Mammies and li'l sisters by practising with them until they could shoot out all the black in the Ace of clubs with three consecutive shots at twenty yards.

'Jus' watch me, boy, an' you'll learn real good 'n quick.'

'Gee, mister, will I be just as good as you, one day?'

The boy usually learned just quick enough to have let the instructor ingratiate himself with the remarkably handsome widow woman who was the boy's mother. That was the stereotype we took to the range with our new weapons. But, practise as we might, we would never be that good. Perhaps our instructors were not that good – though, for all we knew, they may well have had designs on the local widow women nonetheless!

Feet apart, both hands locked over the butt in classic fashion, we suddenly found out that a Colt .45 gained weight even faster than Billy Bunter. The foresight wavered uncontrollably in the merest breeze and as the trigger was pulled, the wretched thing seemed to leap up and offer to shoot out the stars, or commit a passing pigeon to a short back and sides. At best, the wretched thing was only accurate (even if we could hold it on the target in the first place) over a mere twenty-five to thirty yards. Holding fire until we could see the whites of our enemy's eyes was not a drama – it was a necessity – and we were unconvinced that a chivalrous opponent would throw down his rifle or machine pistol when he saw that we were only equipped with a Colt and do the decent thing by using only his pistol against us. However, for flyers, the Colt was the only weapon that could be carried with us on an aircraft and was intended more to boost our confidence and perhaps bag a rabbit or two to aid our survival were we to be shot down over enemy territory.

In actual fact, I did find that in close quarter shooting, my efforts with the revolver fired from the hip were every bit as striking, if that is the word, as were the more formal target performances when we were standing up properly. It came as something of a relief when we all handed in these weapons to the armourer at the end of our drills. As cadets, we did not retain them, even unloaded.

The weeks slid busily by. We would wander into town in Stamford or Grantham when we were off duty at weekends and found ourselves sneaking rather more frequent and somewhat ambivalent glances into Gieves's, the military outfitter's, window. There, tucked away behind the resplendent gold on the peak of a Group Captain's cap or the enormously wide braid on an Air Commodore's sleeve, we could see the more anonymous barathea of a mere Pilot Officer's 'best blues' with that exiguous strip of blue braid on the forearm. At this distance in time from the actual events of these days, I forget now whether it was optional or not for National Service officers to purchase 'best blues'. It was certainly advised. No CO was going to take too kindly to a scruffy PO turning up in the Mess at a Dining-In Night in the coarse cloth of his 'working' blouson and trousers, when all the other more senior officers were poncing around like something out of a Gilbert and Sullivan operetta. So a few of us bolder spirits actually crept in and had Mr Gieves's man establish the length of our inside leg and a few other necessary parameters so that we would be the prompt recipients of the 'full works' as soon as our Passing Out Parade was over. We had, of course, to pay a deposit against our order – which would be forfeit were we to fall by the wayside in these last few weeks.

That was done by cheque. Having been an impecunious but financially rather careful student for several years before being called up, I had a perfectly good bank account. Many of us, however, had not, for the simple reason that we had never had as much money as would make holding an account worthwhile. At OCTU we were told that the bank used to sustain the RAF's business was Cox's and King's and that we were to open accounts therein. Our pay, both as cadets and officers would be paid in monthly to that bank. As a Northern Scot, I had never heard of this establishment and had a naturally deep suspicion of effete southern 'chancers' and usurers with double-barrelled names. The Bank of Scotland, the Royal Bank of Scotland, the Clydesdale Bank and so on were solid, dependable, rooted in the traditions and commercial acumen of the north. This lot could be a bunch of real 'fly by nights' who would offer me no interest and probably charge for every letter they wrote to me to cut down my overdraft. But, again, we did as we were told, and it turned out all right.

Little by little, we were gaining in confidence, knowledge and skills and had to admit that the combination of lectures, practice in the technical tricks we had to master and sheer physical fitness, led to most of us beginning to feel that we might have some of these mysterious OQs after all. Even when we went over to Cranwell to use their pool for dinghy drills, we behaved ourselves a bit better than we had expected to and were suitably impressed by the traditions of that fine RAF establishment. Only the prospect of our final assessment on the Saltby battle course had us fighting back sneaking feelings of inadequacy. This was largely because we had expected the RAF to train us in how to go about things in the air and on and around airfields, GCIs and so on. We had not reckoned on doing all the things that were in the province of 'pongos' – that ruffian band in khaki, the PBI ('Poor Bloody Infantry'). However, some of us on Course 44 had been already, and were likely to finish, in the RAF Regiment whose task it was to ensure the effective ground defence of RAF airfields and other establishments. In this specialised work, RAF Regiment personnel would be expected to outperform the Army. The rest of us, in certain circumstances recognised by the military mind, might also, in combative times, have to take to similar rough work – and in any case our mentors thought it would be good for us.

It was said that instructors would be firing live rounds over the top of us as we crawled under the various barbed-wire entanglements which we would have to get through or over and that the liberal application of thunder-flashes would both shatter our eardrums and the darkness during the night exercise. In the event, the thunder-flashes were real enough but we concluded that the firing over us as we crawled about under the wire was noisy but that blanks were being used. None of us were hit, though all of us were temporarily deafened.

Even that was less threatening than had been some of the training battle courses we had been put through (at the double) prior to this final challenge. These were not for the claustro-, or any other kind of phobic. The battle courses we remembered from our first square-bashing days had not been so long, so strenuous nor so competitive as were those we now trained on. Often the first obstacle was to crawl, always with one's rifle, under a huge tarpaulin pegged down to the ground at the edges. It was, of course, completely dark under this and as a result it was all too easy to get the boot in the face from the struggling chap in front, just as one thought one was heading in the right direction for the exit and the next stage in the torture. Next, there were slippery longitudinal logs to run up and along before grabbing a rope and swinging over a pond like a cesspit. Rope ladders which twisted all the wrong ways with an apparent life of their own, some high and uninviting brick and wooden walls which had to be surmounted either with the cooperation of one's mates or not, and a series of transverse logs which were just a bit more than a long step apart, were waiting hazards.

In plimsolls and running gear these would have been hazardous but manageable. In full battle order of ammunition boots, webbing and rifle they became serious threats to the integrity of one's person. Most of us finished with more than our fair share of bruises and cuts, sweating like pigs and our whole bodies shaking as if we'd been stood on a concrete vibrator for half an hour. It was a miracle that we were able to aim our rifles at anything, to say nothing of making a certain minimum score on the targets. For myself, the worst moment came in the crawl through a zigzag two-foot diameter earthen tunnel which ran for some twenty feet underground and which had also accumulated several inches of water in its middle reaches. The trick was to hold your rifle by the muzzle with your thumb over the bore (to keep out the water) and rest its length on the inside of your knee and lower thigh as you crawled along on your side. When one came to a zigzag turn, one rolled on to one's other side, still keeping the rifle dry, to negotiate the bend and so on to the end of the tunnel.

It was just my luck to have in front of me in the middle of this very hazard the fattest, least athletic and most claustrophobic cadet in the bunch. In the damp pitch dark and with the next chap crawling impatiently behind me, I was trapped between him and this fat oaf. Jammed between the muddy walls of the tunnel, he was by now using up far too much of his oxygen, as well as ours, by bawling that he was stuck. Panic-stricken and kicking, his flailing boots and his expansive bum were far too close to my nose for comfort.

We had been told that the supervising officer and NCOs were on the lookout for this sort of emergency and that, when the stream of cadets ceased for a few minutes to emerge from the tunnel, they would proceed to open up the tunnel with spades from up on the surface. Not being at that stage quite the trusting soul I might have been, I decided to try a hearty thrust with my rifle up the arse of the blockage together with a firmly intoned instruction to the fat bastard to turn on his other side and get moving. It seemed to work. As I passed him at the exit, I enjoyed the small pleasure of hearing him get a mouthful about not following his instructions from the supervisors. It was not, however, a pleasant experience for a minute or two – and seemed a lot longer! I marked him down as one to be avoided at Saltby.

When, towards the end of our course, we, in khaki denims and full battle order, were piled into the inevitable three-tonner Bedfords to enjoy limited views of the old English countryside on the way to Saltby, we knew that greater subtleties than simple dark tunnels awaited us. The exercise started in the afternoon and ran through till the evening of the next day. Several of us would be told that we were the Platoon Commander for various stints and would be expected to show appropriate 'leadership' and battle competence in achieving the specified goals.

As attackers, we were to infiltrate and capture the 'HQ' which would be set up in and around an old crumbling barn in what could be described as broken scrub and partly wooded country. The defending force would be deployed both in fixed positions and as scouting patrols for which we would be constantly on the lookout. They would also be defended by a variety of booby traps for which we were expected to be on our guard. Broken down into eight man platoons, we were turfed out of our lorries a good mile or two from the target. Iron rations, a couple of magazines of blank rounds each, camouflage cream for our exposed faces and hands and enough net to stretch over our steel helmets were dished out to each of us and the three-tonner disappeared into the distance.

We knew that it was a deliberate ploy not to name which of the eight would be Platoon Commander. We also knew that the officer 'observers' could sneak about the area at all times to examine, among other things, which of us would assume, and by what methods, the leadership of the group. By this time, all of us were committed to reaching our pass-out parade successfully. To have suffered all we had, only to be 'rusticated' as AC2s again, was by now unthinkable. But there were the seeds of real conflict being sown. We knew we had to show 'leadership' but that eight chiefs and no indians would produce a shambles. This was probably the first time that our solidarity as a group had come into question.

We held a parley in a dry ditch by the woodside where we had been dumped and were just (after a more acrimonious discussion than was usual for us) coming to the conclusion that each of us would be Platoon Commander for a six hour stint throughout the Exercise and that we would draw for an order of the going. Just as we were doing so, a shadow fell across us as an officer, complete with a clip-board of papers, was studiously annotating our activities from behind a large tree. We would not have seen him at all had not the sun just moved round enough to cast his shadow across us.

'Well, well, gentlemen – not very watchful are we, when a great lump like myself can sneak up on you while you engage in the unwarlike luxury of philosophical discussion. And you're far too close together for mutual cover and lines of fire. Come on, waken yourselves up a bit!'

He asked who was Platoon Commander just as we were reaching our own conclusion about that and before we could indicate that Bert had drawn Number One for the first stint, the officer simply pointed to the man nearest him and barked, 'You'll do!' We mentally adjusted the running order in our heads for later and waited for instructions from the new incumbent. His reactions were far from lightning fast. Some of us just have greatness thrust upon us!

The details of all that ensued over the following forty-eight hours are lost to me now. Only episodes remain with any clarity and it is now much clearer to me how, in actual ground combat, situations can so easily become a total shambles if good communications break down. We needed to coordinate our activities with two other platoons which we knew must have been dropped off within a mile of us, but we carried no radio and had therefore to find them without their thinking that we were 'the enemy' and loosing off a magazine of blanks at us. That would surely have failed the whole blooming lot of us. Four of the smallest and quietest movers among us were sent out as scouts to find and make the necessary contacts, while we larger specimens spread out in cover and lay back under our camouflage for a 'quiet hour'. Actual sleeping time was not programmed into the Exercise so we took the chance when we could grab it. Unfortunately, the Red Indian propensities of the chosen scouts exceeded even Bert's expectations and the crackle of a broken twig announced their return with the information that one of the other platoons had already scouted an area of 400 metres all around them and found it clear of 'enemy' activity. In the course of so doing, they had met our scouts very quickly – hence their prompt return. Their Platoon Commander clearly was stacking up OQs at a frightening rate so we decided to work on our own initiative rather than simply joining forces with him. We therefore moved away to the south. (We had sussed out that we must be on the northerly extremity of the battleground because we could see a beautifully maintained farm and orchard stretching out to the north behind us. The authorities would not have us skulking about at night in an inhabited area.)

There were still a couple of hours of daylight so the risk of disturbing either sentries or missing trip wires and so forth was relatively low. We found good cover from where we could finally ascertain our targets and plan an attack and dug ourselves in to wait for darkness and eat a sandwich or two. A chap I hardly knew – not one of the 'FPs' – but a Flight Sergeant Regular and myself were designated to reconnoitre the woods and broken area up to a low ridge about half a mile away with a view to assessing a good line of approach to the enemy base which we had already suspected to be in the dead ground behind the ridge. Our 'intelligence' was partly based on the fact that several of us had seen at least three observing officers sneaking about near the top of the ridge for about an hour now and we guessed they would not wander far from their Mess tents.

We crawled out just as the last light was failing only to find that the rich nightlife of the heath was revelling in the damp of a recent shower and the pheromone call of our warm bodies. In spite of puttees over our boots and tightly buttoned wrists, these enterprising creatures wormed their ways (the metaphor is used advisedly) up our legs and arms to find solace and a gentle meal in the undress circle around our scrotums. The camouflage net over our helmets, daintily dressed with bracken and grass, formed a trap which ensured that only the more aggressive gnats and other creepies found their way to our faces, eyes and necks. Curiously, they seemed to have more difficulty finding their way out. I was on the point of laying down my rifle, the better to scratch at an unbearable itch, when suddenly there was a commotion and a curse from the direction of my mate fifty metres on my left. I froze and pressed myself, itch and all, into the bosom of mother earth. I heard the clipped but quiet tones of one of the observing officers who seemed to be another ten yards or so further away.

'Right, laddie, you're out of it for now. You're officially dead. Follow me to HQ'.

He strode off with our chastened and bedraggled Flight Sergeant in tow as the RAF Regiment 'defender' who had jumped him crawled away in the opposite direction. Aware that the success of my whole platoon depended now on my getting both to the observation point on the ridge – and getting back safely to the platoon position – I crawled on, wishing I had opted for a Colt 45 rather than a Lee Enfield rifle as my personal arm. The rifle was awkward and 8lb heavier and the shoulder strap kept getting caught on sticks and other obstructions.

Over an hour later, I was greeted warmly on my exhausted return to the platoon.

'Jesus, Clarkie, where the hell have you been. At least you're the first back. Got any gen?'

'All very well for you bastards,' I responded, 'sitting on your fat arses while I bloody torture myself crawling through thistles and cow shit only to get jumped by a bloody patrol. Chiefy got nicked.'

I began to relay all I had seen of the defenders' positions and buildings and to report the route I had taken which was clearly free of booby traps and trip lines. Danny, who was next in line for Platoon Commander, cut in.

'Listen, you guys, Clarkie's got all this gen in his head now. Instead of him trying to get it to penetrate you guys' thick skulls, why don't we let him take on the next Platoon Commander stint instead of me and I'll take the next one after that, OK?' Nobody demurred.

It would be too tedious to recount all that became of us that night, even if I could remember it. Perhaps one of the worst experiences of the whole exercise was, after crawling for ages to recce the sound of some voices, we squinted from our cover to see nothing more than a couple of the observing officers having a relaxed meal by a field kitchen. We sniffed the air like Korky the Cat to try to catch the rich aroma of the soup pot since we had approached, properly, upwind. For a moment we did think a thunder-flash in their mince would have livened up the party a bit but decided, reluctantly, to slink away as quietly as we had arrived and explain their narrow escape to them later, especially if we required some spare OQs to compensate for any gaffes we might have made earlier.

Later in the night there was much more crawling, a cacophony of thunder-flashes, some within feet of us, the crack of rifle fire and the acrid smell of smoke bombs as we pressed home our first attack. Then whistles blew. Officers and clipboards reappeared and we were stood down for an hour or so while an analysis of our efforts so far was made and reported to us – in a rather disparaging manner we thought. Our 'prisoners', who had been harshly interrogated, were released back to us and we were told to bivouac for a couple of hours before being briefed for the next series of tasks to begin at 4 a.m.

We found some shelter amid rocks and bracken, indulged in a brief assault against the insect life, wrapped our gas capes round us and slept. A minute later, it seemed, more whistles and we began the same old story again, but as defenders this time.

In some ways, that was an easier task. Our territory was defined and we could set up our lines of fire, booby traps and trip wires as we chose. It sounds petty now but I distinctly remember some of the lads actually collecting cow-pats and placing them just where bodies would fall if the trip wires worked. Unfortunately, the only ones that could be carried any distance were already hard and lacked the soppy green squelchiness and richer bouquet of more recent jobbies. There were not too many of the latter because the local farmers were well warned about these exercises and no animals bigger than a fox or badger wandered the heath while we did battle.

By the afternoon of the next day, we were filthy, dog-tired and our hunger was matched only by our thirst. The final whistles found me bruised, slightly bloodied but unbowed and not giving a monkey's cuss for OQs. Some of the lads who had been captured, 'killed' or been caught making bad tactical decisions were heavily despondent and we did our best to reassure them that that set of wankers (the observing officers) didn't know their arses from their elbows and we were sure that they must have scored some good marks some of the time. It all seemed a long way from aeroplanes. Somebody said, 'And to think that these bloody pongos do this sort of thing all the time!' I wasn't sure that they actually did but it was perhaps the first time anyone had a sneaking sympathy for any of our mates who had had the misfortune to join the Army.

The three-tonners bumped and trundled some very hangdog cadets back to Spitalgate where we handed in the mud encaked denims for laundering and repaired to our billets to clean our rifles and blanco our webbing for the morrow. We turned in early and dreamt of huge brimming pints ... and other things.

Saltby signalled the last big physical effort before we were to emerge as officers and gentlemen. The last big mental effort was the final examinations including, as I remember, both essay and multiple choice type questions. This was a time when we noticed the sharp division between the 'FPs' and the cadets who had come from other ranks and a miscellany of units. Some already had their wings as Sergeant pilots or navigators and some had been in technical trades. All of them, however, faced the prospect of written examinations with much more trepidation than did those of us who had, only months before, written examinations at university for up to ten hours at a time. Several of us took them in hand for brief seminars on examination technique, how to plan and lay out an answer and the value of storing information under headings and sub-headings. They always seemed to be embarrassingly grateful and we were glad that most of them came through in the end.

One day, just before the end of the course, we were lined up for parade in front of the assembled instructional officers. I remember the sun shining brightly but it did not seem in any way to be a portent. We knew what was about to happen. We would be sirs or serfs within the hour. With typical military exactitude and only slight regard for any personal sensitivities, our final overall marks for all activities, airmanship, ground combat, technical proficiency in the air and on the ground, knowledge of military law and what was required of an officer and a gentleman were added up and the final result announced. Those who had not passed at this late stage had been told privately before the parade and their marks were not announced. Some of course had fallen by the wayside much earlier but they had been RTB'd weeks before. One of our cadet swots was the Sword of Honour winner. Strangely, I was announced as the runner up and as such would be a sword-bearing officer of one half of the squadron at the Passing Out Parade before the Air Officer Commanding. Nearly all of the 'FPs' made it. The relief on hearing the results for the successful cadets was huge. The disappointment on the part of the others was deep and we were really sorry for them. They had gone through all the trials and torments we had and had nothing to show for it. At least we would all get drunk together in the evening. We did.

That evening in the billet, we sewed the narrow little blue and black rings denoting our new-found status on to our uniforms with as much alacrity as was consonant with neatness. We also made something of a point of getting out on to the Station roads as soon as possible just to see if the Warrant Officers and NCOs who had been so scathing about us not so long ago would actually salute us. They did, and we did not forget to reciprocate the salute. Actually, we were not gazetted as officers at that time and we were chancing our arm. The ethos of the RAF, however, is such that we had eventually become quite friendly towards most of them and they were indulgent of our little conceit. Perhaps they felt that they'd made the best of a bad job.

Those of us who had ordered 'best blues' from Gieves's were quick to confirm that we'd be picking them up as soon as possible. We did so with a flamboyance which belied our anxieties that we would not have enough cash to pay for them, especially after the booze-up which our final marks presaged. We also began to anticipate the diaspora of the 'FPs' with a measure of gloom and despondency. The world of junior officers in the RAF is not so large that we thought we would lose touch with all and sundry for ever but the chances of more than a passing contact in the months remaining of our full-time Service career were low. On the other hand, for those of us in the General Duties Branch, there was a more limited range of operational Stations to which we might be posted and it was likely that several of us might be posted together.

So we hit the town in Grantham that night for appropriate rejoicing, commiseration and maudlin recapitulation of the joys of Service life – so far. It became harder and harder for me to remember my role as the sword bearing Flight Commander in the forthcoming Passing Out Parade. Naturally, my pals kept coming up with ingenious suggestions as to where I might stick the blooming thing. The Drill

Manual, however, compelled me to be conservative with my thrust and parry.

In the event, heavily dozed with Alka-Seltzer and buckets of water, we all put on a bit of a show for the sake of the lads whose parents, wives and girl friends had travelled the length and breadth of the land to see them pass out. As it happened, only one did! A Sergeant picked up his rifle and did him the kindness of letting him lie until the AOC had finished his speech of exhortation and congratulation. I seem to remember the Air Vice Marshall's steely look as he congratulated me on managing to sheath my sword without castrating myself and some muttering of a quotation from Pirandello to the effect that 'Anyone can be heroic from time to time but a gentleman is something you have to be all the time. Which isn't easy.' Being an officer can be equally difficult, we were assured.

'Gentlemen, dismiss!' and we fell out to mingle with the camp followers. A last visit to the Orderly Room to find out where we were to be posted to, collect our travel warrants for a few days' leave and a final brief *au revoir* to our friends from Course 44 marked the end of an era. The next stop would be at an Operational Station.

CHAPTER 6

Operations

We turned up at the Orderly Room, the eager anticipation at hearing of our postings (and hearing the SWO address us as 'Sir') all too apparent on our shining faces. There was an exotic island in the Indian Ocean with an RAF base on it where we might live like lotus-eaters in the endless sunshine. At two bases at least in 2nd TAF in Germany, the beer was said to be remarkable in its quantity, quality and accompanying bar girls, and of course, there was RAF Akrotiri in Cyprus, an equally sought-after exotic posting. We could hardly wait.

'Ah, yes, Pilot Officers Clark and Farmer, I did see your papers here a minute ago.' We beamed at hearing our titles and were almost salivating in anticipation.

'You will be posted to RAF Macmerry for radar duties and detached to Leuchars (151 Squadron) with effect from this day week.' He smiled drily. 'Well, you should be pleased. You're both Scots aren't you!'

We sagged. 'Join the RAF and see the world!' had proclaimed the posters. Lying bastards! The chap in front of me was grinning inanely at his posting, Hong Kong! His fantasies were already burgeoning with visions of endless Chinese meals and the considerate attentions of lissom waitresses with splits in their cheongsams up to their armpits. The reality may well have been a further quick trip to Korea and a much more Spartan and warlike lifestyle. Another was looking rather dispiritedly at the name of RAF Bircham Newton where he was to become something in the Admin Branch. That Station carried a certain cachet among RAF personnel at that time, so we warned him not to turn his back on anyone when he got there. We cheerfully reminded him that luckily he'd be sitting down most of the time and the whole lot of the Admin Branch were a lot of bum polishers anyway. For ourselves, well, at least we'd been spared RAF Saxavord in Shetland or Grimsetter in Orkney where we would, as reputation had it, have had to live and work amid endless horizontal rain and snow, assaultive Great Skuas and where even the sheep were standoffish.

George reminded me of the famous wartime poem about Orkney, the first few verses of which he said he could just remember but which I came to hear recited with some passion one night in the Leuchars' Officers' Mess. The performance was laid on by a junior officer who had had the misfortune to be a Londoner, somewhat given, in his prior civilian existence, to a life of the bright lights and endless social whirl of Mayfair and Soho. An admin error had led to his spending an unusually long tour of duty up there, so he had most certainly not forgotten the words:

'This bloody town's a bloody cuss -
No bloody trains, no bloody bus,
And nobody cares for bloody us -
In bloody Orkney.

The bloody roads are bloody bad,
The bloody folks are bloody mad,
They'd make the brightest bloody sad,
In bloody Orkney.

All bloody clouds and bloody rains,
No bloody kerbs, no bloody drains,
The Council's got no bloody brains,
In bloody Orkney.

Everything's so bloody dear,
A bloody bob for bloody beer
And is it good? – No bloody fear,
In bloody Orkney.

The bloody 'flicks' are bloody old,
The bloody seats are bloody cold,
You can't get in for bloody gold,
In bloody Orkney.

The bloody dances make you smile,
The bloody band is bloody vile,
It only cramps your bloody style
In bloody Orkney.

No bloody sport, no bloody games,
No bloody fun, the bloody dames
Won't even give their bloody names
In bloody Orkney.

Best bloody place is bloody bed,
With bloody ice on bloody head,
You might as well be bloody dead,
In bloody Orkney.'

These dyspeptic sentiments rather belied the actual hospitality, and even the weather, currently afforded to all the Services, in summer anyway, in Orkney, or Kirkwall in particular. Some of us also knew a couple more verses, both in coarser vein. However, it reassured us that our postings to bases more than a couple of hundred miles further south of Kirkwall were nearer to the bright lights and the action in Edinburgh where in off-duty times we would ponce around the Royal Mile and the Rose Street pubs in our smart new blazers and flannels. For some reason it didn't quite work out like that. The fact that we were now workers and not trainees had somehow eluded us. Worse still, much of our work, attached to a night fighter squadron, was at night.

Our first Officers' Mess was at RAF Macmerry, an old Battle of Britain fighter station to the east of Edinburgh. It was being used largely as a domestic site for a GCI radar station some miles away at Dirleton which was mainly underground, apart from the aerials. Macmerry was little changed from its wartime days and both the Mess itself and our quarters were Nissen hut designs. These were essentially horizontal half cylinders of corrugated steel on a concrete base and with brick-built end walls. The junction of steel and brick turned out to be the perfect home for myriad beetles, spiders and especially, cockroaches.

When George and I turned up at the Guardroom, it became immediately apparent that our advent was unexpected both by the SWO and the guard commander. The Adjutant had gone to Haddington so we would have to wait in the Officers' Mess anteroom (as the general lounge was always called) until he turned up and found our documentation. The anteroom was furnished with a small bar in the corner and a variety of rather well worn easy chairs and on the wall hung a number of Squadron badges, some in-flight pictures of WW2 aircraft and an extremely heavily used dart board. There was a panoramic view of the Firth of Forth from the windows. A rather dapper young LAC behind the bar (one of the batmen) offered to find us a cup of tea and we settled to await our official welcome.

Plate 12: Pilot Officers Farmer & Clark (right) at Macmerry (author)

A broadly-built Flight Lieutenant pilot wandered in and we dutifully shot to our feet, thinking this must be the Adjutant. 'For Christ's sake, take it easy, chaps!' he said with a grin, pointing to the two rings on his sleeve, 'I'm only the SADO (Senior Administrative Officer). The Adjutant will be back with the grub in a minute or two. He'll get you sorted out.'

We were still hypersensitive to rank, forgetting that we need only leap up when a Senior Officer (i.e. Squadron Leader or above) entered the room. The fact that the Adjutant, who happened to be Mess Officer at the time, was away shopping like a housewife for food, also brought home to us that we were now in a right Mess, so to speak. We would have Mess bills both for anything we drank as well as for a pro rata (by rank) contribution to the food in question. This was bought in and delivered to the cooks so that we could enjoy a rather better standard of cuisine than would be afforded us by the strict Air Ministry rations. Some degree of food rationing was still in force after the war and right into the early fifties. The drinking was optional but the food contribution was not. We wondered, not as yet having been paid as officers, whether we could afford the lifestyle of gentlemen.

At that point, in wandered a shortish, bespectacled Pilot Officer who looked to be about the same age as ourselves and who turned out to be a National Service officer with a number only a few hundred short of our own but who had succumbed to the offer of an extended three year 'Short Service' commission. He was at first sight, 'busy', jolly and helpful. We found out later that he was seldom busy, but usually remained jolly and helpful.

'Ah, yes, you're the two sprog officers we've been lumbered with.' He turned to the SADO. 'They say that some of them are almost human, you know, Johnny.' Turning back to us, 'You're just the chaps we're looking for to take over a couple of inventories – excellent!' Green as we were, we thought that sounded quite important and grinned fatuously. Little did we know the tribulations that awaited us.

'We'll get you a proper room along the corridor in due course but for the moment we'll have to park you out there. Anyway, you'll be up at Leuchars a good deal of the time getting to know the chaps in 222, 43 and 151 and it's much posher there. You'll need your best blues for Dining-In Nights.' He waved his arm vaguely in the direction of the Firth of Forth and bawled, 'Pasquale!' A rather dapper young airman materialised from behind the bar. 'Sir?'

'Pasquale, meet Pilot Officers Clark and Farmer and guide them with your ineffable skill and aplomb to Hut 6 where they will be temporarily domiciled.' He turned to us. 'Pasquale will be your batman, do your buttons and all that.' He meant polish them, not fasten them.

'Good chap, Pasquale. Look after him and he'll look after you. Come down to my office after you've dumped your kit and we'll see to your documents.' We envied him his buoyant assurance and followed our guide to the door.

Some fifty yards from the Mess proper stood a single Nissen hut of early Forties vintage. The gloom of its hang-dog air and the sight of the rust forcing the paint from the corrugations was confirmed by the bedraggled mustiness of the interior. It contained a few rooms, the end one of which (ours) contained two beds, two upright chairs and two wardrobes, the doors and catches of which had seen better days. There were basic toilet facilities, but just as at Kirkham, the light bulb did not work. 'I'll tell the electrician', said Pasquale, as he saluted and left. He did this because we were still wearing our greatcoats and caps from the trudge across from the proper Mess. Officers without caps on are not saluted and officers do not go outside on their Station without their hats on.

For once it was a pleasant change not to have a rifle to lug around and we would only be issued with our revolvers from the armoury if and when we might require them. We sat on the beds and began to shift our gear from kitbags to wardrobes. I pulled an old and yellowing sheet of newspaper from the top shelf to put my shirts on it. As I dragged it out, there was a minor snowstorm of lightly rattling dark carapaces which fell to the floor. The sturdier specimens scampered off to find a dark corner before we could despatch them but the heavier bodies of a few beetles, earwigs and especially cockroaches, which seemed to predominate in this entomological paradise, were firmly crunched under foot and shovelled outside. This did not bode well. We thought wistfully now of our past 'bull nights' at Kirkham when even two specks of dust were not allowed to rest in peace anywhere in the billet. If we couldn't shift them, then we had to polish them.

We began to examine in closer detail the nooks and crannies of our new home. A few of these at the junction of wall and corrugations were not so much suspicious crevices as great gaping voids through which a near gale force wind was whistling. Around the architraves of the door and behind the skirting boards, there was a veritable sussuration of insect exoskeletons as cockroaches by the hundred shrunk from our wrath. If there was to be one protected species in this hut, we immediately decided it would be us. George lit the stove with amazing efficiency and a murderous gleam in his eye.

'Right, Dave,' he said, showing at last the wealth of OQs he was surely endowed with, 'Away and see if that bugger Pasquale can find any DDT powder. I'm going to heat up the poker and roast out these beasts before I bed down tonight. Leuchars may be a better place later on but we're stuck with this right now.'

I padded over to the batmen's room in the Mess on what was to be a vain quest. When I got back to the billet, clouds of blue smoke were billowing from the window and door and George was dragging a red hot iron poker down the sides of the architraves and along the skirting boards to the accompaniment of a kind of Gregorian chant, a litany of curses and imprecations such as I had never personally put to music. The refrain seemed to be something like 'Fry, you bastards, fry; you must die, tiddley-eye-tie, die!' He was, after all, a slightly devout Roman Catholic and a teacher of music to boot – at least in his former civilian existence. His success at extermination seemed to be rather less than at extempore choral composition. The smell of underdone cockroach, overdone paint and blackening woodwork was revolting.

'Come on, George, if the poker doesn't do the trick then your singing will. They'll all die anyway with the cold blowing in these cracks. If they don't, then we bloody will!' I added lugubriously. Our official day was nearly ending and we marched briskly down to make our number with our new CO, Squadron Leader B before retreating to the Mess for a snifter before dinner.

The CO was affability itself. 'Relax chaps. Have a seat and tell me a bit about yourselves. These bloody documents are too boring for words. I hate 'em! This easy-going stuff's just for in here and when I tell you, though. Outside and on duty you'll be just as smart and officer-like as I want all my officers to be. No monkey business out there – OK? Right … ' He pushed his chair back and got his briefing from us. He then outlined our own programme of duties, starting next morning at the nearby GCI for a week and then up to Leuchars for some more flying.

During the war, old B had flown Hudsons in Coastal Command, mainly on strikes against shipping on the west European coast. We were later to hear that he had been of rather more senior rank at one time but had made the fatal error of 'shooting up' (at an extremely low altitude) a solitary citizen who was walking a sandy Suffolk beach. B was only celebrating his crew's safe return from what had been a very tough operation and relieving the tension of a pretty scary day.

They came in low, having sustained a bit of flak damage, and were looking for the nearest useable airfield. B was piloting the aircraft when he saw this erect figure stalking along a wide sandy beach, apparently enjoying a danger-free day in the sun.

'Let's scare the shit out of this bonzo on the beach,' he proposed as he came in ten feet over the wave tops and aimed straight for the walker. The latter was not obviously impressed, but could be seen to wave his fist as B went round again and came in again, even lower. This time, the soldier (as it turned out to be) dived face down in the sand. B chuckled, climbed to height and headed for home.

Apparently he was court-martialled a few weeks later and a ring came off his jacket sleeve. Unfortunately, the 'bonzo on the beach' had turned out to be a very senior Army Staff Officer inspecting a minefield who was naturally reluctant to stretch his length on the sand but who had also enough presence of mind to take the aircraft number and report the episode to Air Ministry.

That evening, we met all our fellow officers, several of whom were also National Service chaps of fractionally greater seniority. The Regulars were, almost without exception, ex-WW2 aircrew, engineers, signals or admin officers and several had been decorated. A few were completely mad and had reputations for exploits both in the air and on the ground which had us wide-eyed every time we heard the stories. For legal and other reasons, most of these tales are unrecountable here, and would in any case, be better and more colourfully told by the originators. But, like all such tales, they had no doubt become embellished by the years and only detailed scrutiny of these officers' records would reveal the promotions gained and the promotions lost because of them. One Flying Officer Fighter Controller, originally from New Zealand, had been once a 'three ringer' (Squadron Leader) until, among other things, he was said, when serving as a flying instructor, to have been caught unscrewing and waving above his head to the watchers the joystick of a Tiger Moth on take-off, while the student pilot in the front cockpit, blissfully ignorant, struggled with the plane. On that first night, our own tales, even after a drink or two, were decidedly low-key and mostly referred to our civilian existence. A year or so later, it was a different story!

Work in a GCI is divided into Watches, usually of eight hours. Sometimes, however, for operational reasons, fighter controllers and their teams might have to do a double shift. Within these times, of course, there had to be breaks for relaxation. Sitting at a radar tube, watching with unremitting attention the blips which represented both friendly, 'hostile' and civilian aircraft, working out their courses, speeds and heights and correctly identifying each, is concentrated effort. It has to be done in near darkness, with a jumble of R/T messages from several sources coming through the earphones and/or loudspeakers. It is all under the control of a Chief Controller who sits overlooking the plotting table and his assistant, known as OpsB. They have direct lines to Sector Control which will decide which Squadrons to scramble for a particular task, to the ROC and to the Army AckAck (Anti-aircraft) Gunnery Liaison Officer.

The actual fighter controller sits with his radar operator/plotters at tubes down below and speaks to the pilots directly as soon as they've taken off and subsequently until they have visual or airborne radar contact with the enemy. There is an unmistakable smell of re-circulated air, hot electrical circuits, and sweaty bodies. It is from holes in the ground at various points round the British coast that the air defence of the Kingdom is coordinated. At the time described here, just after the Berlin Airlift and during the Cold War, fighter airfields were at readiness and GCIs were operational twenty-four hours a day, every day of the year. Soviet bombers and reconnaissance aircraft then had the habit of attempting quietly to intrude into NATO airspace, usually to the north and east of Shetland, just to check that we were 'on the ball'.

Several controllers would go on shift together, each at his own console and have fighters allocated to him, as soon as they were airborne, by the chief controller upstairs. The whole show was deep underground and we would turn up at this unimpressive looking brick and concrete shed in a field, a few hundred yards from the rotating aerial arrays, and go through the steel doors and down by lift or stairs to the Ops Room and cabins. There was also a secure 'Coding Room', radar engineers' workshops, toilets and restroom. We were struck by the change in atmosphere from our training days. This was now patently serious stuff.

Some of the aircraft on certain missions would be 'gunned up' (i.e. armed) and any errors could not now be written off as training mistakes. Everything we had learned was now to be put into practice expertly, carefully and most noticeably, much more quickly than before. This was for real and we immediately needed to know much more about the aircraft, their flight characteristics and their armament.

RAF Leuchars was, and probably still is, a Master Airfield, that is, an airfield that can accept aircraft for landing and take-off at all times and in all conditions, by GCA (Ground Controlled Approach) if necessary. It is a large, permanent, well-established fighter station, usually the base for a Wing strength force of both day and night (later described as all-weather) fighters. Excellent Messes, good married quarters for those who required them, a wide range of on and off duty facilities and its own RAF Regiment Ground Defence Unit differentiated it massively from the humble set-up at Macmerry.

The aircraft with which the Squadrons were then equipped consisted of two squadrons of Gloster Meteor 8s (always described as 'Meatboxes') and one of De Havilland Vampire 10s, later swopped for Gloster Meteor NF 11s and 12s. There were several Meteor 7s used for training purposes because they had dual controls in a two-seat tandem cockpit. There would also be a variety of other Communication Flight aircraft, the occasional 0xford or Anson or Varsity for navigational training, a Hawker Hunter or two for aerobatics practice and occasional visits by so-called experimental aircraft like the English Electric Lightning from Warton (not far from dear old Kirkham) where it was then being developed and tested, or a Canberra or two for radar calibration or photographic reconnaissance duties. From time to time, a Flight of American B-47 atomic bombers would fly in from Boston to sponge a bite of lunch for their crews in the Mess before they flew off again to resume their worldwide patrol. There was a time when it was NATO policy for there to be at least one of these aircraft, armed, in the air at all times. It was amazing how often their crews could squeeze several golf bags into the bomb bays, and find an hour or two to explore the thrills and hazards of Royal and Ancient St Andrews in the bygoing. There were even a few clapped out ex-WW2 B-17s dropping in to refuel after some long and tedious 'fighter affiliations' up and down the east coast of both England and Scotland. Their crews were notorious for their poor R/T discipline – and for their frankness when they watched and listened in to the controllers vectoring the fighters on these occasions.

If the controller's final vectors left the fighter with a hopeless tail-chase, this would be obvious to the B-17 crew acting as 'hostile' and they'd come up on the control frequency with something like, 'Oh Jesus. sonnyboy, that sure was a bum steer! That Limey fighter's goin' to be runnin' up my ass all the goddam day!' The RAF equivalent would be something like, 'Uniform, (the GCI call-sign) Striker 22, breaking off – tailchase.'

RAF operational stations such as Leuchars would usually have been commanded by a Group Captain or Air Commodore in overall charge of three Wings, each under the command of a Wing Commander, the WingCo (Flying), WingCo (Engineering) and the WingCo (Admin). We referred to the first of these just as did the Squadron and Flight Commanders. In practice there was the closest relationship between aircrews and the chaps on the ground who serviced their aircraft, the riggers, fitters, instrument and radar mechanics and armourers. Even in the fifties, fighter aircraft were highly expensive and technically sophisticated pieces of machinery and both, indeed all, the WingCos were capable of reminding us all of these great truths in a relatively forceful manner at regular intervals.

On arrival at Leuchars, we met the WingCo (Flying) and the Adjutant and this time we were expected. 151 Squadron had some flying time allocated to let us familiarise ourselves with Vampire NF 10s and 222 would use the Meteor 7 a couple of weeks later since their Meteor 8s were, of course, single-seaters. First we would sit down in the crew room with Pilot's Notes and draw flying suits and chutes from the appropriate stores. It represented a substantial advance from Oxfords. The power available in these combat aircraft compared to trainers was immense. Take off and landing speeds were 40 knots or more faster and the rate of climb (slow by the standards of contemporary interceptor fighters at the time of writing) were stunning to us greenhorns. Accordingly, we read assiduously. These were our first jets so we began to think in terms of pounds of thrust rather than revs and manifold pressures. We discovered new things about dive brakes and spoilers, to say nothing about armaments and air gunnery.

We also discovered, rather unnervingly, that the early Vampire10s were not fitted with ejector seats and Pilot's Notes kindly told us what to do in the event of 'abandoning the aircraft', as it is always put. The phrase has a kind of wistful feel to it, as if one were heartlessly discarding an adoring lover. In any circumstances that would have compelled one to do so, it would not have seemed like that at all. However, we were firmly of the opinion that the phraseology was carefully chosen by the financial wizards at the Ministry of Defence to ensure that we would use our best efforts always to bring these expensive items back with us in one piece after we had played with them.

The procedure was that the crew would release the overhead canopy, the pilot would invert the aircraft and the crew escape each by banging the release clip of his Sutton harness and letting the slipstream suck him out. What we came to realise later was that there was a very good chance that you would very smartly come by a pair of broken femurs or a broken neck as your body hit the tail-plane between the twin booms of the fuselage. It was less than encouraging, especially when we knew the frequency of 'flame-outs', i.e. engine stopping, in the engines currently fitted to that plane. According to one of the experienced pilots I spoke to, it also had the 'glide characteristics of a brick-built shithouse'.

In the event, I never once experienced a 'flame-out' – although we had a couple of 'flames-in', so to speak, when the radar transponder (code word 'Canary') burst into flames a long way from base. These units very often tended to overheat if they had to be left on too long. Mostly they just created smoke and went U/S but a cockpit full of smoke is seldom pleasant and the box was a bit close to the fuel tank for comfort. We learned accordingly to make very quick identifications on aircraft we had asked for 'Canary' from when we were controlling. When it was switched on, the blip on the radar tube on the ground showed little castellations, thus distinguishing it from an enemy aircraft which would have none. But in the Vampire, a manoeuvrable aircraft which responded to a light touch on the controls, there was good visibility from the cockpit, side by side seating for the two crew and the turning circle was good until you were at or about 40,000 feet where it ran out to about a six nautical miles radius at attack speed. The armourers used to grumble though. The aircraft was so low on the ground that they had little or no room to clean, demount or re-load the guns in the nose. Still, they always managed it.

Plate 13: Meteor T7 and Vampire T11 in company (© Crown Copyright MOD)

Those who flew in the RAF were, and are, always very aware of the teamwork necessary in keeping aircraft at readiness, safe and fully functional. Many aircrews formed quite close friendships and bonds of mutual trust with the latter and were unhappy when teams were from time to time broken up. Len Woodrup, describing an overhaul of a 'Meatbox' illustrates very well the separate but wholly integrated roles of the ground crews.

' ... *the first aircraft from 245 squadron was towed in. Airframe riggers jacked it off its wheels onto castored stands and scaffolding and started to remove the ailerons, flaps, rudder and elevator control surfaces, also the cockpit canopy. Ground equipment mechanics removed the wheels. Engine fitters and mechanics removed the jet engines. Armourers took out the twenty millimetre canons and the ejector seat.*

      Radar and radio mechanics removed radar and radio sets. Electrical mechanics removed starter panels, generators, control relays, gun and rocket firing mechanisms, bomb release switches, landing lights and so on. Instrument mechanics took off the bits which interested them.

The aircraft soon became an aluminium skeleton, containing only control cables, fuel tanks and fixed wiring. As another aircraft was brought in to the hangar, the first was moved to one side and the stripping process started again. Eventually three rows of Meteors were moving down the hangar in various stages of dis-assembly and re-assembly.

As the weeks progressed, the original Meteor was rebuilt with many of its original components, although some new spares were used from the store's stockpile. In theory, the stockholding was always two aircraft sets.

The aircraft was finally towed out of the hangar and filled with fuel. The engines were run up and tests were made to check engine jet pipe temperatures and synchronise power output.

The next day a pilot examined the aircraft externally and checked the operation of the control surfaces. Finally he removed the red and white sleeve from the pitot head tube and climbed into the cockpit. Before he sat down he removed the safety clip and disc on top of the ejector seat. The attendant mechanic helped the pilot fasten the parachute/seat harness straps before he climbed down from the side of the cockpit.' (War Games, pp114–5)

Our main training flights were, however, mostly in the dual controlled Meteor 7s. There was a good deal less cockpit space than in the old Oxfords and take-offs were much more thrilling. Being jet powered, they were also less noisy and, so far as we could see, the only disadvantage in them was the fact that they were not pressurised and we would be flying at much higher altitudes and higher speeds than an Oxford could even look at. In consequence, the ground crews would make sure that we were properly strapped in, and the radio lead from our 'Biggles-type' helmets plugged in before the canopy was closed and take-off checks began. The surge of acceleration as the brakes came off at the end of the runway for take-off forced one back into the seat with impressive power and was just the precursor for the experience of 'g' forces, gravitational and centrifugal forces, we would come to take for granted during aerobatics and combat exercises.

It would be hard for anyone who flew in these early jets not to be exhilarated by their performance relative to initial training aircraft and not to revel in the swooping, rolling and corkscrewing in clear blue air or between banks of cloud which gave three dimensionality to the upper environment. By contrast, the relative tranquillity of a climb to altitude on a fine sunny day alongside your Number 2 never ceased to amaze me. As we climbed into the troposphere at 30,000 feet or more, above the cirrus wisps, the upper sky would seem to assume a darker blue coat and the sunbeams would spark off every rivet and tiny fold in the aluminium wings and fuselage of the plane fifty yards on one side of you. And then, as you broke formation, would come the sudden awareness of the huge emptiness of the wide sky – especially if a layer of stratus happened to cover the earth. It was easy to understand how so many pilots who had written about air battles during WW2 would describe them as a few hectic seconds or perhaps a minute or two of aircraft all around you, converging and diverging in a chaos of airframes and bullets, only for everything to seem to evaporate into an empty sky and leave nothing but specks on the horizon and a few pillars of cloud.

Plate 14: The author in a Meteor 7 at 30,000 feet (author)

Like all young men, however, when complete concentration on what we were doing slackened, we'd lapse into the usual ribaldries about what was happening in our gut as we climbed. As the pressure of our body gasses sought the much reduced atmospheric pressure of the cockpit and upper air – something happily not much noticed in modern airliners which are usually pressurised to about a 10,000 foot level – the tendency to fart repetitively was only made bearable by the fact that we wore our oxygen masks all the time after take-off. It was habitual to set the oxygen feed to 'Normal' at take-off and to switch to 'High' at 20,000 feet and above.

A much more painful, and fractionally more unpleasant, phenomenon was noticed by any aircrew with catarrh or a cold which blocked their sinuses as they gained height in an unpressurised aircraft. The severe pain of the high pressure air in the bony cavities which could not be released to let the air pressure equalise could be truly crippling, enough to prevent proper management of one's duties on the aircraft. Something similar could also happen if one had a biggish cavity under a filling in a tooth. I have suffered from both on several occasions. It is not funny. The only cure is to dive quickly to a lower level to equalise the air pressure and abort the flight if it necessarily required high altitude.

For obvious reasons, nobody would fly with a bad cold or blocked sinuses and RAF medical officers would delight in the none too pleasant operation of washing them out for you if you complained. Similarly, regular visits to the dentist were well worthwhile. It was at RAF Leuchars that, for the first time in my life, I experienced near painless dentistry from a young and relatively newly qualified Dental Officer. Along with a pilot and a fighter controller, I went to his caravan surgery at the base and explained that I was chicken-hearted so far as dentistry was concerned.

My abject, grovelling fear derived from a series of very unpleasant dental experiences I had endured in my early boyhood. There was no dentist in my own town so every time that 'the De'il o' a' diseases' came to visit me, one of my parents would accompany me in the bus to Elgin where my mother had, to me, a wholly unwarranted faith in the skill and competence of a barbarous old chap, just about to retire. After a couple of hours in the course of which the bus completed a mystery tour of every fishing village along the Moray Firth coast, I would hold my face in miserable apprehension of what was to come. The old dentist never used anaesthesia on children.

'Their teeth are quite soft, Mrs Clark,' he would intone to my mother, 'and in any case they're better to get used to a bit of pain.' So saying, he would reach for the menacing cord-driven drill. This was driven fearsomely slowly and erratically by one of his aged feet on a contraption like a bicycle pedal. As he tired, and he always seemed to be doing so because we never could arrive until late in the day, the drill ran slowly and painfully, taking an eternity to cut away the carious dentine and exploring every nerve-ending in my head while I bawled unashamedly with the pain. Techniques such as these were later used in the war by the Gestapo as torture to extract information rather than teeth, but at my age, and brought up in a Calvinistic manse, I simply assumed that I must have sinned most terribly in my earlier childhood to warrant such a hideous 'cleansing'.

Having thus explained my gibbering apprehension to the young Flight Lieutenant dentist, I was advised to come round to the front of the dreaded chair and watch the whole procedure, while my mates, Gus and George, fearlessly had their cavities drilled and filled. The dentist explained to me his every move from the initial local injection to the final smoothing out of the amalgam. Both his patients, though somewhat stiff-jawed, were happily planning a pint with me in the Mess in quarter of an hour's time. To my discomfiture, they hung about in the surgery while I was 'done'. It was, however, a revelation to me. A little prick, which I am sure was what the dentist thought I was anyway, as the anaesthetic was injected, a minute or two of idle chat, a couple more of the whirring of the cord-driven drill (but by an electric motor), some more poking and packing, all painless, and the dentist was saying, 'Right chaps, off and get your pints. I'll have one myself off your Mess bills in an hour, but I've a couple more patients to see to before that!' My indebtedness to that RAF dentist is enormous for I have never had the slightest qualm about visiting any dentist since then.

Many of the most pleasant hours in the air were when we were on tasks described as tail-chases or 'local flying'. In the former, a Flight Commander or some other experienced pilot would lead us all around north Scotland at varying speeds and altitudes while we had to keep right on his tail as he tried to shake us off. It could become quite competitive. On the other hand, local flying (especially in VFR conditions) was more relaxed and could give opportunities to fit in (literally) flying visits to home or girl friends, and, if we were confident that we would not be seen by anyone who mattered, to 'shoot up' their ménage or work place. Janet, now my wife, used then to work as a schoolteacher at a country school near Brechin and I remember vividly one fine day looking back as we climbed out of a steep dive low (but not too low) over the school to see her headmistress, I think, gesturing vainly in our direction.

Some of the most dramatic landscapes I have ever seen were when we flew out of Leuchars just after the terrible January gales of 1953. There were, I think, two Vampires which broke their ground tethers and were damaged during that gale and innumerable tales, across the length and breadth of the country, of civilians and Servicemen alike being blown off their feet. Looking down on the terrain from a cross-country flight a week later, there were Highland valleys where whole forests lining the hills and glens, especially on each side of a loch along the length of which the gale had blown, were laid in a herring-bone pattern along the ground, flattened by the storm. So widespread was the damage that some of the valleys looked as if they'd been combed to look like the central parting of a member of a barber's shop chorus.

Plate 15: Photo taken over Brechin by the author from a Meteor 7, having just made a pass over his girl friend's home (arrowed) (author)

Back at Macmerry, the daily (and nightly) routines of watches on and watches off at the GCI at Fidra continued as we persisted in the learning of the new skills we required as controllers of better and faster aircraft flown by more highly skilled pilots and crews. Best news of all, however, was that we were now using centimetric rather than metric radar. This gave the controller the great advantage of working at a PPI which had less central clutter (round the aerial position) and which showed the aircraft as dots on the screen rather than as 'sausages' at the centre of which the aircraft was presumed to be.

This had the effect of enabling us to analyse and predict tracks with much greater accuracy as well as define with more assurance the geographical position of the aircraft. Altitude measurements of targets still gave us some problems because the aerials for this scanned in the vertical plane with a narrow beam width in both dimensions. This meant that the aerial could only relay to the controller one brief signal in each 360° rotation. Because of the size of the aerials and their dual movements (rotation plus a reciprocating vertical scanning movement) if the plotter missed the plot first time through it, then it could be dodgy confirming, perhaps half a minute later, the aircraft's height. In that time it could have flown four or five miles and the plot might not even have been of the same aircraft. Some controllers could become almost intuitively inspired with their identifications of plots. Others would be utterly nonplussed and on the edge of panic. Some pilots could become very shirty with fighter controllers who were either slow or uncertain with their vectors and other instructions – until they came down to the GCI and tried it themselves! It was one of the great strengths of the RAF that its most senior officers were always prepared to arrange plenty of airtime for controllers and at least a modicum of GCI experience for pilots and navigators.

The most senior of officers to make an impact on me during my National Service were the AOCinC of Fighter Command at that time, Air Vice Marshal Atcherley and an Air Commodore Lott, who was Sector Commander, based mainly in an underground Sector Operations Unit near Edinburgh.

So far as the first of these was concerned, he came to RAF Macmerry to carry out the annual AOC's Inspection. This was a serious occasion when every man jack of us, from CO to the most junior Admin Orderly, had to be on his best behaviour, impeccably turned out, keenly aware of all his duties and responsibilities, and with any paper work for which he might be responsible, up to date and correct. The AVM was a hugely respected ex-wartime pilot who was known to be both strict and clever on duty but charming and convivial off duty.

For days the CO had us organising extra kit inspections, chasing around when we were on duty as Orderly or Duty Officer ensuring that the Station would, of a sudden, become as 'bulled-up' as a recruit training camp. 'If it moves, salute it; if it doesn't, whitewash it!' was the universal cry. The SADO and Adjutant spent more time in their offices than we had ever known them to and the CO's prowess on the dartboard was, for once, somewhat below par. Like many operational units, we were, on the whole, more concerned with the primary task – the air defence of the United Kingdom – than with the frills and flummeries more associated with the likes of Cranwell or even Spitalgate and Kirkham. Consequently, for a week or so, everybody was edgy, and those of us who had been on duty for night flying and had therefore enjoyed less sleep than usual, were all the more so. If we came off shift at, say, 0600 hours, we could grab some breakfast at 0700, dive into our kip for about five hours and then run a ground combat exercise for some of the airmen or do a kit inspection of some of the huts in the afternoon.

The big day dawned grey and miserable – and to all our discomfiture, it stayed that way, and even got worse, in several senses. Apart from a few necessary bods who had to stay on as telephonists, firemen and so forth, the whole camp was lined up on the parade ground. As the AOC's retinue of staff cars with ensigns flying from the front mudguards slowly drove through the main gate, we called our various Flights to order and to present arms for the General Salute. The CO and Adjutant greeted the AOC and his aides with due formality, and the guard of honour was appropriately inspected in the steady drizzle.

In spite of the rain, the bricks which edged the roadways and paths around the camp were resplendent in their new whitewash. The limply fluttering RAF Ensign (brand new for the occasion) on the flagpole gave an air of ceremonial and we thought the initial parade had gone quite well. The AOC's group and the CO wandered off to do their esoteric business in the Admin block while we junior officers dismissed our Flights and shot off to ensure that all was in order and would meet the eagle-eyed scrutiny of the AVM Atcherley and his pals in the Sergeants' and Officers' Messes, the Armoury, MT Department and so on. We would then wait in the Mess to be introduced to the AOC at the end of his formal rounds.

Apparently the CO, had had a rough time of it about some of his paperwork, duty schedules and so on, but was blustering his way out of it quite well with one of the Aides. The real damage was done when the AOC apparently slipped away on his own to examine the cookhouse. All the tables, furniture and the cooking utensils had seemed not too bad and they had at least swept the floor after lunch. But when the imposing, gold-braided figure of the AOC crept into the dining hall, there was a very junior and not too bright AC2 padding up and down with a bucket of water on his arm, into which he was dipping his free hand to scatter water droplets around him on the floor like the solitary reaper.

'Laddie! Come here! What in the name of the gods do you think you're doing?' bawled Atcherley.

The little erk was significantly perturbed at the sight of so much gold braid, but dropped the bucket and saluted as best he could without showering the AOC in an arc of shimmering droplets. His next words were to bring upon our heads a stream of polysyllabic opprobrium such as that particular airman had never heard and were to consign the whole camp to another complete AOC's Inspection exactly a week later.

'Sir, I'm just laying the dust, Sir.'

'Laying the dust ... laying the bloody dust ... in a cookhouse? There should not be a bloody speck of dust in a cookhouse, laddie, and you and your Catering Officer should be well aware of that simple fact!' The AOC strode from the building, shared a brief but pointed conversation with our poor CO (whom we all liked well enough to back him to the hilt) to the effect that he would discontinue the Inspection there and then and re-run it in exactly a week's time. If everything was not entirely to his satisfaction on that occasion then heads would indubitably roll, including, perhaps even especially, the CO's!

The very special Dining-In Night for all the officers which had been planned for that evening had to be summarily cancelled, or at least postponed for a week. Most of us, when the news got around about the episode in the cookhouse, hid away in our rooms rather than face old Ben. When we did eventually assemble in the anteroom for a routine dinner the poor man was standing at the bar with a double whisky, head in his hands, muttering, 'Pray God I never clap eyes on that silly wee bastard in the cookhouse or I'll pin his balls to the dart board! Who the hell wants an AOC's inspection every week of the f****** year?' We made sympathetic noises and retreated numbly to the dining room. Fortunately our esteemed CO had not survived all of the war and a bit more without being a resilient man, so by the end of the evening we had assured him of our solidarity in the matter and that we would move heaven and earth to get everything, absolutely everything bang-on next week. Perhaps more importantly, we had all toughened our resolve with more than a few pints and drams after dinner. That night we might have been, in the patois of the northern Scot, 'fair fleein'' but there was certainly no night flying!

After a week of hectic activity and rehearsal, much cajoling, several dire threats and a certain amount of speculation as to the consequences for all of us if the AOC, yet again, took umbrage, the whole procedure was re-run. Happily, this time the AC2 laid the dust before the AOC arrived, the whitewash was even whiter in a glimmer of sunshine, the stores were in order and the books were all properly cooked. The AOC declared himself satisfied and repaired to the Officers' Mess where he showed himself to be, not only worthy of all the respect that we had afforded him, but also a most open and friendly man who took some time to acquaint himself with us National Service officers and our respective academic and other backgrounds as he did with our senior officers, some of whom he had known during and since the war.

By that time I was no longer the most junior officer in the Mess, so provided I remembered to pass the port to the left, I was not in a position to make a mess of proposing the Royal Toast. It started as a resplendent occasion with the Regular Officers all in very fancy uniforms with all medals. I was glad then that, unlike some of the National Service chaps, I had invested in a set of barathea 'best blues' but George and I had to survive an appalling exercise in topology beforehand trying to make a smart job of tying our black bow ties. Clip-ons were very infra dig and we would have been quickly found out during the high jinks that inevitably followed the dinner.

Dining-In Nights are, in effect, the CO's inspection of his officers. They are perhaps one of the few occasions when all the commissioned staff gather together at the same time to come under the eagle-eyed scrutiny of the boss. They tend to be relatively formal to begin with as everyone congregates in the anteroom for a few pre-prandials and there is some conversation with the CO and other senior officers. This is thinly disguised as social, but in reality, when reviewed later, is really aimed at allowing one's seniors an opportunity to 'suss out' what problems, difficulties or successes their junior officers might be experiencing. Most of us found that the conversation was less probing when we found ourselves able to offer the WingCo or Squadron Leader another whisky, or two, before the chat got properly under way.

Even in a simple Nissen-type Mess, the silver and crystal will come out and the long table(s) will be clad in snowy linen. At a large and long established Station like Leuchars or Cranwell, it will be even more impressive. The batmen and stewards, neatly clad and on their best behaviour, line the wall ready to serve and the assembled officers will stand, awaiting the CO and his entourage to take their places at the top table. When the CO sits, so do we. Then the Padre (if the Station is large enough to sport one) says Grace. If not, another officer will be asked to and there is a bustle of activity as the soup or *hors d'oeuvres* is served.

It was a strange thing that while the dinner was in progress, we all felt a bit constrained – largely because we knew we were always under the close scrutiny of our seniors, sometimes very senior, whereas the capers we (including the senior officers) got up to later in the evening and night were often a bit outrageous. They were not for sensitive minds. It was interesting to note how the more introspective and guarded of the commissioned, or would-be commissioned, narrators in the very interesting book, *Called Up*, by Chambers and Landreth, often remarked with some distaste on the rowdyism of an Officers' Mess on a Dining-In Night. For myself, it did seem to be a bit over the top at times but I was reconciled to the thought that traditions take many forms and can have strange origins and subtle functions. It was easy for me, who had lost a cousin, a Sergeant fighter pilot shot down in the then recent war, to see that a bit of wildness in the Mess after a few drinks might have been one way to cover the stress of repeated operations and the loss, sometimes daily, of one's friends and colleagues.

There would be a bit of rugby with the chair cushions, rough checking to see whether bow ties were properly tied and Don A, one of the Regular controllers, like myself, the son of a clergyman, would settle to the piano for a choral rendition of 'Eskimo Nell' or the 'Ball of Kirriemuir' complete with some rather graphic and exaggerated mime from the more vocally challenged (amongst whom the CO was included). Perhaps our greatest fear was that that same CO would indulge one or another of his worst after-dinner habits. The first was, by pulling rank, forcibly to enrol any three of the junior officers into a game of Canasta, a card game to which he was then addicted and which regularly would last through the night and indeed on till breakfast time. Worse still, he nearly always won the money.

His other vice, more commonly demonstrated when he was a bit depressed and after rather more booze than normal, was to decide suddenly that the party had ended. When that happened he would disconcert us all by making as to shoot out all the Anteroom lights with his Service revolver. 0.45 calibre bullets have a tendency to ricochet alarmingly after hitting the inside of a Nissen hut's corrugations so there would ensue an immediate retreat to one's bedroom or a dive to the floor behind the chairs. I have been able, compulsively even, to count up to six (when the magazine would be empty) shots in every American gangster film or Western I've ever watched since. The barman, face as white as his linen jacket, would duck into his storeroom and crouch anxiously behind the steel beer barrels we had emptied earlier in the evening. It was not surprising that we were inevitably and regularly horrified at the size of our Mess Bills and barrack damages after every Dining-In Night.

Old Ben's marksmanship was no better than ours with the .45 Service Colt. He was, however, a complete dead-eye at darts and carried his own set at all times. These were formidably heavy arrows, even for the well-built six-footer he was, but there was nobody in the Mess who could compete with him at 301 up. At lunchtimes or before dinner, he would bounce into the Anteroom, fix one of us poor Pilot Officers with his blue eyed, steely gaze. 'Right, Dave – play you for a whisky. Middle for Diddle!' and so saying, one of his brass and feathered missiles would wing its way to at least the twenty-five spot. My own feeble feather would languish somewhere nearer the treble nineteen. Occasionally one of us would prevail but such would be our consequent celebrations that our Mess Bills suffered even more than if we'd actually lost.

Lest it be thought that our daily lives as junior officers were an unending round of sinful pleasure, the reality was that we were worked quite hard. There was always some shuttling around from Macmerry to Leuchars and vice versa, and occasional detachments to radar units at Crail or St Abb's Head. We had our first of many experiences of flying night PIs and many more of controlling them. The AI mark 10 airborne radar on the Vampires and Meteor NF11s was not entirely without defects. After all, it depended on a small rotating dish aerial in the nose cone which could, in a variety of aerobatic manoeuvres, be subjected to considerable 'g' stresses. It did mean, however, that the navigators had their hands full after the initial vectors from the controllers on the ground had brought the aircraft into a favourable position to pick up a good plot from their airborne gear and which would allow the attack to be pressed home. Missiles do much of this work themselves nowadays, but then it was still necessary to bring the attacking aircraft into cannon or machine gun range (a few hundred yards rather than miles!).

It was also about this time that the tacticians at the squadrons were trying out a new line in head-on attacks. Up till then, the usual attack was originated from the enemy's beam, the attacking aircraft being directed from a position somewhat ahead of, and to right or left of, the target but such that by the time the attacker had completed his 90° final turn, the target would be close in front of him and on the same track. Matching speeds for this task was not too difficult given good radar estimates of the target aircraft's speed. Some Russian aircraft of the time were, however, known to be very fast and might out-run an attacker even after a good intercept. For this reason, the head-on attack was aimed at nullifying the speed advantage but it did, of course, mean that closing speeds of around 1,000 mph would give little time to aim and fire (and avoid hitting the enemy with your own aircraft). Again, this is a situation which becomes easier with modern guided missiles but was quite hairy in the fifties – and a total dead loss if the heights were not right. So we practised hard at these both by day and night.

In the middle of a long night at the GCI, I had been controlling two aircraft from 151 squadron on a series of PIs, both 'traditional' and head-on attacks, when, very suddenly, all the radar went down and we were left with VHF radio only. It was to prove to be an adventuresome night.

Fortunately, I had a good radar plotter behind me who had been marking on his tube with a Chinagraph the positions of both attacker and target and their tracks. ('Tracks' are the representation of the aircraft's position in relation to the ground, whereas 'courses' are the compass directions given by the controller – corrected for magnetic variation – which the pilot steers through the air. Since the body of air through which he moves is itself moving, in any direction relative to the aircraft's course, then the resultant is the track over the ground). This meant that when I called up the pilots, I could advise them of our problem and give them approximate courses and distances back to Leuchars. However, the Sector Commander had to approve of the exercise being called off, so when our chief controller called him up, he wanted to know how long it would take to fix the radar. Could the aircraft simply orbit where they were till everything was fixed? Accordingly, I called the pilots and asked them to stand by and orbit at their present positions. They were both a bit huffy about it since there was turbulence in their area and their remaining endurance was running low.

Hank, the Engineering Officer, was flapping around with a couple of Chief Technicians, one in the bowels of the consoles and another away across the fields at the aerial array. I asked him how long it would be. 'How the f*** should I know?' He bellowed. 'It's only just happened. We think it's a total HF power failure to the aerials, but we've got to know why!' and he scampered out of the control cabin. Meanwhile a quick conversation on the ground line between the chief controller and Sector had resulted in the exercise being aborted. I called the crews again. 'Suitor 21, Suitor 22, this is Uniform. Sector instructs exercise to be aborted. Transmit for fix. Over.'

There was a useless whistle as both pilots tried to transmit at once, then, 'Uniform, Suitor 21, understand exercise aborted and RTB. Suitor 21 transmitting for fix, orbiting at angels 27, indicated airspeed 320 knots, above all cloud, good visibility. This is Suitor 21 transmitting for fix. Out.'

That form of chat on the VHF was usual to allow the chaps at RDF (Radio Direction Finding) stations scattered over Scotland (or the whole of the UK for that matter) enough time on the air for them to spin their directional receiving aerials toward the transmitting aircraft. Each RDF then phoned in the direction of the transmission relative to that station and these were triangulated on the central RDF table map. Usually three RDFs at good relative angles to the aircraft would enable a 'cocked hat' to be drawn on the map within which the transmitting aircraft might be thought to be. If the 'cocked hat' was nice and small, that would be an 'Able' fix. If it were large and loose, that would be a 'Charlie' fix and correct only to about twenty-five miles. It was always comforting to get an 'Able' fix. That would be expressed in Georef notation to allow the pilot to check it on his map.

The GCI controllers would also hear the fix and immediately work out a course, allowing for conditions, wind speed and direction at the relevant altitudes, and pass it to the pilot.

'Suitor 21, Uniform. Do you read? Over.'

'Uniform, Suitor 21. Roger, strength 5. Over.'.

'Suitor 21, Uniform. Vector 273. Make angels 10. Over.'

'Uniform, Suitor 21. 273, angels 10. Thank you. Out.'

The heights advised would be determined by a number of factors including the distance out from base, the nature and amount of cloud cover and the positions of other aircraft. Other instructions would follow when the aircraft had reached that level. The other aircraft would then follow the same procedure with minor variations in instructions. Normally, the controllers would follow them down on the radar, monitoring drift and so on as well as other traffic, but we still had no radar on this occasion.

At that point, one of our Chief Techs who was an absolute wizard at dealing with electrical and electronic faults of every kind came into the control cabin to show us how the whole of Scotland had been without a radar defence system for an hour. He held up a funny, crispy, dark brown object about four inches long. It was still smoking a little. It had been a mouse which had inadvisedly explored the concrete tunnel through which the very high voltage (something like 11Kv) to the aerials was transmitted along exposed pairs of copper wires supported on low ceramic insulators. At intervals along this were small air gaps across which the voltage had no problems in arcing. It allowed the technicians to see that the current was flowing, and to keep clear of it. The adventurous mouse, however, had managed to sniff one of the wires just as its tail brushed across the other, thus short-circuiting the system. The mouse, in a flash, was done to a turn and Scotland's air defence system was in a shambles.

Nor was that the end of exciting episodes for that particular night. Having sent the aircraft back and been stood down for a tea break, we were back at the consoles half an hour later when, around 0300 hrs, everything came on line again and the technicians descended on us to effect their calibrations before we again used the apparatus. We were impressed by their skill and stood back admiringly. Unfortunately, just at that point, one of the other senior NCO Technicians appeared, rather white-faced, at the control cabin door to ask if any of us were skilled in First Aid. He held up his thumb and, right through the nail, the tip of the metacarpal bone and the soft tissue at its end was a neatly bored and cauterised hole through which we could see the light of the corridor behind him. He had managed, while checking on the damage possibly incurred by the late lamented Mus Musculus, to slip his thumb tip into the gap between the high-tension carriers and the arc had done the rest.

We concluded that it was a nice clean job and a simple dressing in the First Aid room would see him fit to continue, for the meantime at least. There was much chat about teaching him to get his finger out, and several more or less accurate quotations from, appropriately, Burns, about 'the best laid plans o' mice and men' tending to 'gang aft agley'.

If these were the scenes in the GCI associated with night flying, they never matched the excitement and glory of being in a fast and manoeuvrable aircraft as the well-defined lights of the runway and airfield buildings disappeared astern. The soft glow from the instrument panel and the deep darkness outside as one climbed through a cloud layer somehow emphasised the privacy and yet completeness of the cockpit. The restricted visual boundary determined by the navigation lights on the wing tips and the occasional flare of St Elmo's fire along the wing, would suddenly, as we broke cloud, give way to a limitless but sparkling indigo universe. Any moonlight might just catch the cloud tops below with silver and on a clear night, there might be the odd momentary shimmer of a breaking wave or a ship's wake far below. The romance of the occasion, however, could only last a few minutes while we gained height. Thereafter it was business as usual, a sharp lookout for other aircraft and close attention to the AI radar and VHF messages.

Most of the aircrews found low-level PIs much more taxing than the same exercise at 20,000 feet. At 300 or 500 feet, there is much less room for error at high speeds and the risk of unwitting loss of height in steep turns was significant. Occasionally, the tensions of the moment would be given away by a pilot failing to lift his finger from his transmit button at the end of a message, or even pressing it when he had no message to transmit, thus blocking the channel for himself and anyone else on the same frequency. Neither the chief controller nor the Wing Commander (Flying) would be best pleased at that. But it was well understood.

I remember vividly one night when I was on duty in the GCI when two of 151's Vampire NF10s were undertaking a series of low-level night PIs. The attacking aircraft had just been given his final turn-in vector and acknowledged it. We were then puzzled to hear nothing from him for some minutes. His target aircraft colleague then called to ask if we'd heard from him because he should have been in clear sight of his target by then. The eerie silence continued. It turned out that they'd gone in, probably dipped a wing in the sea as they turned at high speed and very little was ever found. Everyone was pretty depressed about episodes like that. Fortunately they were few. Another dramatic crash about that time killed a new CO for RAF Leuchars as he was actually flying up to take over the base – and that was in daylight.

The busy day and night schedules we were engaged in at that time had wholly put paid to the regular athletics training and competition I had been involved in at OCTU. There, I had been one of two or three reasonable athletes who were eventually picked to run for Group and then for Command. I still have a few paltry gongs to prove it! That would involve trundling off in a bus or three-tonner to some other RAF Station with a good athletics ground like North Weald, Halton or Duxford early in the morning, competing, in my case in the mile or three miles, and then, after tea, returning to Spitalgate, usually too late to get into Grantham for a pint or two.

Now on an operational station, the only regular exercise I could manage was a few rounds of golf with the CO on Saturdays, or occasionally a Wednesday afternoon, when I was persuaded by him (not nearly such a good golfer as he was a darts player) to forego the fleshpots of Edinburgh until evening. All my pals, except for one of them who from time to time might be Orderly or Duty Officer, shot off there like a flash at weekends. The compensation was that being stationed where we were, and having the CO's MT pool 'Standard' car, which he drove like a maniac, we would play rounds over some of the best golf courses in the land. At St Andrews, the Old, the New and the Eden, and, nearer Macmerry, Luffness New, Longniddry, and both the Gullane courses suffered from our flailing clubs. It happened that I was a better golfer than Ben by quite a bit, but he thoroughly enjoyed his golf and I saw a much more relaxed side of his personality than was usually apparent on duty. It was prudent always to give him his full amount of handicap strokes and to let him win from time to time. Strangely, the other chaps never accused me of being a creep and it certainly never occurred to me to take advantage in any way of our hours in each other's company.

By this time, I had settled into a busy and interesting routine at both Macmerry and Leuchars, had made firm friends among my fellow officers, had a new room and batman of my own and was gradually becoming better at my job. Although I did not appreciate it at the time, my reading about others' experience of National Service, in whatever arm of the Services, has made it clear to me that the single biggest factor determining whether one enjoyed or detested doing National Service was that of being active and involved. Even the rigours of combat were preferred by many to the endless boredom of being hideously underemployed, especially in some occupation which one had not chosen and which did not stretch one's abilities in the slightest. It is true that there were a few times when poor weather, aircraft or equipment unserviceability would reduce us to finding tedious (and perhaps unnecessary) tasks to carry out. These might have included more kit inspections for some of the airmen, refresher courses in some operational procedures, ground combat exercises, decoding secret signals or equipment inventory checks (most hated of all!).

It was also alleged by our seniors that all junior officers had to become proficient at coding and decoding secret signals. We suspected that the thrust of their enthusiasm for our undertaking this task was contributed to much more by the awareness that it was an ineffably boring task than by any real need for young chaps who would be out of it within the year to become something like the Maestros of Bletchley. When things were quiet, then I might be sent into a signals' room where the pad with the messages would be handed to me, full of mysterious four letter groups. With due ritual, the code book for the day would be taken from the safe and the door had to be locked by me before I opened the code book and began the laborious task. Most of the messages were of such stupendous banality and dullness that one's schoolboy-like sense of romance and excitement at being party to secrets of State was utterly extinguished long before the last group had been deciphered. It was one of the great tediums of Service life from which other ranks were spared. They never knew what they were missing. They also missed being inventory holders.

At one stage I had, as the Adjutant had originally predicted, been the junior officer given the Officers' Mess inventory to manage after the incumbent was demobbed. Being green and inexperienced in such matters, I was easily hoodwinked into accepting the inventory even though it suffered from innumerable deficiencies. As time went by, however, inventory checks by a senior Admin officer were managed by complex arrangements with the officer in charge of the Sergeants' Mess inventory. For example, I was well aware that we held insufficient pots and pans of various sorts, several upright chairs too few, a great deal of cutlery too little, great deficiencies of cleaning brushes and materials and so on. The Sergeants' Mess was in a similar situation. Since it was a physical impossibility for the Inspecting Officer to be in two places at once, and since the two Messes were nearly adjacent, my colleague holding that inventory and myself were no time in arranging for a human chain of Admin Orderlies and batmen to spirit the right number of items between Messes at the appropriate time of the inspection. Their willingness to undertake this task was, of course, in direct proportion to the amount of drinks' money we, the officers concerned, were prepared to lay out in the interests of a 'complete' inventory.

The detached lay observer on such occasions would have found the little crocodile of 'bearers' shuttling in both directions between the buildings, laden with 'pots, cooking, cast iron, 4 pint', 'brushes, wooden, floor', 'chairs, upright, officers, for the use of', 'mugs, pint, plain' and even 'curtains, bedroom, chintz, patterned', quite fascinating. It had to be done both efficiently and surreptitiously, outwith the passing gaze of any senior officer. Junior officers and NCOs could be guaranteed not to spill the beans for they could be in the same boat at any time. Once the magic signature was on the last sheet of the inventory, all could revert to its rightful home for another six months or so. What could be said was that we were all sure there was enough of everything between the two Messes to furnish fully any one of them, with maybe a little to spare!

Very senior officers, Air Commodores and above, did not have much to do with 'sprog' young officers like us. They, braided and be-medalled, would be seen at the top table with the CO in large Messes like Leuchars, hogging at breakfast time, for the page three girls or the sports news, the *Daily Mirror*, the *Sketch* or the *News of the World* on Sundays while we 'sprogs' struggled with the *Times* or the *Guardian*. Breakfast was the only meal at which the reading of newspapers at table was, for officers, condoned in the RAF.

Then one night, because of a shortage, through leave or other duties, of more senior officers at the GCI, I was, for once, fulfilling two roles of both Fighter Controller in the cabins and Chief Controller in the Ops Room. There was little air activity and I was congratulating myself on how well the night was going. One control cabin was active with a pair from 151 which had just taken off when the Pilot Officer who was controlling them contacted me on his internal phone to the effect that he had two or three plots on his tube away up north of Shetland which looked as if they were Russian 'Bears' or 'Badgers' intruding on our airspace, very high, flying east to west and north of Unst. At that range, plots could be unstable and could come and go a bit so I went through to have a look myself. Sure enough, two and possibly three 'blips' were right at the edge of the screen. There were no civil or RAF flights scheduled for that area at that time (0130 hours) so we had to take the view that they might be hostile. The Cold War was still very real at that time and there were NATO provisions for dealing with such threats.

This was serious stuff. We were supposed to intercept, with armed aircraft, such intruders and warn them off – shoot them down if they persisted. But this was well outside the authority of the GCI controller. It had to be cleared with the Sector Controller in his hole in the ground at Barnton. In recent times we had intercepted other stray Soviet bombers in that general area but they had always veered off with a wave to our crews.

We believed that they were simply checking out our readiness and efficiency of our equipment. But more than one plot was more problematic. Then I thought that it could be 'anaprop' (anomalous propagation) or a kind of false signal which the radar picks up from time to time in special circumstances due to reflections from the Heaviside layer. It was not a decision I relished. If it was not 'anaprop' and I disregarded it, I was in trouble, perhaps we all were! If it was and I sent a couple of fighters after it at what would be extreme range, I could endanger the crews for nothing.

Straight away I scrambled a couple of Vampire NF10s, gunned-up and with wing tanks. The cabin controller put them on a northern vector to make all height as fast as possible. Simultaneously I had OpsB call Sector and waited to hear the Sector Commander's reassuring tones on the headset. I was tense and feeling the responsibility rather heavy.

I could hear the phone being picked up at Sector.

'AC Lott here!'

I was flabbergasted, a wretched airman on the blower at Sector in a situation like this. I gave him a right mouthful.

'AC Lott, for God's sake! AC Lott! This is the Controller at Dirleton here and I don't need a bloody aircraftsman. Shift your bloody arse, Airman, and get me the Sector Controller pronto or you're on a fizzer!'

There was a significant pause. Then, 'Air Commodore Lott here. To whom am I speaking?'

'Oh, Christ', I thought, 'now I'm really in the shit!' Visions of a court martial for insubordination, bad judgment, lack of awareness of the identities of my senior officers and eventual dispatch, stripped of my commission, to Cape Wrath flashed through my mind. However, the matters of the moment were more pressing so I actually said, 'Pilot Officer Clark, Sir, duty GCI controller. We have a problem … ' and I went on to brief the Air Commodore on the situation. He immediately authorised the scramble to press on and intercept and agreed to be 'on tap' throughout the episode. I went through to the cabin to see how the controller and the aircraft were doing.

By this time the two aircraft were still climbing since the plotters had given us a target height of angels 41, close to the aircrafts' operational ceiling, and there seemed to be several targets, though their position was indeterminate. They seemed to appear and disappear. It was beginning to look more like 'anaprop' but we could not be sure. I called Hank, the engineering officer, to take a look at the tube and see what he thought of the echoes. He could not be sure either.

The two pilots were getting anxious about fuel. They had faced headwinds on the climb and had had to use a lot of throttle to make speed on the climb. They were nearly at the point of no return. If they passed that, they had no guarantee of having enough fuel to RTB. In the OPs room I called Sector again and asked for the Air Commodore to make the decision as to whether the two crews had to press on. They were still not in range of the target plots with their airborne radar and were yawing a bit in the thin air at that height. The leader called the GCI to ask us to check out alternate landing facilities if they could not get back to Leuchars, and just as I was checking with Lossiemouth and Kinloss that they were open, I heard the radio repeater in the OPs Room.

'Uniform, Suitor 17, nothing in sight or on our AI, some turbulence. Probably 'anaprop'. Request immediate RTB. Over.'

The plots of attacker and targets were converging and both were erratic and uncertain at the extreme range. It had to be 'anaprop'. Not a Russian 'Bear' or 'Badger' in sight!

'17, Uniform. Affirmative RTB. Call Kinloss on Channel (giving the appropriate frequency).'

The two aircraft turned for home and the cabin controller gave them a vector which optimised their track for either Kinloss or Leuchars. From where they were, there was only a 10° difference anyway between them and the two bases. We all relaxed briefly but knew that getting back to base was going to be dodgy for both crews.

Sector was informed and the Air Commodore, very civilly in the circumstances, thanked us for our services. He would be up on the morrow to Macmerry to speak to our CO and he advised the duty controllers and myself in particular to be available to speak to him. That did not exactly cheer me up.

Our relief that there was no national emergency was soon tempered by the next call from a rather tense pilot in the second aircraft on the sortie.

'Uniform, Uniform, Suitor 19. I have about ten minutes flying time fuel left. Commencing descent to Kinloss. ETA twelve minutes. Please clear with them that I must get in first time round or ditch. Over.'

'Suitor 19, Uniform. Roger. Confirm ETA Kinloss twelve minutes, with tanks expected empty. Stand by. Out.'

There then followed a hasty phone call to Kinloss Tower (Air Traffic Control) in the course of which I made it plain that no other traffic should get in the way of 19 and that their emergency crews should stand by. Fortunately their night flying schedules were completed so we were able to reassure 19 that he would get straight in and he should contact Kinloss Tower now. Suitor 17 then came on to say he was descending with 19 who was still under power but that he would soon break away as he thought his fuel would allow him to make it back to Leuchars.

At that point, 19 left our frequency, just before, as it turned out, his engine stopped and he was forced to glide for the last few miles and made a good landing without power – a considerable feat of airmanship! The other aircraft was vectored in by the GCI and landed at Leuchars with not much more than a smell in the tank. We expected the Sergeant pilot of 19 to be refuelled and to fly home after he and his navigator had had a few hours of sleep at Kinloss. Or so we thought! It turned out that they did not have the right sort of key to open the fuel tank of a 'Vampire' at Kinloss and another aircraft had to fly one up from Leuchars next day. That's modern technology for you!

The bus drove a weary watch up to the domestic site at about 0430 hours of the day after we had gone on watch. What had started as a quiet and uneventful night had escalated into a crisis situation that was right on the edge of the competence of someone as junior as myself. I was not looking forward to the repercussions from Sector and my own CO later in the morning. All that I could hope for was that the CO at least would not wish to be wakened until breakfast time and that I would have time both for a few hours' sleep and a chance to review and organise my thoughts and memories of what I had done throughout the episode before facing him.

I resisted the temptation during the morning to telephone the two crews at 151 Squadron. If there were to be an inquiry about the episode either by the WingCo (Flying) or by the Sector Commander, then it would be better if I were not to be thought to be influencing the views of anyone at all. I knew both crews and that they would be fair and factual in their de-briefings. George and 'Tommy' Atkins, two of my PO buddies had got to hear of the excitement by mid morning.

'Hear you nearly lost us a couple of aircraft last night, Dave!' they greeted me over coffee. (I was off-duty till evening.)

'Bollocks! It was a masterly performance. Jim (the actual cabin controller) and I handled the whole affair with aplomb and consummate competence. It was just a good job that some of you wankers weren't on or the whole bloody squadron would have been dropping out of the sky all over Scotland!'

They knew perfectly well how fraught it had been and were just glad that they had not in fact been on duty in a situation like that. At that stage, none of them knew of my unwitting insubordination of an Air Commodore. Unfortunately, George said, 'Why are you not still in your steaming pit pushing out the zzzzzz's, anyway. You must be knackered.'

Jim chipped in too quickly. 'Because he's carpeted in front of the CO at 1400 hours. You should have heard him bawling out the Sector Commander last night. Called him a 'stupid bastard' or something so the

Air Commodore's coming over from Edinburgh at two to tear a strip off him. Still, I've booked him for my batman when he's back as an AC2 tomorrow. At least, compared to you lot, he's house trained and sometimes clean.' There was a sudden hush of disbelief.

'Jesus, Dave, what did you say to him?' So I told my side of the tale as best I could. It would be a useful rehearsal for after lunch.

I knocked on the CO's door at 1400 hours exactly. I had even changed into my best blues. It seemed tactful – and it might be the last time I'd wear them. When I entered, both Ben and the Air Commodore were standing at the window behind the desk but they asked me to take a seat and sat down themselves. The amount of blue braid on the arms and medal ribbons on the chests in front of me was substantial. Ben said, 'I think you've made the acquaintance of Air Commodore Lott, Dave, haven't you?' I concurred.

'Pilot Officer Clark, I'd like first of all to hear your appreciation of the tactical situation in Sector airspace between the hours of midnight and four a.m. this morning. I have of course heard all the recorded transmissions and seen all the logs.'

So keyed up was I with trying to marshal my facts after only a few hours' sleep that I forgot to apologise for my outburst. However, I recounted the events and procedures of the night before as best I could. The Air Commodore nodded a few times but gave no clues as to what view he was taking of the whole thing. Eventually he said, 'You seemed a bit rattled when you greeted me on the phone last night. Were you?'

'Yes, Sir. Normally Flight Lieutenant T would have been Chief Controller and I would have passed some of the decisions to him.'

'Quite right, Clark, but he wasn't, was he?'

'No, Sir.' Just as I was going to stammer out some sort of an apology to him personally, he cut in again.

'In the circumstances, Ben and I have come to the conclusion that you handled the whole operation with a competence beyond your experience. There were difficult decisions to be reached and although it turned out to be 'anaprop' you did what was necessary – although I must say that I shall expect to be treated with more deference by junior officers in future. Incidentally, I do agree that it was stupid of me to say A C Lott rather than Air Commodore Lott. It was misleading.'

This was not what I had been expecting and my relief must have been palpable. 'Thank you Sir, I do apologise for shouting at you. I am unlikely to repeat it.'

'I should bloody well think so, Clark.' He smiled, 'Anyway, we one-ringers[*] have to stick together!' My guess is that that sort of resolution of a situation could only have come about because of the general ethos of the RAF – although I may be doing the other Services an injustice in saying so. I felt a great weight had come off my shoulders and marched briskly up to the Mess to embellish the story and extract a few drinks from my mates on the strength of it.

Imperceptibly, my second winter and spring in the RAF wore on with only a few longueurs to mar the daily, and the nightly, round. Those events which were sufficiently far, in their content, from our usual working routine at airfield or GCI did, however, illustrate the range of activities that a young National Service officer might have to tackle.

1953 was well under way when the Adjutant called me one morning when no flying was planned to accompany a young eighteen year old AC2 to the Sheriff Court in Haddington as 'Airman's Friend'. That is the role assigned to the officer who speaks for the accused in a civil court when no matters that might give rise to a court martial are involved. In this case the poor airman had been 'nicked' for some relatively unimportant road traffic offence to which he would plead guilty.

As we were driven by one of the MT pool drivers to the court, the poor chap was desperately in awe of what would become of him. Since his offence had been outside duty hours, from our point of view he would have no charge to face in front of the CO. Both he and I knew that he was a first offender and that any penalty would be relatively light. At eighteen years of age, however, the lad needed reassuring that people were not hanged for that sort of offence nowadays and that any fine and endorsement of his licence was something he could reasonably be expected to live down within the year. My task was simply to be identified in Court as the officer representing the RAF as the accused's employer. Up till then I don't think I'd ever been in a court of law in my

---

[*] The badges of rank of an Air Commodore and of a Pilot Officer both consist of a single band of two-tone blue and black braid. That of a Pilot Officer is about a third of an inch wide whereas that of an Air Commodore is about two and a half inches wide.

life. Even my parents, who had moved in thoroughly middle class circles, were somewhat in awe of the local Sheriff themselves. With that background, I was all too aware of my youth and inexperience in the presence of a judge and perhaps less sure of myself than I appeared to the poor airman.

I might be asked for a report on the accused's military record (which was uninspiring but without major blemish) and the Sheriff might ask me any ancillary questions about the man as he thought fit. I carried the airman's personal file and some notes from his section NCO. Once more, the best blues were out and I was called on to report on the airman and answer a few ancillary questions. The colour gradually returned to the wee white face in the dock as I talked and he got away with a minimal fine and an endorsement of his licence. Coming back in the car, he was relieved beyond belief at the penalty and that the whole episode was behind him. Waiting to hear when he would be called to Court had blighted the past few months of his Service.

'Sir,' he asked, as we drove back to the Station, 'do you think it'll be in the papers?' I told him there might be a snippet in the local Haddington press but that it would not get banner headlines in *The Times*. I asked him why he was concerned and he rather shamefacedly told me, 'If ma grannie gets tae hear o' this, she'll gie me a awfu' beltin'.'

As he was a west coaster I told him that she would not hear anything from us (the RAF) and he could perhaps choose his time to tell her, if ever. He was even more relieved than when we came out of court. I doubt very much whether contemporary eighteen-year-olds would either worry as much about a speeding offence (I think it was) or set such store by his granny's reaction to the matter. In my mind, that was to his credit.

The second major event to stand out in memory as being outside normal duties was much more dramatic and tragic. I happened to be Duty Officer one day and was more or less confined to the camp from morning till the flag came down at night. It was early afternoon and I was on my way from some errand to the Guardroom when I noticed a bright yellow painted 'Firefly', which I thought might be from a nearby Royal Naval air station, doing a series of relatively low-level power dives at a fairly steep angle a couple of miles to the west. It did seem a curious set of manoeuvres and I remarked on it to a passing fellow officer. He said he'd seen this done some days before and that he thought, though it was no more than hearsay, that the aircraft was on lease to Ferranti as a research aircraft on which to test new radar or other electronic gear.

Halfway to the Mess the engine note changed, (the aircraft was propeller driven) and there was a great bang. I looked across the fields and there was a column of black smoke rising near the edge of a wood about a mile away. It was obvious that the plane had crashed and it looked serious. I rang the SADO and asked whether we had any responsibilities as the nearest RAF Unit. He thought we did, both for rescue and for mounting a guard on any wreckage. 'It's all yours Clarkie-boy,' he said. 'I'm far too busy' as he pushed away some papers and stretched his legs languidly on the edge of his desk and grinned. 'After all, I'm not Duty Officer today. You are. You'd better get a truck, call out the guard and a few of the Sick Berth chaps and get over there. If the Rozzers call, I'll tell them you're on your way.'

Fortunately, the 'Rozzers', as he called them, did call a few minutes later and it was fortunate that they did. Although I had organised a truck, the personnel and equipment for the job, there was the small matter of confirming the exact locale of the crash. The Police had got that from the local farmer on whose ground it had occurred. We were advised that it was probably fatal. At the age of twenty-three, I had not up till then even seen a dead body, no less extract one from a crash. Once more, it was a case of putting a bold face on it and doing my best to assume an air of command. I remember wondering as the three-ton Bedford trundled toward the scene whether this was what 'OQs' was all about.

We drove across a field and alongside a small wood to reach the site and I remember thinking that it was my good fortune that the crash had not occurred close to a main road. The sightseeing ghouls would then have given us a good deal more trouble – and we might have revealed our own squeamishness in a way perhaps not terribly flattering to ourselves. As it was, when we reached the crater at the foot of which the remains of the 'Firefly' were still smoking and steaming, there were only a couple of farm workers whom we had to send back out of the immediate area and they were not enthusiastic anyway about going any closer than fifty yards. They asked me whether there was any ammunition in the aircraft and I had to say that I did not know. Up to that point it had not occurred to me that there would be. I had simply taken it for granted that it had a role only as a research vehicle, but now I began to wonder. I thought that if it had been going to ignite, it would have done so by now.

The guard Corporal and a 'Whitecap' (RAF Policeman) quickly strung out a boundary tape and a few airmen with rifles at points around it. I knew that the rifles were unloaded but the public did not, so it was quite effective. A few more adventurous characters had by now crossed the field and were watching from a distance. I took three chaps from the Sickbay into the hole and close to the wreckage immediately, since our first task was to get any surviving crew out as quickly as possible. As soon as we got close, it was obvious that there was no life left for the two poor chaps, pilot and navigator/radar operator. There are two separate cockpits in tandem on that aircraft and the side of the pilot's in front was broken off. I thought I could release his harness and extract his body from that side. I asked one of the chaps to help me but he turned away retching and as pale as a sheet. The other two were not much better and it looked as if they were going to pass out. I urged them to put their heads between their legs for a minute till they felt better and then help.

On my own, I reached up toward the dead pilot who had suffered terrible facial and head injuries, grasped his, still not really cold, hand and pulled his arm to get the body nearer to a position from which we could get it out of the aircraft. The whole arm came away in my hand. It had been severed at the shoulder under his uniform jacket. He was in Naval uniform and I grieved to see the wedding ring on his swollen and broken finger. It was all I could do not to be sick myself but I was brought back to my senses by the arrival of a proper Rescue team of firemen, I think, who took over the business of retrieving the bodies. The pilot's features were unrecognisable and of course he had multiple other injuries. The only consolation was that he must have died instantly, as must his navigator.

The latter presented a more serious problem to the rescue squad. He was not facially damaged nearly so much, probably because he had put his arm over his face at impact, but such is the curious effect of sudden impact that much of his abdominal skin and tissue had burst through his flying suit and wound itself in strips around the control column in front of him. It was impossible to find the release clasp of his harness so he had to be cut out of his cockpit and the human tissue unwound from the controls. We laid the two bodies as reverently as we could on and under a couple of Service blankets. I sent my obviously suffering airmen back to the truck and handed the bodies over to the Ambulance and Police. The guard had to be scheduled for reliefs through the night since there was secret apparatus, albeit smashed, in the wreckage, and until further notice that the wreckage had been removed. I returned to the Station on the truck to find most people on day shift coming off duty so I went straight to the Mess and ordered a large brandy. I felt I needed it.

A couple of fellow officers came in, took one look at me and one of them said, 'Good God, Dave, if that's what being Duty Officer does for you, I'm never going to do it again. Have you seen a bloody ghost or something?' I caught my pallid complexion in the bit of mirror behind the bar. It hadn't occurred to me that I still looked like that an hour after the worst of my experience was over. I said I thought perhaps I had seen a couple of ghosts and was not keen on the experience.

At that point the SADO came in for his pre-prandials and explained to the others what I'd been up to. So I had to go over the gruesome details again. But we were young and resilient. In other circumstances, I might have taken a few drinks more than usual that night but I was still Duty Officer and had to be stone cold sober later for other duties like visiting any airmen on charges in the Guardhouse and the flag lowering ceremony at 2100 hours. University had not taught me any useful tricks for dealing with these sorts of exigencies. Curiously, and in retrospect, I think aspects of my Service training at OCTU and otherwise had.

It was not lost on me many years later that I had had no post-traumatic stress counselling after my gruesome experience but that I had myself in my later professional career often given such counselling to others who, by any reckoning, had themselves been subject to less stress. I found myself wondering whether the contemporary citizen is inherently less stress-tolerant than we were then. Perhaps we were, to some extent, stress-inoculated, both by the particular jobs we were in on National Service and because we had just lived through the privations and hazards of war. Perhaps, and I think more importantly, we expected less support in such situations and there was also high pay-off in our Service situation in being self-sufficient and having our own coping strategies when things got 'a bit fraught', as we would say.

There was also the advantage of great support, largely tacit, but deriving from the fundamental understanding and comradeship of one's fellow Servicemen of all ranks. The chaps who had been sick at the crash site knew I would never divulge it to anyone, officer or airman, and, had it been the other way round, I knew they might have had a wee chortle about it among themselves but they would not have made fun of me or 'spilled the beans' to their pals about me. Moreover, in spite of the apparently light-hearted banter and raillery about stressful situations both on the ground and in the air, which was 'par for the course' both among junior officers and senior NCOs, all of us were aware that it could all happen to any of us at any time. The chat, the exaggeration and the bravado were all a cover for a constant low-level anxiety which was never far from consciousness.

It is more than likely that those writers quoted by Royle and by Chambers and Landreth who metaphorically raised their eyebrows and sometimes were explicitly scornful at some of the high jinks that some officers got up to at Dining-In Nights had endured a National Service in very boring but usually stress-free occupations. It is possible too that some who involved themselves in those same high jinks did so for different reasons, conformity, insecurity or simple stupidity rather than, as I am postulating, for some, to release pressure. It is equally possible that others again avoided the anteroom rugger etc and went off to their room with a book or spent more time in the gym as their means of release. All were legitimate adaptation methods and could, of course, be inter-mixed as the occasion demanded or the individual felt appropriate.

Plate 16: Meteor NF11 on the approach (Paul Crossley)

Plate 17: Vampire NF10 starting up at RAF Leuchars (Andy Thomas)

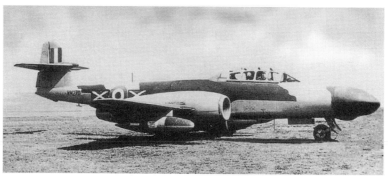

Plate 18: Meteor NF11 of 151 Squadron at Leuchars (author)

CHAPTER 7

Abroad

About this time, the Vampire NF 10s of 151 Squadron were being replaced by a tandem seated, pressurised, 'all-weather' version of the Meteor 7, the NF 11, with an elongated nose to accommodate the AI mark 10 radar. It still had the long, heavily metalled, side-opening, canopy of the '7' though later versions, the NF12 and 14, were fitted with a nice, long, clear Perspex canopy. We were to become familiar with the two slightly later versions, the last of the variants of that worthy workhorse, the 'Meatbox', also with the longer nose to accommodate the airborne radar, but only when we had been demobbed from full-time Service and were doing our required three and a half years part-time airmen in the Royal Auxiliary Air Force. The performance, especially in climb and at high altitude, was improved, but the armament was still essentially four 20mm cannon. That meant we had new aircraft with somewhat different flight characteristics for us to familiarise ourselves with.

The day fighter squadrons were still stuck with their single seat Meteor 8s but just as the night fighter chaps of 151 were all agog to get the new delta-winged Javelin, so were 43 and 222 squadrons waiting for Hawker Hunters and/or English Electric Lightnings. But as ever, in the Service, National or otherwise, there were always longer waits for new equipment than the crews would have wished for. The Javelins arrived at 151 after I had been demobbed. Worse still, after a few years, 151 Squadron was disbanded and new homes had to be found for our mascots, a pair of rather cute little owls, normally kept in a little aviary at Leuchars. Yes, they were cute little Little Owls, to be exact.

In the high summer of 1953, a major NATO exercise, 'Operation Coronet' was to take place in Germany. Apart from the squadrons permanently on station at places like Brüggen, Rheine and Wahn, several others, including 151, were to join 2nd TAF (Tactical Airforce) in Europe. Mobile Fighter Control Units would also be necessary to back up the permanent control staff in West Germany. A substantial representation, both of aircraft, crews and controllers from our Group was therefore instructed to prepare for some weeks on the continent. Fantasies of cool German Pilsner by the banks of the Rhine, of fresh-faced German girls who might want to practise their English, and of a genial, warmer summer, all found a place at the back of our minds as we scuttled off to collect our warrants for a brief period of embarkation leave.

It is not the Service way, however, to make things too easy for its junior officers. Along with my travel warrant was a further buff envelope pressed into my sweaty hand by the SADO. He obviously knew its contents, and yet again, his knowing grin filled me with the deepest apprehension. Before I left the office, I had opened it to scan the contents. It seemed strange to issue orders like this just prior to leave taking.

We had looked forward to a relaxing week's leave in the north with parents and girl friends before a brief and comfortable flight from Leuchars to the appointed airfield in Westphalia. But no, it was not to be. The signal in the buff envelope said that Pilot Officer Clark and a certain Pilot Officer Evans, from another unit and whom I had never clapped eyes on, had been designated as officers in charge of a train load of airmen who were to be shipped out, along with a number of senior NCOs, from Lytham St Anne's to various bases in Germany. On my return from leave, I would collect overnight baggage only from the Mess and would proceed to Lytham by train where the local RTO (Rail Transport Officer) would introduce me to my colleague, Evans, and our 600 young charges. My other kit required in Germany would be sent out to my designated base at Sundern, Westphalia, along with that of my fellow officers selected for this duty who would monitor it on its way there and meet me again after I had delivered the 600 to places like Wesel, Osnabrück, Celle and Münster. This whole programme, I thought, had all the hallmarks of an impending massive cock-up.

The easy bit was getting myself down to Lytham from Edinburgh by train. Now that I was an officer and gentleman, there was none of the sweaty crush of a third class compartment. I revelled in what was only my second experience ever of travelling first class in a train. The first time had been when I travelled from Grantham to Aberdeen on leave after being newly commissioned. On that occasion the elation of having become an officer had masked the details of the trip.

I met Evans on the platform at Lytham with sufficient time before the train departed for us to have a chat about our strategy of management. In spite of the fact that he was an admin rather than an operational branch officer, I got the impression that he was even less senior than I was and was reluctant to take the lead in organising things. It was then that I imparted to him the lore I had gained about the consummate art of successful delegation – especially to competent NCOs. This was immediately reinforced by the sight of three or four Flight Sergeants and a Warrant Officer briskly lining up the 600 airmen on the platform for a head count. We were right. They all had one each! It turned out that the WO was present only to report that everyone had got aboard the train so he need not be included in our grand plan. Fortunately, it was a special troop train so the distracting presence of civilians would not embarrass us. Evans had by this time confirmed that I was the senior officer and thus would hold the nominal roll and sign for the receipt of 600 bodies. He had already himself discovered the art of delegation.

Covertly, I had been observing the NCOs at work as they sorted out the airmen and their kit on the platform. Two of them seemed, although I must have been going on minimal cues, to be slightly more positive and analytical than the others. Accordingly, I moved quietly toward the first of these two and waited till there was a lull in the proceedings. 'Flight Sergeant! – A quick word, if you please.' 'Sir!' he acknowledged, and had a quick word of his own with the men in front of him – something to the effect that he'd have anyone who moved from their spot castrated there and then. He did an immaculate left turn and marched, business-like, toward me. It was hard for me to think that a year ago I'd never have dared to speak first to a Flight Sergeant and equally hard to suppress the thought that the 'Chiefy' must be thinking 'What's this greenhorn, jumped-up wanker of an officer up to now?' If he did, he showed no sign of it. He was a big fellow with a pleasant smile as I introduced Evans and myself. Next to the departing Warrant Officer, he turned out to be the most senior NCO. That must have conveyed itself to me in a subliminal way as I watched his earlier performance. That made it easier to discuss matters with him since I would not be offending any of the other NCOs present. They could be a bit touchy about such things.

His orders had been more detailed than my own. There were to be brief breaks in the train journey at Crewe and Rugby when the men would be allowed to disembark briefly to go to the toilets and collect tea and a wad. We were due to arrive at Harwich in the evening where emigration and customs' rituals would be observed and about two hours later we would board the regular ferry to Hook of Holland. We decided to cut the breaks to fifteen rather than the twenty minutes scheduled on the orders. That would give us some leeway to round up stragglers and get away on time. After all, the train, although a special one, was still running on track that had to be cleared for normal traffic as well.

There were enough Sergeants and Flight Sergeants to allocate one to every two carriages although we felt it better for them to be separated in a carriage of their own midway along the train for the journey itself. They would simply patrol the length of the train from time to time to keep order and check that there were no mishaps. Evans and I would take our turns at this too and we sat in a compartment next to the NCOs. We were all in agreement about these arrangements before the train drew into the station at Lytham St Anne's. I offered up a silent prayer of thanks for some decent NCOs.

About 550 or so of the troops were sensible and orderly. To cater for the inanities and indiscipline of the rest, we decided that the NCOs and ourselves would get off first at all the stops and station ourselves at intervals along the length of the train before we allowed any other doors to be opened. We would then impress the men about noting which carriage they were to return to and indeed to which train. It would have been all too easy for some of them to have dashed off into a lavatory, exited by another door or platform and piled into the wrong train. Indeed some of them might have had something of the sort in mind! We cleared it with the Station Master that we could use whistles to signal disembarkation and re-embarkation. We did not want to face the spectacle of three or four trains suddenly chugging off prematurely to the four corners of the land, full of mystified passengers, just because our Sergeants were making free with the whistles.

At the first whistle, doors swung open and an inchoate mass of air force blue in boots rattled across to the Crewe station toilets and buffet. The official distribution of tea and wads was not scheduled to happen till we reached Rugby. Some even took the fleeting opportunity to use the old cast iron embossing machines which, for a few pence, punched out on aluminium tape one's name and address, or anything else. They would use the output to mark their kit or bed space later. Nowadays you can buy hand-sized plastic versions of the same apparatus in any newsagent's. Then, the machine, cast iron and usually painted red or blue was a totem worshipped by many a youngster on every major railway platform.

Three shrill blasts on Flight Sergeant F's whistle a quarter of an hour later brought them all, more reluctantly, chewing food and supping tea from cardboard cups, back to the train and into their places in the carriages. The count began again – and again – and again. I was worried. It was not so long ago that I had bawled out an Air Commodore, and I had neither lost an aeroplane nor a crew. What would happen if I lost an airman, even 2nd class? The Flight Sergeant had checked very thoroughly and reported to me that there was one man missing. We had 599 airmen properly *in situ*.

The train was now necessarily delayed while two of the NCOs, PO Evans and myself scoured the hidden, and in many cases, none too salubrious recesses of Crewe railway station. The miscreant was eventually found curled up asleep on a waiting room bench and was marched none too ceremoniously back to his place on the train. One more episode like that and he was on a 'fizzer'! Five minutes late, we settled back for a quiet read as the train lumbered through the English countryside, confident that the departure of the night ferry would not be compromised by this brief delay.

Troop trains do not speed imperiously across the land on their military business. They meander at a boringly leisurely pace by way of branch lines and iron byways, always ready to halt, wheezing and puffing like a bronchitic old man, while smug civilian expresses thunder past exercising their priority in a blur of steamy windows.

Sometimes we thought that the signalmen must have gone to sleep or forgotten about us altogether, then, with a jerk and a shudder, we would start up and struggle along for another twenty miles or so to the next hiatus. Perhaps it was just because we were crossing the industrial heartlands of England. Travelling sophisticates had once advised me that, in the UK at least, journeys from north to south and vice versa were always quicker and easier than trips from west to east. This was always said in such a way as to imply that it all had to do with deep mystery, lines of magnetic force, or other occult matters rather than just with poor organisation or the local topography. I was rapidly beginning to lose the healthy scepticism with which I would normally have treated such sallies. Worse still, we were still not at Rugby, the stop for snacks, and, as they say in the best Westerns, my 'tape worms was really hollerin''. The schedules had not allowed me any lunch before boarding, organisational matters and my concerns about our laggard airman at Crewe had prevented me getting a cuppa and biscuit there and the afternoon was already well spent.

However, no sooner had these morale-eroding thoughts entered my mind than Rugby hove in sight. This really was a twenty-minute stop. Everyone was to collect from a number of official trolleys a wad of sandwiches and yet another large paper cup of tea. Evans, myself, and the senior NCOs leapt out with surprising athleticism, bawled out every carriage with the time aboard again and blew the whistles. This time we were better catered for. My trusty Flight Sergeant simply exercised *force majeure* and stood forbiddingly over one of the trolleys and its awe-struck attendant, deftly deflecting to each side or to the next trolley down, by a glower here and a well muscled arm there, the wave of bodies until the officers and NCOs got their fair share of the goodies. 'Take a couple, Sir', he muttered, 'This bloody train's going to be all bloody day getting to Harwich.' He was right, and I did. The old tale about sensible officers enlisting the aid of good NCOs was being thoroughly endorsed.

The last of the trolleys was just being wheeled away, totally empty, when the three blasts called all to order again and the head count was repeated. The Chiefy came up to me yet again. 'You're not going to believe this, Sir, but we're short of one stupid bastard again – and we think it's the same guy. We've double checked.'

'Thank you, Flight Sergeant. Take two of the Corporals and check all the public buildings on and around this platform. If he's off the platform he's a deserter and we'll leave that to the MPs. PO Evans and I and the other SNCOs will search every bit of the train.'

Three minutes later, another of the NCOs came up to me just as I was checking the toilets at the end of each carriage. 'We've got 'im, Sir, same chap, but I think you ought to see him Sir. He looks ill or drugged.'

I trotted along to the luggage van at the front where all the spare kit was stacked. Lying on some canvas bags was the same airman lost at Crewe. He was pale and unable to explain himself. He looked as if he had been deeply asleep and suddenly wakened up. That turned out to be the case. For all that I had once cured a Drill Instructor's sick dog with a dose of warm milk, aspirin and brandy, this did not seem to be quite the same sort of problem.

The NCOs, hardened to many forms of lead swinging in their charges, seemed to think I should put the poor chap on a 'fizzer', shackle him to a carriage door handle and hand him over to the Military Police at Harwich. I was not so sure. Evans was non-committal. Even when I asked the airman whether he was feeling unwell, he seemed to have difficulty grasping the question and he certainly looked very unwell. He muttered something about a bad headache and being sick. I decided to give him the benefit of the doubt and arranged for one of his mates to look after him till we got to Harwich.

As we trundled on across the flatlands of East Anglia I spent less time on my paperback and more trying to remember whether an exigency like this had ever been the subject of a lecture at OCTU. Neither Evans nor myself could remember anything like it. The papers I held for the journey contained only a nominal roll for each disembarkation point in Germany – so many off at Rheine, so many at Osnabrück, so many at Celle and so on. I would collect the signature of the RTO (Rail Transport Officer) at each station as the appropriate men were checked off. There were no helpful little notes on the back page saying what happened if 'n minus one' men were delivered rather than 'n' men. Perhaps our ailing airman would recover enough to be counted out, so to speak, and I'd not have the problem of explaining a deficiency, either in myself or in the numbers delivered.

The neat red-brick houses of Parkeston, with their flowerbeds and burgeoning vegetable plots on the one side, and the flat expanse of the estuary on the other, proclaimed the approach of Harwich just as the sun was reluctantly glowing its last over behind Dedham. For a young man who had never before been out of his own country, the sight of several vessels of different sizes manoeuvring just offshore, their navigation lights twinkling red, green and white in the gloaming was an unmistakably romantic sight. For a few minutes I let my mind wander in pleasurable anticipation of the new sights and scenes I was about to experience.

My twelve year-old grandson told me a year or so ago that he was about to experience his twenty-eighth air flight abroad in the summer. I was suitably impressed. Most present day young people of twenty-three (the age I was then) will have taken already at least one holiday in a foreign land by boat or plane, almost as a matter of course. In 1951, however, foreign travel was mostly the prerogative of government officials, journalists, Servicemen like ourselves, and the rich. Moreover, only six years before, the world had been ravaged by war on a scale unknown in human history. Aboard ship it was still necessary to keep a watch for the occasional un-swept mine bobbing to the surface, tensions still reigned between the Western European nations and the Soviet bloc and much of Germany remained a ruined and blasted wasteland where we could not be sure we would be welcomed. The tensions of the Berlin Airlift were still fresh in our memories. The Iron Curtain and Checkpoint Charlie were realities for us rather than the stuff of films and novels.

My reverie was abruptly terminated as the train squealed to a halt in Harwich port. This time there was every sign of other military activity, not perhaps on our scale, but there was a liberal sprinkling of naval and army personnel of all ranks busily rushing hither and thither in and around the sheds and ships. For a change, I had to keep my eyes peeled for senior officers of any Service lest I failed to give them the salute to which they were entitled. The whistle blast this time was for our chaps to form up with all their kit right on the platform and to keep together and in good order until I ascertained which Customs' shed they were required to muster in for clearance before boarding the ship.

Yet again, the head count was of 599 bodies. This time, however, we knew where the 600th one was. He was clearly in a bad way, semi-conscious and lying on the carriage seat on which he had travelled from Rugby. I decided that the situation called for medical attention reasonably urgently so I left PO Evans to direct our chaps to the right Customs' shed while I explored the possibility of getting a doctor to see our invalid. Fortunately, there were at least two RAMC doctors readily available (in case some troops required various inoculations) so I persuaded one of them to see our man in the train. He wasted no time. An ambulance was called and the airman was carted off to hospital directly. I heard some months later (though not through official circles) that the poor chap eventually died of a brain tumour.

My greater difficulty was then getting the doctor and the Harwich RTO, an Army Captain, together long enough to have them sign an affidavit vouching for the fact that I would be delivering only 599 airmen rather than 600. For once there seemed to be no official numbered form for such a purpose (there may have been, but in the rush nobody knew what it was) so I simply had a blank piece of foolscap with the Harwich RTO stamp and a scrawled note signed by the doctor and the RTO. Unfortunately, neither scored highly on penmanship, nor did they print their names and numbers below their signatures. I was too green and junior either to insist or to recognise what difficulties such an omission would lay up in store for me next day.

A couple of hours later, we were all successfully aboard ship, counted out and the gangways removed. Evans and I had a four-berth cabin shared with a couple of army Lieutenants. There was no porthole and it was steamy hot but we would be glad enough to get our heads down for a few hours in due course so there were no complaints. Just as the ship cast off, I went up on deck, met my two or three best NCOs of the day and bought them all a drink. Since it was essentially a civilian ship only used by the military, who comprised the vast majority of passengers, it was possible for us to drink together in the bar without breach of protocol. Anyway, they thoroughly deserved it.

For a couple of hours more I stayed out on deck. It was a calm cool night, refreshing compared to the cabin below decks and relaxing after a rather hectic day. I found myself wondering whether some AC2 would fall overboard and complicate my life even more but decided that that would have to await the dawn. Meanwhile, I would savour the novelty of the situation.

Hundreds of other National Servicemen must have shared moments like these as they left their native shores for the first time, many on a much longer and more threatening voyage than mine. I spoke to a few who were on board returning to Germany after leave. They had all the blasé indifference of the hardened traveller in spite of the fact that only eight months or so ago they had wandered for the first time into foreign fields just as I was now doing. It was encouraging that most of them seemed to have enjoyed their postings in Germany.

Most had come to take for granted that being in another country to serve part of their two years was not much different in their eyes from serving the same time at home in the UK. They had little to remark on the present political or social conditions in the land of our erstwhile enemies. Some had learned a little German, but few mixed to any significant extent with local German people. The chaps I spoke with were mostly Army and they simply enjoyed the beer and the copious, if sometimes rather stodgy, meals in the restaurants. Gradually, these conversationalists wandered off and I was left to ponder the verities as the last lights of Harwich and of what was probably Southend faded into the night. I found myself wondering whether there really would be any chance to mix with the German man-in-the-street if we were there, working irregular hours on exercises and even then, watching what we said within the constraints of the Official Secrets Act. The steady throb of the engines and the occasional 'ding-ding' of a bell buoy brought me back to the present and replaced the chatter as people turned in. I watched the hypnotic blue and silver phosphorescence of the wake spread and diminish with the distance.

My three cabin companions were already enjoying a fitful sleep when I turned in so I never got to know them at all. Come morning, we all had our duties organising our own men. I grabbed a simple breakfast and a few passing glances over the side as we tied up at the pier in Hook of Holland. All was bustle and movement. Cranes swung their loads from ship to quayside and vice versa while trucks and longshoremen scuttled about the pier side. A cacophony of shouts and commands from the pier in two or three languages mingled with the more measured instructions to shipboard troops and other passengers on the Tannoy aboard the ship. Made slightly uneasy by the apparent confidence with which everybody else seemed to be going about their business, I looked around anxiously for any sign of my NCOs. My relief was huge when I saw some of them chatting to Evans near the top of the gangway.

The train we were to embark for the trip to the east was already standing on a nearby siding so, in due course, we formed up for the tally just outside it and all 599 climbed aboard a much more salubrious transport than we had been used to in England. The small boy in me found it romantic just to read the names of the towns where we might stop on the carriages – Arnhem, Apeldoorn, Hengelo, Rheine, Osnabrück, Hannover. I really was abroad after all. The officers and NCOs had the use of a pleasant restaurant car where coffee and eventually lunch were served as we watched the flat polders of western Netherlands and then the heath lands of the east roll past. Groups of cyclists of all ages and sexes pedalled their way along the roads on top of the dykes and waited in groups, one foot on the ground, another ready to pedal again, as the train negotiated level crossings. The occasional sight of the sails of a windmill or of local fishermen in baggy trousers confirmed the stereotypes we held of this pleasant but over-crowded land.

At Arnhem, the bridge still showed pock-marking with shell and small arms fire and in many of the small towns both bomb and shell damage had left gaps and ruins in the streets. Some windows showed all too dramatically that perhaps a sniper had used them. Bullet holes in the stone and plasterwork converged in their dozens at the lower corners. In the rural areas, more especially as we approached the German border, there were areas of green and pleasant tranquillity. Belled cattle grazed in small fields surrounded by woodland and a few peasants would lean on their implements and stare at the train as we passed. Their characteristic Dutch farms, the domestic part at one end of the large, usually two-storey building, were attractively thatched and painted while the barns and the animals occupied the other end.

Soon the train was slowing for the border beyond Hengelo where our papers would be checked by German customs and police. I felt a strange qualm of emotion which was neither guilt nor anxiety but related to both as I watched the grim and rather punctilious olive-grey uniformed German officials march down the train towards us, checking everyone's papers. Less than a decade after the war, I, in full uniform, still felt strangely exposed in this land of our former enemies. Perhaps our earlier training in escape and evasion techniques had created a certain mental 'set' which had me unconsciously planning an avoidance, disguise and escape route from the train. In the event '*Alles in Ordnung. Danke, meine Herr'n*', from the German assured us that we could proceed, after a change of engine, into his land.

Crossing the border from Scotland to England and vice versa had never seemed of great significance to me. I did not expect a sudden transition in the topography, the activities of the locals, the buildings or the atmosphere. Crossing the sea to Holland with its customs' formalities, the distinct break of the sail across the North Sea and the early morning awareness of a subtly different atmosphere, a different language and traffic on the other side of the road was another matter altogether. Being 'on the Continent' was now defined for me. The crossing from Netherlands into Germany was, by contrast, not so sharply differentiated as had been the prior one. There was no immediate obvious change in the lie of the land, the clothing, activities or bearing of the inhabitants. Dutch cows seemed utterly similar to German cows. Dutch poplars and German poplars were identical. The slow flowing canals and streams on either side of the border were completely similar. The bicycles disappeared, however, and the farmsteads were progressively less colourful and 'ethnic' as we progressed into Westphalia.

As we rattled over the points near some of the towns, there were still some signs of past bombing and shelling eight years into the peace. In the larger towns like Osnabrück and Münster, it was even more marked and later in my stay I saw total devastation, acres wide, around Essen, Düsseldorf, the famous marshalling yards at Hamm and in Köln. The thousand aircraft raids of my Bomber Command predecessors must have been truly terrifying for the local inhabitants and seriously disruptive of the transport and manufacturing capacities of Nazi Germany. Like many others, I had heard, at first hand, the radio reports of these from war correspondents, some of them in the bombers at the time, and I had read fuller and perhaps more balanced historical accounts subsequently. This immediate observation, even eight or nine years after the events, conferred a harsh reality to my fantasies of what it must have been like. Gradually and quite subtly, I was beginning to assume the attitudes of a member of an Occupying Force rather than feeling the irrational sense of threat I had experienced at the Customs' check at the border little more than fifty miles ago. I began, simultaneously, to wonder how the local indigenous population might react to RAF personnel, especially in uniform.

We had already dropped off a small contingent of our 599 at Rheine, a once active Luftwaffe airfield during the war, and my ruminations were temporarily halted as we now approached the slightly less flat country around Osnabrück where several hundred, the right several hundred, that was the tricky bit, would be disentrained. My NCOs yet again showed their experience. I began to appreciate their long and well-established habit of treating all 'erks' as if they were idiots. For myself, I might well have credited, mistakenly, a bunch of AC2s, LACs and SACs with a certain amount of autonomy, even initiative. That, averred Flight Sergeant F, was the stuff of which chaos and cock-up was made, and, having tactfully 'encouraged' (i.e. 'instructed') me to take up their plan, the NCOs had already, nominal rolls in their hands, sorted all the Osnabrück contingent into two or three carriages by themselves.

One of the Sergeants, along the corridor of the now slowing train, was declaiming, 'Right, you lot, you are about to enter Osnabrück Hauptbahnhof.' He was proud of his German pronunciation. 'You will open the doors when I say so, not before. Meanwhile, nobody will move from his present position alongside his kitbag until I say so. I do not care' (pointing to an airman squirming embarrassedly) 'if you crap yourself or wet your knickers waiting here. You had plenty of time to see to all that in the last hour – so stand still, you!' He fixed the squirmer with his gaze and completed his instructions about their onward travel.

I could not but reflect on how things had changed for me in the course of the last year. Once irked by, and scornful of, the seemingly mindless disciplines imposed on us as 'erks' ourselves by these paragons of the drill square, I was now entirely grateful to, and full of admiration for, the 'Chiefies' and Sergeants who had smoothed my way all these two days. They had quietly prevented Evans and myself from making a total shambles of an exercise which carried all the potential for disaster. More particularly, they had done it in such a way that they neither eroded nor disregarded our nominal authority and left us feeling we were still in charge. They knew perfectly well we were fearfully inexperienced in such matters but they lent their skills ungrudgingly to the completion of the exercise. It is more than possible that it was not all done out of altruism or *esprit de corps*. They no doubt recognised that the quicker and the more efficiently the task was carried out, the quicker they would themselves get to their billets and out on the town or into their beds. Nevertheless, by the end of that long day, I was more than glad of their cooperation.

Hour by hour we off-loaded airmen, eventually in total darkness in Bückeburg, about thirty miles west of Hannover. As it happened, that was where our missing man had been posted to – and he was not there! I had my piece of paper with signatures but the receiving RTO clearly thought I had lost a man and had fabricated the paper and signatures. I pointed to the Harwich RTO stamp. 'Anyone with a bit of nous could get hold of that!' he snapped. It was a late night for him too. 'You're a bloody man short, Pilot Officer Clark, and you don't leave this office until this is sorted out. I'll have to get the Adjutant!' He reached irascibly for a phone. 'And he'll not be too chuffed having to come down here at this time of night either.'

By now, about 2230 hours, there was no train, no helpful NCOs, no Pilot Officer Evans (He had gone off to Celle) and no transport for me to get to RAF Sundern which had been my original personal destination. I had only an overnight bag and found myself wondering what had become of the rest of my kit which had been sent out with my officer colleagues from Scotland. I started, wearily, to tell the story of the sick airman for the third time, hoping perhaps that sheer persistence would wear down the RTO's scepticism. It did not. He simply stumped out of the office muttering, 'Where's that bloody Adjutant?' while the Sergeant at the desk behind him shook his head hopelessly.

I hung my uniform raincoat and hat on a hook behind the door and perched myself uncomfortably on an upright chair to await developments. The Sergeant tapped away self-consciously at something probably quite inconsequential on his typewriter. I asked him about getting to Sundern.

'No chance tonight, Sir. The officers' bus dropping off at Sundern went three hours ago, but you'd missed that by the time the train from the Hook got in anyway. You might get a lift in a three-tonner in the morning, though. It's a stores' lorry but it's just the driver aboard.'

My heart sank at the prospect of sitting on that chair for the next eight or nine hours. And I was beginning to feel tired and hungry. The day had been long and testing.

Then the door burst open and the RTO and a brisk RAF Flight Lieutenant with a navigator's brevet came up and introduced himself. 'Pilot Officer Clark? You've lost a man, I hear, for Bückeburg, was he?' I showed him the man's name on the nominal roll I still held. I showed him the paper with the signatures of the RTO and the Army doctor at Harwich. The Adjutant turned to the RTO. 'What's the problem?'

The RTO was peeved. 'That's not a proper manpower deficiency form. It could have come from anywhere. We're responsible for the missing man. He was posted to us and he's not here. I've heard nothing from either Lytham or Harwich.'

The Adjutant was undaunted, and the same rank as the RTO. 'Well, Jenks, all you have to do is ring up this ... whatsisname ... at Harwich Port Sickbay and verify that our man went to hospital in England. I'll take Clark up to the Mess and get him a bed for the night. He must be knackered. We'll get him to Sundern in the morning.'

'But look at the bloody time. The medics will be on a different shift at Harwich by now,' grumbled the RTO.

'Well, somebody'll be on duty all night there and they'll have some record of the episode, and anyway you can confirm the signature on that paper.' Turning to me, the Adjutant said, 'Give him your bumff, Clarkie. I'm sure we'll get it sorted out by morning. Come and have a drink – oh shit,' (looking at his watch) 'the bar'll be closed. I'll get you some tea and biscuits.' It was by now nearly 0200 hours of the next day so I dumbly followed, cogitating, as I was to do on several subsequent occasions, on how varied were the styles and approaches of my fellow officers.

Happily, the night, or morning, ended on a high note. I was taken to a spare room in the rather fine Officers' Mess building where, within minutes, an absolutely lovely, dark haired, neat and slim German civilian chambermaid came to make up my bed with a fresh pillow and duvet and with a tray of tea and biscuits. The least I could do was to converse with her for a little in what, in the end, turned out to be, for the purposes intended, my somewhat inadequate German. She was, of course, still there in the morning, and with more tea. To my regret, however, I never saw her again. But a posting to Germany did not seem so bad after all.

A much more workaday German steward came to advise me over the breakfast table that my three-tonner was waiting at the front door. I grabbed my bag and signed out. The young LAC driver was a fresh-faced Midlander who'd done this stores' run umpteen times and was utterly unabashed at driving on the right with a right-hand drive truck whether on rural byways or on the Autobahn. At that time, the latter were only two-lane, paved with granite blocks we would have described in Aberdeen as 'cassies'. On this occasion the driver was apologetic.

'It'll be a bit of a bore for you, Sir, but I've got to use country roads mostly because there are some outlying temporary Fighter Control and DF units dotted about for 'Coronet' which I've got to drop stuff off at. But you should be at Sundern before lunch.'

I pretended to accept this with calm resignation. Inwardly I was glad of the opportunity to see something of the country, especially off the beaten track. It turned out to be not unlike the farming lands of north-east Scotland though there were more horse-drawn carts and tricycle-type motorised trucks – apparently ill-maintained with two-stroke engines which produced a lot of noise and exhaust smoke but which we comfortably overtook.

My driver was a personable lad who obviously liked to chat. He almost never had a passenger. He was also a National Serviceman who had never been away from home until he was called up. After 'square-bashing' he had done a driver's course at RAF Weedon, I think, not that far from where I had been at Kirkham. Now he was seriously thinking of signing on for at least another year. 'It would boost my pay a bit, and I like it out here. I never had a steady job after school at home and I've got some good mates out here. I'm not sure if I'd get a job as a driver in England and I'm not trained for anything else, so I might as well sign on.'

After a comfortable silence while we negotiated some stray cattle in a village where the roadside cottages crept in on us a bit, he obviously steeled himself to ask me whether I was National Service or Regular. 'I've never spoken to a National Service Officer in GD before. The only ones I seen were Education branch or doctors an' that. Are you goin' to sign on, Sir, do you think?' The thought had not crossed my mind since my square-bashing days and it brought me up short. I had always assumed that the two years followed by three and a half in the Reserves would do me perfectly well. But … if truth were told, I was now quite enjoying myself.

'What did you do in civvy street, Sir?' asked my driver, politely ignoring the fact that I had still not answered his earlier question. I told him I had just come from university with a degree in psychology but that

I would have to take post-graduate training for up to three years after I got back to civvy street before I was fully qualified to work as a professional psychologist. He was nonplussed.

'Does that mean you can tell everything that's in my mind an' that, Sir? Jesus, I hope it doesn't.' He involuntarily burst out laughing. 'Half the time there's nothing very much an' the other half it's all crap!' Echoing his laugh, I reassured him that he was under no sort of scrutiny and that I was enjoying my drive with him. I didn't really believe his self-deprecating exclamation. He drove and comported himself with an assurance that suggested to me that he had, perhaps for the first time in his life, found a niche and was beginning to discover himself. One up for National Service! At RAF Sundern, he leapt out to get my bag out of the back of the truck. I wished him well and we exchanged salutes. It had been a pleasant few hours.

In the Mess there, and somewhat to my surprise in view of the exigencies of the Service, I collected the rest of my kit and was advised that my journey was not yet over. My Unit was under canvas at a site adjacent to an ex-Luftwaffe airfield near a village called Handorf, south of Münster. The sooner I got there the better the CO would be pleased.

For me, camping had always carried a touch of romance. It hinted at a closeness to nature and a relaxation of the usual constraints, imposed on a more youthful me by parents and other adults, to fall into the cotidien domestic routines of cleanliness, order and regularity of hours and habits. The last time I had been under canvas had been either at Boys' Brigade camps in the highlands of Grampian or in my own wee tent in the hills around Aviemore or Tomintoul during the last year of the war. Then, we had lived on snared rabbits, fish from the burn and vegetables from a friendly crofter. We had cooked over a fire of fir cones and fallen timber, washed in the streams, risen with the sun and slept in the dark, soothed by the wind in the pines and the purling water of the burn. Because it was wartime, we had to camouflage our tents, tell the Police where we were and could show no lights after dark.

Our domestic arrangements for Exercise 'Coronet' in the heath and woodlands around Handorf were not quite like that. This was a tented peripheral Unit spread out among mixed birch and pinewood near a former Luftwaffe airfield. There were a couple of larger marquee-type camouflaged tents to serve the purpose of HQ and Officers' Mess, the usual hessian-screened pit latrines and wash stands with bucket-cold water showers and several two-man bivouac-type canvas tents for the officers. The NCOs and men had to tolerate greater mutual proximity by being crowded, six or eight at a time, into a miscellany of bell and other bivouac tents. One of my fellow officers found me gawping at one of the larger Mess tents and greeted me lugubriously.

'Hi, Dave! We thought you'd never get here. You'll see you're not in bloody Leuchars or Macmerry now. We got ourselves sorted out in pairs for our tents when we arrived yesterday, but you're going to have to rough it with a pongo, I'm afraid. He's a bit odd. He's the AckAck Liaison Officer, a First Lieutenant from the Gunners. He's got two bloody great wooden boxes in the tent apart from his kit and we've no idea what's in them. He's been in Germany for about a year but he doesn't say very much. Best of British luck!'

I found my flapping brown canvas home for the next few weeks and shoved my kit under the camp bed which lay along the length of the tent. It was obvious that the one on the other side was occupied in that it had been slept in but not made up and a leather 'Sam Browne' and gloves were lying on the end. But there was no sign of the occupant. Introductions would have to keep.

We were to be immediately busy setting up a fighter control unit, complete with mobile control cabins, aerials, generators, VHF units and mobile Ops room before inspecting the airfield. In this setting, there was to be no sticking to our usual job descriptions and all that nonsense, we were told by the CO. Every man who was warm and vertical was given a task by our Engineering and Signals Officers, and only after the first flights had taken off from the nearest operational airfield and all the necessary calibrations of the gear had been done, would we be free to enjoy the alfresco life of this particular limb of 2nd Tactical Airforce in West Germany.

Our cooks had done a remarkable job in their new field kitchen and we dined, belatedly but well, in the 'Mess'. It was there that I met Lieutenant B for the first time. He was an ex-Public School boy from a minor English establishment which had had a cadet unit associated with it and he intended to make the Army his career. To our concern, he seemed to know very little, and to care even less, about the deployment of the guns about which he had to liaise with us. Normally, the anti-aircraft liaison officer in an Ops room would be responsible for ensuring that no live firing took place if and when our aircraft were operating in the airspace covered by these guns. What he seemed to enthuse about most were the very attractive regional coats of arms and other badges which embellished the beer glasses in most Westphalian Biergärten and pubs. Apparently he had been 'collecting' (i.e. pinching) these from establishments the length and breadth of the Ruhr, north as far as Hamburg and east to Hannover and intended to cart the whole lot back to England when his tour of duty ended. The secret of the two big wooden boxes was out. They were packed with dozens of attractive beer glasses, some goblet-type with stems and others of the simpler mug design.

When we went to turn in after a few (incredibly cheap, in comparison with UK prices) drinks in the Mess-tent, he shamelessly demonstrated to me the quality of his acquisitions. Whether it was my rather severely moral upbringing in a Scottish manse or not, I could not really enthuse about his prizes, knowing they had all been stolen. 'It's no big deal', he would say. 'I just go in and order a beer or two – better if there's a few of you – and pop one of these in to my pocket or up my sleeve as I leave.' The fact that he could be bothered arranging for those two great boxes to go with his normal kit on the train and boat amazed me. Most of us preferred to travel as light as possible. The local beer mats were interesting and several chaps collected these in large numbers, swapping them like schoolboys with postage stamps, but they were disposable anyway and we knew that the Kellermeister was not bothered about them. The glasses, however, were something else. When he was not enlarging on his plans to secrete away further 'trophies' or ruminating aloud on what his erstwhile chums from school would be doing back at home, our Army friend said little or nothing either of more general or of more personal interest. Fortunately, our duty hours seldom coincided, so our acquaintanceship was fleeting. I did not feel deprived.

The pattern of our lives was fairly broken over that period because of the nature of the Exercise. On the whole, flying weather was quite good both by night and day. There were considerable control problems with some of the Dutch and Belgian squadrons which were participating along with ourselves. These were partly due to language difficulties compounded with poor VHF reception and partly to a combination of internal rivalries between the two former nationalities' pilots, especially among the day squadrons, and our unfamiliarity with their rather less disciplined flying habits. One of the Dutch squadrons found out where our tents were and delighted in trying to blow them down by coming in low and climbing at full throttle as they reached us. Their popularity waned when we were at the time (early morning) just getting our heads down after a long night-flying duty. In due course we were forced to reciprocate until our respective commanders clamped down.

At night, our aircraft would stooge about along the Berlin air corridor, ensuring that no Soviet intruders came too close. Of course, their pilots were doing exactly the same thing. It never came to much. We reckoned they were just chaps like us doing a job and when we did get close enough, the aircraft would just peel away with a wave from the crew. From our point of view, Exercise 'Coronet' was largely to examine our (and NATO's) capacity to deploy mobile control and attack/defence systems in unfamiliar country quickly and efficiently and effect good coordination with the existing permanent forces.

We did have some free time, however, usually at weekends, and would get a truck into Münster or some of the neighbouring villages where there were pleasant little beer gardens by the riverside – I think it was a branch of the Ems. One of them was a favourite of mine and two or three of us, minus our soldier, for obvious reasons, would enjoy the ambience of the place. We were well aware that our Luftwaffe predecessors must have lounged at these selfsame café tables with their beers some years before, wondering how many Lancasters and B17s they might be faced with in an hour or two. The same willows dipped and rustled over the greenish water. The same colourful summer flowers overflowed from the tubs round the buildings. Perhaps the ducks were a younger breed but the beer was much the same, a Düsseldorfer Pils, and the landlord assured Johnny T and myself, the only German speakers in our group, that we were disarmingly like our former Teuton equivalents both in style and habits. We had always thought we were quite civilised but did not know quite how to take that last opinion. Having heard some German ex-officers carousing in Münster the week before, we considered such a comment to be a bit ambiguous.

Münster itself had been severely bombed during the war and still bore many scars. So did some of the people. Occasionally, I had had to visit the city in uniform and there were several people of both sexes who would turn away very deliberately and spit as I passed. From time to time too I would pick up some resentful comments directed at British airmen particularly. The vast majority, however, seemed to be prepared to let sleeping dogs lie and were polite and helpful when I had to approach them, for directions for example.

We had found a good restaurant adjacent to the Rathaus in the city centre and a free Saturday night would find us putting away a few beers and a huge mixed grill. *'Mehr Kartoffeln, mein Herr?' – 'Jawohl, bitte, aber nicht so viel für meinem Kamerad, danke. Schade dass er kein Deutsch spricht.'* Thus could I pull the occasional fast one over my less linguistically facile mates who would look wonderingly as I was served three spuds to their one. Johnny T, one of my Flight Commanders, and the CO both seemed to take some interest in how my facility with German was improving. It later transpired that they were lining me up to do the shopping in town for a few extra goodies for the Mess. Having heard of my weekend visits to the Biergarten and elsewhere in Münster, the CO greeted me loudly at the bar one evening in our woodland Mess tent with, 'Well, Dave, so how's your German these days?'

Knowing perfectly well what he meant, I enjoyed the trace of ambiguity in his question and achieved a small score in front of my fellow pilot officers by replying, 'Fine, Sir. She was ever so much better the second night!'

What we did in our free time on these visits to the city depended on how long we had before the truck, which had delivered us in the afternoon, left Münster again at night for Handorf. There was no other way to get to our base. Thus there were times when a tardy airman would get close to even time for the last hundred yards to catch the departing three-tonner. On a free afternoon, we would sometimes settle for a walk round the old city with its tall and ornate high gabled Hanseatic buildings and arcades. On other evening occasions, we would frequent another quiet little Biergarten where a pleasant little trio of accordion, violin and drums played at weekends. There were coloured bulbs slung from the trees around the concrete dance floor which was the centre eight metres or so of the area surrounded by tables, chairs and rustic benches. A few attentive waiters scurried about replenishing schnapps and Steine. The regular patrons were of all ages and nobody seemed to resent the few British and other Servicemen who frequented the place.

One evening there had been a group of young students at two or three tables, one of which was only half occupied. I was looking in vain for a free place to sit with my beer when one of the students invited me, in English, to sit with them. They were keen to practise their English but varied widely in their expertise and I too was glad to use such German as I had. They were a fairly self-confident bunch and though some were a bit brash, it was congenial enough. We bought each other beer and danced from time to time, in my case with a rather attractive but quite shy young student of pharmacy. Being a year or two younger than myself, Kristina remembered little about the war, only the noise of the bombing in Münster, because her mother and grandparents had lived in a village outside the city and her father had been a prisoner of war in Scotland for several years till 1945. She volunteered that he had been no Nazi (although it was the fashion to disclaim any such affiliations at that time) and that he had been well treated as '*ein Kriegsgefangener*', working on a farm much of the time. Although she spoke very little English, we got along very well and we met several times (quite by chance, as I explained to my mates) subsequently.

We had been warned in our briefings before leaving the UK to be cautious about fraternising with the locals although none of us was very clear about why, in 1953, we should be. There had been a time about five or six years before when the authorities were worried about the apparent ease with which troops could purchase all manner of favours, including sex in its various expressions, for a tin of Nescafé or a few bars of perfumed soap or NAAFI chocolate. There was also some anxiety, especially in the case of officers who might have access to classified information, about the possibility of their being suborned by women in the pay of or sympathetic to the Soviets. It was not our impression, however, that these were substantive reasons for undue caution now, although we were not unaware of some risks and those of us who were on the operational side were very careful about what we talked if the conversation ever got round to our aircraft, equipment or what our duties comprised.

Some Servicemen who were stationed in Germany for a longer term than we were had formed firm relationships with German girls and there had even been a number of marriages. Others, if the bar-room chat were to be believed, did seem to enjoy a colourful, even hectic, sex life but among the National Servicemen, officers and men alike, many had girl friends at home, and in any case, were not particularly inclined to be simply sexual adventurers. There was no contraceptive pill in those days, the risk of venereal disease, especially where casual sex was concerned, was reckoned to be quite high, if only the available 'ladies of the night' were to be the partners and a significant proportion of Servicemen were, like us, only abroad for a brief period of weeks or months on exercises. In these circumstances, there were, amongst men in my own and similar units, periods of romance snatched between long hours of duty, temporary and fleeting but warm friendships with cuddles and kisses and many promises for the future, never likely to be fulfilled. Most of these pleasant little episodes were simply part and parcel of the adventure of being abroad in the comfortable warmth of a Westphalian summer. The pressures and tensions of night flying over unfamiliar country, not that far from a possible future enemy, whether in the aircraft or in the control cabins, soon pushed such matters far from consciousness.

Apart from the novelty of living in tents and experiencing the vagaries of adapting to being in another country, especially one against which we had waged total war only eight years before, our activities whilst on duty were almost identical to those we had come from a month previously. Compared to the north of Scotland, the airspace was a bit more crowded at times, what with international civil air liners going about their normal business and the various activities of the fighter aircraft of the other NATO countries we were trying to coordinate and collaborate with. In some ways, the events of that spell with 2nd TAF which made a greater effect on me, had nothing to do with the technicalities, boredoms and excitements of our RAF life. They were concerned more with the nature of the German mind and the hidden history of the war which emerged subtly and incidentally to our daily life there.

Two episodes early in our stay defined something of the former and a third revealed the latter. The first of these occurred because our encampment was in sheltering woodland several miles from any major township and was entirely unfenced. On our first and subsequent weekends, we would be going about our usual business, in or out of our tents, but with the brailing rolled up, the better to ventilate and dry out any dampness. We became aware first, of the occasional stray dog sniffing around and uninhibitedly cocking a leg here and there among our bits and pieces. That was followed or accompanied by shouts and childish chatter and the sight of locals of every age and style peering at us through the trees. Our privacy was entirely forfeit to a random visitation of German families from the neighbouring village of Telgte. Curiosity whetted by the noise of our trucks and generators in the woods, our aircraft flying low overhead and perhaps the cooking smells from our field kitchen, they had decided to satisfy it by making a scrutiny of our settlement, perhaps in the hope of picking up the odd treat such as a bar of chocolate or 'finding' some useful spare bits and pieces with which to mend their cars or loose cable to rewire their electrics. The guard at the main entrance would hustle them away but they simply re-appeared elsewhere on the perimeter and infiltrated among the tents. My AckAck liaison friend became ever more anxious, ironically, about his collection of glasses being stolen and there were, of course, some firearms about as well.

The CO was becoming increasingly irascible about it. 'There I am, up all bloody night for the night flying and I get out of my scratcher for a quick visit to the bog. So I'm sitting there in my hessian heaven thinking lovely thoughts and this little Jerry bastard pokes his head round the corner and quietly surveys my performance! It's bloody diabolical!' We rather enjoyed our own reconstruction of the image but pretended not to.

'Dave', he said, after dinner that evening, 'you're supposed to be the trick cyclist in this mob. What's the best way to keep these buggers at a distance? We can't possibly fence the whole works – no time, no cash, no equipment, no materials – and we're supposed to keep good relationships with the locals.'

Over another of our really cheap evening drinks (even a large liqueur only cost 6d on our Mess bill) I had a chat about the problem with some of my pals and the engineering officer. Three Drambuies later we thought we had the solution. Next morning, a couple of the airmen were detailed to get cracking with the red paint and some boarding from generator pallets. Eight or nine signs were fabricated and planted at intervals on the heathery knolls around our camp. They bore the strange device '*ACHTUNG! GEFÄHR, MINEN!*' in bold red print. Of course there were no mines whatsoever either in or around our camp, but the readers were not to know that – and it completely solved our problem. No intruders bothered us again throughout our stay. Good Germans did what they were told.

It has been said that the German mind is rule bound and inclined to be unquestioning about instruction from authority. Many examples of this had been observed during the war both in military and civilian contexts, so it wasn't surprising that something of a stereotype should arise. They, on the other hand, would describe themselves as disciplined and orderly. '*Alles in Ordnung!*' was not a favourite catch phrase for nothing. It became both the explanation of some of their great successes and an excuse for many of their defeats or misdemeanours – or worse. They were only following instructions.

The second episode was different in content and quality but yet spoke of another aspect of the German lifestyle still lingering in the post war era. We were enjoying one of our usual Saturday evening meals in the restaurant near the Münster Rathaus. The huge mixed grill had been done full justice. '*Ein bischen mehr Kartoffeln und noch einige Pils, bitte*' had come and gone and we were relaxing over the coffee before hitting the town. From time to time we had been aware of some hearty singing, foot stamping and shouting of varied musicality from a room above us. We guessed they had had an earlier start.

Quite suddenly, a leather-jacketed German clicked his heels obtrusively at our table and addressed us with what some of us thought was a rather cool smile. '*Verscheiden Sie mir, Bitte, meine Herren …*' and he went on to explain, wholly in German, that a group of ex-officers of the German forces, Wehrmacht, SS and Luftwaffe, were holding their weekly dinner party and singsong upstairs in a private room. It was not fitting that we ('*weil Sie Offizieren wie uns sind*') should have to share space with the common people, on the floor of the house, so to speak. We were formally invited by *Herr Oberst* so-and-so, the senior officer present upstairs, to be their guests for the evening. We had the slight suspicion that the invitation had been issued only after they had suspected that none of us could outrank a full Colonel and that each of us in consequence would have to be duly deferential to their senior officer, in the event that we accepted their invitation.

Johnny T, our Flight Commander, and myself explained to our non-German speaking colleagues what was afoot, being cautious about how we put it since we suspected that the 'inviting officer' (though he really wasn't all that inviting) probably understood some English while pretending not to. In spite of the initial flattery implied by the invitation, the body language and quick exchange of glances within our group indicated clearly enough that the scenario was not one in which we would be comfortable. Moreover, we were unsure as to whether this was one of the kinds of fraternisation which our seniors would encourage or even consider desirable.

Johnny and I therefore thanked the officer for his kind invitation but explained that we were to be on duty later that evening and would shortly be leaving the city. It was a white lie since we all had a variety of ploys to fulfil before departing, but it seemed best at the time. Looking back from nearly half a century on, that must seem a rather small-minded response to what may well have been a genuine offer of fellowship, but the atmosphere was different then. Unconsciously echoing his punctiliousness, Johnny and I had involuntarily stood up from the table to speak to the German who had remained erect and politely a yard or two away from the table. The young PO next to me waited for the German officer to depart upstairs with his sad news and then burst out, 'Jesus, Dave, for a minute I thought you were going to click your heels and give him the Nazi salute!' We all laughed, pushed back our chairs and set out on our various expeditions before we would meet again at the truck in three hours or so.

It was strange how we tended to avoid that restaurant at weekends thereafter lest we got caught up in the 'Herrenvolk' attitudes of those ex-officers. All the time we had eaten there we had never felt any concern that we were in the midst of what they clearly thought were not the 'officer class'. There was no positive decision to keep away. We just felt there was a certain 'unhealthiness' about that group of German ex-officers which we felt we would like to avoid. That feeling emanated not just from the National Service Officers. If anything, the Regulars amongst us, especially the ones who had fought in, and been shot out of, the sky over there during the war, felt the same unease.

Later that very night, I spoke to my student pharmacist friend and her chums about it. Their view was that most of their fathers or elder brothers who had returned home after the war were just keen on settling down to work and their family life. They did not attend regular meetings like that, whether they had been officers or other ranks and there was some suspicion that at least a proportion of those who did were still Nazis at heart. We did not see it as quite the same as a meeting at home of the British Legion or RAF Association. There were no darts or bowls and in that upstairs room, it was all too evident that there were no other ranks. These former German officers were still very rank and class conscious and we suspected that we would not have had any invitation if any of us had been black or obviously Jewish.

The third episode was, and has to this day remained for me the strangest and most forbidding. Normally we did our ablutions in the hessian-screened camp washing tubs and bucket showers. In his off-duty hours, the Adjutant, however, had been walking in the woods and heath land area surrounding our camp rather than going into town, as we had done. As a result, he had discovered a strange brick and concrete German establishment about ten minutes' walk from our camp which was described by the two or three unarmed but still olive-grey uniformed Wehrmacht soldiers minding it as a former 'Decontamination Centre'.

The Adjutant had snooped around it a bit, asked a few questions and announced at a meeting of all the officers that if we liked we could have the use of it to have showers. It was essentially a great concrete hall with a dished floor which had sprays in the ceiling operated by a large iron wheel near the door. It resembled a contemporary fire sprinkler system in a factory or store. There was running water still in the system though it would be at the ambient temperature only since no plant was operating and the German Corporal there would turn it on for us if we went in groups of five or six at a time. It seemed like an opportunity to have a more leisurely shower than a bucket with nail holes in the bottom of it afforded us. The air temperature was around 70°F most days at that time of year, so we would not be completely gibbering with cold. It would be available only during daylight hours while the Germans were on duty there. What they actually did, or from whom they took their orders, has remained a mystery.

When there was no day flying or when we were scheduled for night duty, we would, in the afternoon, tuck our towels and soap like pallid jam rolls under our arms and wander down the track through the woods to this dull grey, anonymous building. We were, of course, in uniform then and it felt odd to be given a smart salute by the Wehrmacht man at the red and white entrance barrier as he raised it for us. The Corporal in olive-grey, temporarily assuming the role of Gasthaus proprietor, ushered us in to the 'bath house' muttering something like, '*Zimmer mit Dusche – nur für Offizieren, ja?*' as he led us to one of the curious concrete waist-high shelves or loading ramps which ran the whole length of the building on both sides. There we could undress dry.

He then, with studied deliberation, strode to the door just inside of which was a large green wheel which opened a stopcock. A few turns set the showers in motion and we lowered our naked and goose pimply frames over the loading ramps and on to the floor of this great sombre hall. This was no ordinary shower. The whole area became a spray-filled, silver-grey universe barred with fleeting shafts of sparkling light which intermittently shot at us and missed as the sun escaped from time to time from its occluding clouds and penetrated the long narrow central window in the roof above our heads. Each of the six of us could have had a jet to ourselves though we could wander anywhere about the great dished floor and still be showered more than comprehensively. Puny trickles of soapy water made black and white jigsaw patterns in the general run-off into the central drain from each of us as we shouted coarsely to each other about what the surfeit of cool water was doing to our 'tackle'.

In due course we would shout to 'Ferdi', as we had decided to call him, to turn off the water. Just as suddenly as it came on, so with a spin of the wheel, the opaque mist of droplets cleared and we leapt, dripping but fresh, for the dry area at the side. It was all a huge improvement on the bucket showers, even if it did necessitate a bit of a walk and we tried to ignore the semi-ruined or demolished ancillary buildings around the 'decontamination centre' itself. There was even a weed-covered single-track railway which seemed to run up to near the main building from the direction of the village of Telgte. The rich red-brown of rusty iron struggled to show itself from among the mass of pink rosebay willow herb blooms which throve among the scattered ballast.

On the second or third occasion when we visited our new shower room, 'Ferdi' decided he could let us operate the 'bloody great wheel' ourselves and slunk off to have a fag or something round the back. It was then that one of us took a closer look at a large green double door at one end of the hall. Our entrance was from a door at the middle of one side and we had involuntarily just kept to the area near there. There must have been nearly an acre of floor space in the building as a whole so from where we showered, that door had just seemed like another exit which we had no need to use. This time, however, we could see that it was made of solid steel with two swing-bar latches on the side toward us and appeared to be sealed around all its edges, even just above ground level, where there was a raised steel rim also with a broad rubber seal.

We decided to have a look at whatever was on the other side of this substantial barrier and, levering the yard-long bar latches upward out of their retaining brackets, we heaved one side of the doors slightly open. I had just completed dressing and watched what was going on over a steadily closing gap as I approached the two who were the 'prime movers'. Amid the jocularity and banter that normally was part and parcel of our visits to the showers, these two stood as if transfixed, wordless.

Somebody else said, 'Come on then, you chaps, let's have a shufti!' and shouldered their way closer, heaving the door a bit more ajar as they did so. Then they stopped too. 'Christ Almighty! Do you know what this is?' breathed one of them, not daring to answer what had become a rhetorical question. I looked in.

Behind the steel doors was a solid concrete room, totally windowless, with a slightly domed ceiling above the walls and, like our shower hall, a concrete floor. There was a complementary pair of identical steel doors, also sealed, immediately opposite the one we had opened, now rusting. Somebody shuddered involuntarily as we almost simultaneously caught sight of the four small, half-inch diameter pipes, each one emerging from the concrete up in every top corner where the walls and ceiling met. Then we looked more closely at the walls. All were covered with scratches, awful, dark brown, almost black, stains by the scratches and on the floor. Here and there was what seemed to have been an attempt to scratch a name or a message. The scratches higher up on the walls were fewer but stronger than the others. We guessed that cyanide crystals produced gas that was probably heavier than air and that the stronger and slightly longer living survivors had climbed on the growing pile of the bodies of their companions to grasp at a few more seconds of desperate life before they succumbed. History records that earlier death camps also used carbon monoxide.

The chill of the Messenger of Death touched our shoulders. We all knew exactly what we had happened upon. It was as if we, simply by opening that door, had, irrationally but inevitably, taken upon ourselves some of the guilt of the terrible events that that deadly chamber had seen. There was not one of us who gazed into its ghastly depths who was unaffected by the awful awareness that, minutes before, we had been joking and joshing around in the very area where the condemned had had to strip and offload their jewellery, watches and other possessions (that must have been what the dry area of the 'loading ramps' was set aside for) before their final cleansing. The awful euphemism of 'Decontamination Centre' was not lost on us and several of us went back into camp and to the good old bucket showers thereafter.

We closed and bolted the doors before 'Ferdi' might re-appear and, very chastened, slipped out. A furtive closer examination of the semi-ruined or demolished building close to the other end of the chamber exposed what might have been large 'boilers' and the stump of a brick chimney. We could not bring ourselves to confirm then from 'Ferdi' what our suspicions about the place were. The following week I tried, but he had suddenly become reticent and he could neither '*verstehen*' nor '*erklären*' when I asked him about the place.

Some of the locals with whom I spoke did say that they knew trains had, during the night, in wartime, come up the line from the direction of Telgte but that they had always assumed that they were serving some obscure military purpose. They certainly claimed to know nothing about Jews or others being killed locally nor of any of the other features of the 'Final Solution'. Just as in the case of our '*ACHTUNG, MINEN!*' notices, they had, a decade before, obeyed the '*Eintritt verboten*' signs down the line and by the roadsides. Even in Münster I found no one who could believe or would admit there was such a place anywhere in the district.

Many times did I, in subsequent years, search for any reference to an extermination camp in or around Handorf, Telgte or anywhere in the Münster area. I have searched in vain. And yet, we saw what we saw and it is difficult to find any other explanation for the particular configuration of special structures such as I have described. One wonders whether there were other such places which were wholly or, like this one, partially destroyed, along with any records that might have been kept. The total denial by the locals has often made me wonder whether the possibility of anything so awful was just too much for ordinary people to accept into consciousness. I have wondered too whether it might have been possible, in a time of total war, for anything similar to have happened, say, within fifty miles of Edinburgh or Oxford and for the local people to have been kept wholly and truly in ignorance of what was going on. I doubt it.

The history books record that although some of the harshest and most remorseless mass slaughtering of Jews and others occurred early in World War Two in the wake of the Wehrmacht's advance to the east, some 'death camps' had been set up by the SS, in Poland, for example, and had been a feature of the Nazi regime even as early as 1933. Even by 1941, over a million had been killed by the SS. Among the first concentration camps were Oranienburg, just north of Berlin, and Dachau, near Munich. One text reports:

'They were originally prison/work camps for communists, trade union leaders, Catholic priests, Jehovah's Witnesses, pacifists, homosexuals, tramps, petty criminals and anyone else who did not conform to the ideals of Nazi society ... In 1939, T-4 was born, totally unknown to most Germans. It was a euthanasia programme to rid the nation of mentally deficient or deformed children and adult lunatics. Probably about 72,000 were gassed, in chambers disguised as shower rooms, by carbon monoxide or by the lethal fumes from a form of cyanide known by its trade name of Zyklon-B.' (p190, The World at Arms: The Reader's Digest Association Ltd 1989.)

We asked ourselves whether we had unwittingly stumbled upon the remains of one such, perhaps lesser-known, perhaps unresearched camp. We asked ourselves whether we had totally misinterpreted what we had seen. None of us thought we had – the effect on us all who saw it ran too deep, and yet, there was the curious phenomenon that part of the place was apparently still both manned, albeit minimally, and that some of the Services to it still worked. The denial of the locals that they knew anything about it was as telling as the bloodstains on the chamber walls. If it had been a simple decontamination centre, what was being decontaminated that they need worry about or could not talk about? Why the *'Eintritt Verboten'* signs? Why did the trains all come and go in the dead of night?

Again we saw the phenomenon of a Wehrmacht Corporal and a few ordinary soldiers (unarmed though they were) still hanging about the place as a symbol of the German hang-ups on routine and the persistence of orders. They had probably been long forgotten about by any senior officers but their pay came in and the local billet was still there. *'Alles in Ordnung!'* yet again. Apart from our few showers, there was no evidence that the place functioned in any other way the whole time we were there.

As the time to return to UK approached, I found myself wondering at the wide range of, and hugely contrasting experiences, a short stay in Germany had afforded me. A shake of the kaleidoscope of memory could bring into sudden apposition a whole series of intense images: the steady hissing throb of the aircraft as the vast starry vault of the sky rotated around the cockpit hood and the glow of the instruments cast an unearthly aura on my hands; the Army Lieutenant sitting on the edge of his bunk in the tent, serially admiring his latest beer glass prizes; the steady chatter of the VHF in the GCI cabin as the greenish-yellow spots on the PPI came together; the pumping arms of the German students as they danced a vigorous polka or foxtrot round the concrete floor of the Biergarten while the gentle Kristina made me feel guilty about my girl back at home. They all pursued each other round my head until another shake of the kaleidoscope rearranged the images; now of the CO being scrutinised in his 'hessian heaven' as he did his daily duty; the Gunner and I heaving ourselves from our flattened tent and shouting abuse at the 'Flying Dutchmen' as the day fighters climbed hard into the fracto-cumulus; the sudden gasp as we opened that dread steel door; the click of Teuton heels and the chorus of *'Der Wacht am Rhein'* from the upstairs room by the Rathaus.

One more shake of the mirrored cylinder of memory and now we were sweatily identifying an Aeroflot jetliner with no reported flight plan which had seemed for most of the interception to be a 'Bear' bomber well into NATO airspace; then admiring the gentle countryside and quiet farmhouses of the West German border and the neat and serried rows of the Ruhr and Moselle vineyards on their sunny hillsides; now the comradeship, the burps and the boasts and the endless noisy rattle in the back of the three-tonner as we were carted home to camp from a Münster night out.

Normal Service routines had, of course, been sustained day and night, but there had been, for almost all of us younger officers who had not before been abroad, a wealth of new impressions which were perhaps the richer for not having been predicted. Perhaps more to the point, we were now engaged in working out how best to smuggle home some of the duty-free booze that had made our tented Mess something of a canvas heaven in our off-duty hours. We knew that if a few bottles of Macallan malt whisky, brandy or liqueur could be smuggled aboard the returning aircraft (though there were few accessible and safe spots where a bottle could be jammed) the ground crews could get them stashed away on landing before the Customs' chaps saw them – for a consideration! In the end, we did have some success.

Only days before the end of 'Coronet', I had just come off a long night flying session and slumped into my camp bed. Perhaps because of bugs in the showers or drinking water I was suffering a nasty sore throat, with thrush and a headache. A couple of aspirin had helped to propel me into a deep sleep when two minutes later, it seemed, I was suddenly being shaken awake by the Adjutant. 'Dave, you're going to have to look slippy. We've just had this despatch rider in with a signal saying you have to report for an interview to the Civil Service Commissioners at Burlington Gardens in London at 1630 hours today.'

For a moment I was befuddled with sleep. 'C'mon man, up, up, up!' he reiterated. 'I've cleared you off duty for today – special leave for this sort of thing – and I've a truck lined up to take you to the Münster *Hauptbahnhof* in ten minutes or so.'

I should have been grateful for his efforts on my behalf but it was taking time for me to remember that, back in the UK, some months before, I had written a letter and filled in application forms for a number of jobs for psychologists in the Civil Service, in particular, for one at the RAE in Farnborough, to work on the ergonomics of instrumentation and cockpit design. It was just my luck that the interview should come up at a time like this when I was out of the country, well under the weather and now desperately short of sleep.

'What do you mean, the *Hauptbahnhof*? Can I not scrounge a lift on one of our own aircraft?' I pleaded, a bit petulantly.

'Sorry, old chap. The Comm Flight aircraft is away on a job and all the serviceable squadron aircraft are fully committed to 'Coronet'. I've made out a list of train departures from Münster to Köln for the next couple of hours. You should be able to pick up a civil flight out of Wahn for London about midday.'

I was grateful to him for the work he'd already done for me. It was, after all, still 7:30 in the morning. I had only dropped into bed at about 0530 hours. In spite of that, I got up a bit sluggishly, envying the Gunner, still sleeping like a babe on his camp bed, got myself into my best blues, grabbed some breakfast and leapt into the staff car to take me to the station. Luckily, I remembered my chequebook for I had very little actual currency, either German or British. This was the sort of situation in which you incurred expenses but could only claim them after the event.

Things went well at first. There was a train just about to leave which wandered through the Ruhr before reaching the Rhine and Köln with its damaged but still beautiful *Dom.* There were few passengers and I was able to drink a more leisurely coffee while the train picked its way rather gingerly from city to city amid a wasteland of bomb craters and twisted metal. Hamm, the famous railway marshalling yards which were carpet-bombed, night after night, by 'Bomber' Harris's Lancasters during the war, still presented a picture of total desolation. Some water-filled craters were thirty feet wide and still showed spikes and snakes of twisted railway lines poking mournfully from their depths.

The names of the other towns and cities the train passed through rang solemn chords of memory. Night after night in the war I had listened to BBC announcers proclaim the 'Targets for Tonight' – Dortmund, Bochum, Essen, Duisburg and Düsseldorf. Now here they were, laid out before me, nursing their scars as the lifeblood of new commerce began to revitalise them. The initial wounding must have been fearsome to leave, eight years on, a cicatrice as raw as this. As the train rattled across the bridge over the brown, wide Rhine toward the station, quite near the cathedral, I began to regret the waste of war – this and other fine cities half ruined and thousands of their citizens, theirs as well as ours, slaughtered or permanently disabled. I became rather self-conscious of my uniform as I hunted for an information desk where I could check on flights from the airport at Wahn.

A brisk, English-speaking woman at the desk advised me of the good news and of the bad news. The former was that there was indeed a plane for London that morning. The bad news was that it would take off in fifteen minutes. There was no way that a taxi could get me to the airport in that time and the next one would not be until 1615 hours, a quarter of an hour before my interview. My heart sank. All that hassle, no sleep, little breakfast and a couple of hours in a train for nothing. My throat felt really sore again. She must have read the disappointment in my face because she quickly added that if I could get to Düsseldorf in about half an hour; there was a British Airways plane for London Northolt due to leave there. The airport at Düsseldorf was about thirty-five miles away by the Autobahn but it was just possible that if I were fortunate to find a taxi-driving maniac and I paid him enough he might get me there in time.

I shot out of the station and was desperately looking about for a taxi, waving vainly at two or three already with fares smugly ensconced in the Mercedes leather. Suddenly a VW 'Beetle' pulled up, almost running over one of my feet in the process. A young German about ten years my senior wound down the window. '*Wohin gehen Sie? Ich fahre nach Essen.*' He seemed decent enough and I thought, 'Well, it's worth a try and at least he'll have to go through or near Düsseldorf to get to Essen.' As quickly as my German would allow, I explained my plight. His face lit up. '*Aufsteigen!*' as he flung open the nearside door.

This, for him, had immediately become an irresistible challenge. It transpired that he had actually been a Messerschmitt pilot in *Jagdgeschwader 2* during the war and, having survived it, he still felt something of a bond with the Royal Air Force which had provided him with such doughty opponents. He promised to get me on to that aeroplane in time and pushed the accelerator to the floor – and we were still in the centre of Köln.

In the course of my life subsequently I have experienced some pretty 'hairy' taxi rides. One was in Sri Lanka where the wheels of a Morris Minor were welded on, eccentrically – in both senses, and had to be burned off to mend a puncture. Another was in India where the driver in Madras had no idea where to take me and we did a hair-raising mystery tour of some incredibly 'ethnic' low-life dives and back streets while he jabbered in incomprehensible Tamil. In neither of these, however, did I ever seriously question that my life expectancy would be more than fifteen minutes. As we tore through the northern suburbs of Köln, little old ladies in lace-up boots, fair young mothers with prams and butcher's boys on bicycles scampered out of the way and I fully expected our progress to be inhibited by the wailing of a police siren. The little air-cooled engine in the boot was screaming in agony while *'mein Flieger Freund'* lifted one or both hands from the wheel to show me his Rolex or his fine leather jacket on the back seat. I hastily admitted to being impressed, looked firmly ahead and hoped that he did not see the little white summits on the Alpine ranges of my knuckles.

We hit the Autobahn flat out and continued that way till, to my huge relief, a slip road signposted *'Flughafn'* suddenly appeared and probably as many as two wheels were actually in contact with the ground as we negotiated the roundabout at the end of it. My offer to pay as we skidded to a halt in front of the Terminal building was genially rejected and my saviour pulled away again with a cheery wave. The clock in the concourse registered exactly twenty-eight minutes since I had left the *Hauptbahnhof* in Köln. As I dashed up to the BEA desk, I could actually see the last few passengers climbing the steps into a twin-engined, propeller driven 'Viking' in British European Airways livery. The charming girl at the desk was quick and efficient. She held the flight for a minute or two by telephoning the Gate and accepted my cheque without any difficulty. In two minutes, I was running out over the apron and was last aboard. It was just after 2 p.m.

After Service flying, it felt quite strange for me to sit with only a lap strap and no parachute or dinghy. The last time I had done that was in the De Havilland Rapide in the 1930s. It felt distinctly unsafe. However, the boiled sweet and the smile proffered by the hostess dispelled all that and I settled to splitting my attention between the view and my watch. It was all going to be a bit 'touch and go'. A rather bumpy and noisy but uneventful flight touched down at Northolt at about 4 p.m. local time and I still had to clear Customs and find a taxi for the longish ride to Burlington Gardens.

In uniform and with only an overnight bag containing toilet gear, pyjamas and a change of shirt, I guessed that Customs would be a straight walk through. How wrong I was. Whether the Customs' man was suspicious simply because I had so little luggage and no Duty-Free goods, and perhaps because he had been appraised of my sudden late entry to the flight in Düsseldorf, he decided to stop and quiz me at length and to search even the cardboard base of my overnight bag and the tissue paper inside the overhang of my Service cap. I tried to get some urgency injected into the proceedings by explaining and showing him the signal which had started my hectic day but some sort of bloody-mindedness had seemed to get into the guy and the more I pressed him the more he detained me.

As a result, it was 4:30 p.m. before I was cleared. I searched for a telephone but found that there was no number on the signal and then had to get that from Directory Enquiries. My frustration knew no bounds as the operator went through all the various Department numbers at that address. Eventually I explained to a secretary that I was detained at Northolt and would turn up as soon as I could get a taxi. Could she please explain my lateness to the Board? It later turned out that she did not.

At 5:05 p.m. I sat down in a waiting room at Burlington Gardens to gather my thoughts prior to the interview. My voice was husky with the thrush and laryngitis, I had a splitting headache and perhaps my temperature and blood pressure were both higher than they should have been for an occasion of this sort. The Board were civilised and pretty high-powered. I recognised one professor of psychology, a Group Captain, and another very senior civil service psychologist with whose academic work I was quite familiar among the six members of the interviewing panel. I felt I was at an immediate disadvantage since they had had to re-arrange the interviewing order and they had obviously been delayed by my late arrival. Halfway through what I was finding a difficult interview, I thought I should try to explain the reason for my lateness. It became apparent that that was the first they had heard of it, but by then I think I had 'lost some ground' anyway. They were genial as well as penetrating throughout the forty-five minutes but I sensed that it had not gone too well. I was right. A month later, a buff envelope confirmed that. In terms of outcome, if not in terms of content, my desperate dash had been in vain.

It was not surprising that I slept deeply on the ferry from Harwich that night. In fact, I may have slept away most of the train journey from the Hook of Holland as well because only at the German border did the Customs check wake me. Medication I had bought in London was beginning to win the battle against the staphylococcus in my throat. In consequence, my 'homecoming' back in camp was convivial. My friends were all off-duty when I arrived so I regaled them with the tale of my trip and drowned my sorrows about the interview. Later in the year, as a civilian again, I faced a similar London interview Board and this time was successful.

Back in Scotland after the exercise with 2nd TAF, my other National Service friends and myself were recognising that we were now quite experienced young officers, utterly at home in our work, familiar with our aircraft, apparatus, techniques and social life in the Mess, virtually indistinguishable from our Regular colleagues. We watched the occasional fresh young and newly commissioned Pilot Officer, National Service or otherwise, display all the early naïveties we had succumbed to almost a year earlier. Incredibly, in the light of our experiences of nearly two years ago, some of us were now giving serious thought to the possibility of signing on for at least a Short Service commission – a year or two more!

We had earned, it seemed, the loyalty (certainly) and respect (possibly) of our batmen, Pasquale and Bryson in particular. My scorn at the stories I had read as a boy about 'fagging' in public schools and so on had caused me some concern about the whole ethos of having batmen at all. They did, however, succeed in smoothing many a passage for us, not only doing unpleasant chores like sewing on and polishing our brass buttons before a Dining-In Night but they would bring to our rooms a most welcome cuppa if we came in at some odd time, knackered or fed up after a particularly trying day, or night. They did, of course get their fair share of drinks and tips from us but they always managed to do their duties without seeming either servile or being creeps. They had a knack of knowing when we wanted to talk and when we did not.

Pasquale in particular had a special skill on which we drew regularly. He was a very competent hairdresser in civilian life and he would 'do' us in our own rooms for a mere florin (i.e. 10p). He had his own white jacket and tools and was in regular demand. His Italian/Glasgow origins showed in his tightly curled black hair, his dark, bright eyes and his dark, bright chatter. His movements were brisk, exact and skilful whether he was pouring a drink behind the bar or clipping our tattered locks. It was rumoured that when he went home to Glasgow for a weekend leave, his alter ego was immediately swallowed up in a glass and chrome salon owned by the extended Pasquale family which presented the visitor or client with a veritable vista of barber's chairs, hair washing sinks and mirrors. And the prices there would have been well out of our reach!

There was one night in the anteroom only a couple of weeks before my demob date when the same Pasquale was serving half a dozen of us, including the CO, who were playing 'Seven, Fourteen, Twenty-One' at the bar. Granted that that is a game which is not played within forty-eight hours of flying and is not calculated to contribute to great clarity of judgment, the CO suddenly turned to me and said, 'Now you, Dave, you should sign on. You've been a bloody good officer and I for one would be happy to recommend you for a Permanent Commission!'

My reaction to such a proposal was, first, to consider that 'the drink was speaking' and second, to wonder whether a recommendation from old Ben was something that would serve me well or not! But then I began to think that in *vino veritas* and a PC could almost guarantee a lifetime career in what was a service for which I had actually developed a high regard. It was true that I liked the operational side of things, the challenges, the sheer thrills, being in the air, mastering techniques and knowing about all 'the bits and pieces'. What was less appealing was the prospect of a posting anywhere in the world every two and a half or three years at a time when I was beginning to consider marriage and in due course, children. The chores of taking squads for ground combat training, doing kit inspections, holding inventories, coding and decoding signals and so on did not quite counterbalance the plusses but were a disincentive at that time. Moreover, I had a good degree and the intention to pursue research in my own originally chosen profession. I could not lightly fail to pursue that Grail. Finally, I suppose that the fact that we had recently lost a crew from 151 when they 'went in' one night during low-level PIs and another pilot from one of the day squadrons had crashed into the hill just west of the airfield soon after take-off, probably because his dinghy inflated on him in the cockpit, had left us a bit depressed.

In the end I was non-committal and we got on with the game. It was an insidious game which I have never played since and would certainly not have the stamina or powers of recovery to play now. I regret to say I learned it from senior officers. Their Mess bills could stand the strain better than Pilot Officers'. The game was so named because it consisted of the players standing round the bar throwing, in turn, five poker dice from a leather shaker. No attention was paid to any faces of the dice other than aces. The number of aces turning up in each throw was counted until the person whose throw produced the seventh ace. At that point, his task was then to nominate some hellish brew to be purchased from the bar, the more zany and unusual, and containing at least three different drinks, the better. An example might be a bottle of sweet stout, mixed with a green Chartreuse and a large gin.

The barman would note this and begin to prepare the fiendish beverage. Pasquale was, incidentally, excellent at reading the signs and tempering his manipulations of the optics and measures to both the condition of a young officer's brain and liver and to that of his Mess bill (which he always knew). Meanwhile, the game continued, the shaker passing from hand to hand until the fourteenth ace was thrown. The thrower thus became the victim who had to drink the hellish potion – though not until the end of the game. The dice continued to roll until the twenty-first ace fell. The poor sod who threw that one was the one who paid for the concoction. Such was the random nature of the game that it could happen that some poor chap would be legless in no time but would never have had to pay a thing. Alternatively, one might have to pay all night and never get a drink and there were even some instances of the nominator being both payer and drinker. *C'est la chance! C'est la vie!* though more often, by morning, it seemed like *C'est le mort!*

As demobilisation loomed, it suddenly dawned on me that I was currently the holder of the Officer's Mess inventory. In the past, I had used every stratagem in the book to swindle the examining officers, just as I, in my turn, had been swindled by my predecessor. Where there should have been four window curtains and there were only three, one was quickly torn into two and the separate fractions checked in at Stores as damaged items on different days so that two whole new ones were issued. The same ploy worked with floor brooms, sheets, drinking glasses and so on. It clearly did not work in the case of wardrobes, cutlery and beds, for example.

So it was that, try as I might, some deficiencies could not be reconciled. I remained short of a wardrobe, officers, for the use of, each, one, and a miscellany of knives, forks and spoons had disappeared forever. We actually found the missing bed in the Sergeants' Mess. They had one supernumerary – perhaps a relic of the hasty and improvised shuttling about at their last inventory check when they had 'borrowed' it from us. They could not, however, help me with the wardrobe or the cutlery.

On the Saturday before my demobilisation, therefore, dressed in mufti as unobtrusively as possible, this particular officer and gentleman could have been found reconnoitring the counters in Woolworth's at the end of Edinburgh's noble Princes Street for the cheapest possible table knives, forks and spoons he could lay his hands on. Several of my hard earned pounds saved from the predatory hands of barman Pasquale were handed over in the cause of remedying that part of the deficiency.

The wardrobe, unfortunately, was never found until after I was demobbed so my final Mess bill had an unpleasant £42 added to it to make that good at Air Ministry prices. I learned much later from an erstwhile brother officer that the wretched wardrobe eventually turned up in a Warrant Officer's quarters when he was being investigated, and eventually cashiered, for dealing in a racket involving beef supplies to the cookhouse.

The last ritual of my full-time service came on the final morning of the two years. In addition to the usual form filling I had to undertake a medical examination by the Unit MO. The night before we had all dined, not wisely but too well, at that estimable establishment, The Castle Restaurant at Dirleton, only to repair thereafter to the anteroom bar for some serious and perhaps at times even maudlin farewell drinking. I was in consequence in that state sometimes described as 'tired and emotional'. The morning light was battering unpleasantly at my retinas. Pasquale, in a final surge of diligence, had polished the buttons and belt buckle on my best blues and the toecaps of my shoes shone like stars in the night. Although the reflections from these items were almost too strong for my weakened state to endure, I had to recognise that Pasquale had shyly excelled himself. I tipped him this last time with what meagre resources remained in my wallet and set out for the Sickbay.

'Ah, Pilot Officer Clark – I observe that you are warm and vertical,' quoth the MO, exaggerating again.

'Yes, Sir'. I muttered, without too much enthusiasm.

'Not much on your card for two years, is there? Generally OK – apart from this morning?' he added. I did not realise he knew of the party.

I lied in the affirmative. By this time I was gasping for a pint of cold, clear water but assumed for a moment a blasé air of suppressed but vigorous manhood. I was afraid he might consider me too fragile to be released unprotected into the wild, catch-as-catch-can of the civilian world. He ran a freezing stethoscope quickly over my trunk, took a cursory pulse and, with the appropriate instruments, peered briefly into my eyes and ears.

'Well, Clark, your eyes are like piss'oles in the snow but then that was possibly last night's little celebration. Otherwise you seem fine. No complaints?' He waited about three nanoseconds for my reply before going on to say that I'd have a further medical examination after being assigned to my first posting in the RAFVR the following summer. At that time, all GD National Service Officers in the RAF had to complete a further three and a half years in the Royal Auxiliary Air Force or the RAF Volunteer Reserve.

'Well, good luck!' He dismissed me, but, unexpectedly, with a smile and shook hands.

'Thank you, Sir.' I saluted and left. The whole examination had contrasted markedly with the rigorous and searching tests I had been subjected to on my entry into the Service. It seemed that the idea now, on my departure, was to ensure only that I suffered from nothing that might now or later warrant any pension payments, so clearly it did not pay for the MO to look too closely for any defects attributable to my Service career. As it happened, over the two years, I had never reported sick and had enjoyed total fitness and good health. A couple of Alkaseltzer, a pint of water and a few hours would again see me in peak condition. Even a dose of Bob Martin's would hardly then improve my shiny coat and cool nose.

All that morning, I found it hard to grasp that the work of the Station went on as normal, utterly regardless of my departure. It was a bizarre egocentricity. I had not expected to feel nostalgic, but both at

Leuchars and at Macmerry word was going around that at long last 222 and 43 Squadrons were to be re-equipped with General Electric Lightnings and 151 with Gloster Javelins, the first delta winged fighters, and with improved equipment and radars. Up till now, we had been impressed only by the occasional sighting of these exotic monsters as their prototypes scampered across our radar tubes with unwonted celerity. As it happened, I need not have been so wistful. The re-equipping of the squadrons took a great deal longer than was then anticipated and even in my final year in the Royal Auxiliary Air Force, we had only moved on to ageing Meteor NF14s.

On the afternoon of 29 October 1953, I packed my case and kitbag, and took a last look round my little room, with never a cockroach in sight. I bade my friends a final farewell, heavily laced with all manner of coarse admonitions about how they should and should not behave in my absence, and strode with a resolution that was more apparent than real to the main gate and out into another world.

For some reason, which I rationalised by saying to myself that my uniform cap and greatcoat would be difficult to pack, and anyway I would be retaining my commission in the Reserves, I travelled home in uniform. It was perhaps a measure of my ambivalence about leaving the RAF that I did not particularly crave to leap into 'civvies' straight away. At Dundee, I watched two of the 151 NF 11s lining up on their downwind leg over Leuchars and wondered which of my friends might be crewing them.

The train journey to Aberdeen could hardly have been more different from the one of two years before to Warrington. No crowded, sweatily apprehensive bodies this time. As I sipped my coffee, I watched the wildfowl scuttering about on the Montrose Basin from the calm luxury of the First Class compartment which my travel warrant afforded me. A couple of business men rustled their copies of the *Financial Times* and *Scotsman* with gentle decorum and, further down the carriage, a Northeast farmer and his wife remarked just as knowingly but with perhaps less *douceur* on the beasts and crops as we rumbled northwards.

At Aberdeen, there was the familiar bustle around the 'Shell' which had been a landmark and *rendezvous* for so many so often over the years and I rejoiced again at the couthy sound of the broad Aberdonian doric voices. There was a strange personal resonance in a fragment of conversation which carried to me in the wind as I crossed the forecourt and headed for the bus station, ' ... aye, so fit are ye gaun tae dee noo?' I had been turning over that very thought all the way up in the train.

An hour or so later, I was greeted by my parents as I dumped my kit in the hall. My father, always with a penchant for the dramatic, said, 'Well, boy, glad to have you back. That'll be the end of another chapter I suppose. This calls for a sherry, I think!'

Not knowing of the previous night's debauchery, he interpreted my precipitate rush to the bathroom as post-travel urgency. But it did allow me to down another pint of water to facilitate my continuing recovery and gave me an excuse to slink into my old bedroom to change into sports jacket and flannels before the crystal glasses were mobilised. It seemed both comfortably familiar and oddly alien at the same time. I had left as little more than a boy and returned as a man.

That was the point at which it became clear that 2536746 Pilot Officer Clark was now an unemployed civilian and nobody would say 'Sir' to him any more. Further chapters were yet to be written.

CHAPTER 8

Epilogue

When one is setting up some experiment in human behaviour or psychology, there is always a primary requirement for a control group. That is, a group of subjects entirely comparable with the 'experimental' subjects but on whom the processes being studied have not been carried out. The effects of those processes are then thought to have been the result of the experimental procedure if they are unique to the experimental group and not found in the control group. Because of the near universality of the National Service 'experiment' on the young men of this country from 1949 to 1962, there has never been the possibility of a contemporary control group of similar size having been studied.

In consequence, it will always be difficult to attribute outcomes differentially to the effects of simple maturation – of 'just growing up' – and to the specific effects of military training and experience. With the exception of processes such as schizophrenia which characteristically cause a progressive deterioration in thought and behaviour and of a few physical illnesses during the very years when National Service was commonly completed, adverse effects on the well-being and psychological adjustment of National Servicemen do not seem to have much exceeded the usual prevalence levels. On the contrary, many who completed their two years are reported in the scientific literature on the subject, and have commented individually though informally, that they thought that the experience was not only generally worthwhile, both to the nation and to the individual, but that it also contributed to a better and fuller development of the ex-National Serviceman as a human being after he had emerged from it.

It is possible of course that such a reaction was sustained as a defence against the inadmissible thought that the whole thing was just an enormous waste of time and effort. His own experience and that of other contemporaries who were National Servicemen and with whom he has discussed the topic, together with his reading of the written accounts of aspects of National Service by others, have led the writer to conclude that the satisfaction of National Servicemen with their experience seems to correlate positively with two factors. The first is the extent to which they felt they had integrated with, and accepted, even temporarily, the mores of the Service to which they were committed. The second was the extent to which they had led an active and involved Service life. Those who found it difficult to assimilate to the style of life, albeit temporarily, and those who were underemployed, were the ones to resent it most and who felt robbed of two years of life. Underemployment might mean either having insufficient amounts of work to do or being underemployed in the sense that the work they were asked to do was well below their level of ability.

It does seem, however, that there were some whom the writer finds it hard not just to describe as 'wimps'. Some were simply mentally or physically tender plants who would, even in moderately pressured situations in civilian life, be inclined to wilt and give up. Others may have lacked the capacity or the motivation to adapt to what must have seemed an alien culture. What was perhaps more remarkable was that so many did actually cope, at least adequately, with the stresses and strains of the early weeks of National Service training in particular. From that larger proportion, however, there was a steady trickle of signings on to the Regular Forces for varying lengths of further service which indicated some feeling that here and there some square pegs had found square holes.

In this writer's experience, Wesker's Pip Thomson would certainly have been well and truly quizzed as to why, having the ability, he chose not to go for officer training. He would, however, have been allowed the privilege of not doing so without the chivvying he was subjected to in the play. In *Chips with Everything* the playwright examines only the atmosphere and activities of the first two of twenty-four months of RAF Service life. His Corporal Hill could be modelled on the writer's second DI Corporal more than on the original martinet, but otherwise the play does reflect the frustrations and resentments, the agonies and the doubts of the 'square-bashing' weeks. The haranguing by junior NCOs, the 'You play ball with me and I'll play ball with you!' bargaining in which the power is all held unilaterally is well caught in the play. The officer characters are, however, rather caricatured – if only just! A few of the Wesker specimens did exist, but in general they were more heterogeneous than the playwright allows and certainly as heterogeneous in attitudes, background and interests as were the men they commanded.

For a large number of recruits, one of the most striking aspects of National Service was their sudden precipitation into very large numbers of their contemporaries. Even in schools, universities and factories, one might, in one's late teens or early twenties, be in peer group populations which, although they might number a few hundred or a thousand at most in all, these groups would be divided into age groups and classes which meant that any one age band would interact only with a limited segment, a few tens perhaps, of the total sub-population. One also had, to a large extent, the choice as to with whom one interacted. There would be a kind of 'assortative mating' whereby in any one of those settings one could settle within a small circle of like-minded colleagues. Initially at least the conscripts found themselves almost engulfed by hundreds in whom the only common factor was the limited age band.

The extreme heterogeneity of the members of each weekly intake into National Service, especially in the Army and the Royal Air Force, made an immediate impact on nearly all recruits. It certainly did on the writer. The mix of social classes, educational level, physical shapes and sizes, linguistic habits, dialects and accents meant that there was a struggle to find any commonality. The Service was, of course, able to use this lack of any obvious common bond by supplying the commonality imposed by King's Regulations, Service values and attitudes and a chain of command which wholly removed the exercise of autonomy and initiative on the part of the new recruit.

The search for kindred spirits, from the very first day, seemed to follow a number of hierarchical steps. I noticed that the process was not unlike that of young men who scan the available 'talent' (as it was called in my young day) lined along the walls of the village or city dance hall. The likely candidates for attention are first subject to a certain amount of direct visual scanning – a clearly physical appraisal. A dance or two and a few verbal gambits then allow of a more penetrating assessment of background, conversational skills, intelligence, interests and so on. Later still, if there is enough reciprocity stimulated by the contact, in several senses, the association/friendship is established and may develop.

In the billet, cleanliness, tidiness and reciprocal eye contact probably weighted the physical appraisal more than analysis of sheer physique or a pleasant rather than unpleasant appearance. Thereafter there was a lot of direct questioning about where one came from, geographically at first, and then more about social/educational background. These initial processes could be seen to occur within hours rather than days of first contacts and went on being refined and being more discriminatory as the days passed. Those recruits who were not active in this themselves, who 'shut themselves off' from these early explorations, tended to suffer by being isolated from the group – and from the support of that group which would become so important in the future weeks. It did not necessarily follow that chaps who were by nature deeply introverted became isolates. Provided that they could manage some responses and met other criteria such as being smart, pleasant and 'knowing', then they would be tagged as being 'a bit shy' but were still incorporated within the group.

My first impression, which may have been erroneous, was that in the initial intake and recruit training stages at least, the Scots and Welsh seemed to be less affected by class differences in their affiliations than were the English. Partly, it may have been that the former simply did not recognise a public school accent or an aristocratic manner when they saw them. An English accent was simply that and that alone. Initially it would be more likely that a motor mechanic and a philosophy graduate becoming friends would be from the Celtic fringes, whereas that would only have happened amongst the English if both had happened to have gone to Oundle or Marlborough.

Later on, by the time 'square-bashing' was well under way, there was a remarkable shift in the structure of these affiliations. Early affiliations which had become quickly established because they were well founded on several compatibilities were not disrupted but a completely fresh analysis of those chaps who could land you 'in the shit' as against those who were 'good chaps' and who would pull their weight when required became prevalent. School, occupational or class background faded entirely from the scene. This metamorphosis was of course facilitated by the progressive detachment from civilian activities and values and the forcible imposition of new rules of behaviour which required cooperative behaviour on the part of the complement of a hut or of a training group to make life tolerable.

For different individuals the whole military lifestyle had the effect of reducing different kinds of autonomy. A recognition of this is partly what fuelled the cry for the re-imposition of the 'disciplines' of National Service on the more unruly members of youthful society in the past couple of decades. For myself, I incline to the view adopted by Len Woodrup and quoted in Chapter 1, that off-loading our 'ne'erdowells', petty criminals, junkies and lager louts on to the fighting Services would be satisfactory neither for the Services, which seek adaptability and intelligent commitment, nor for those at the edge of society who, even in the Services, would probably react much as they do in contemporary civilian life. They would simply not accept the disciplines and would finish up having to be treated, punished or organised in exactly the same way as society now tries to deal with them.

In National Service, the kinds of autonomy which were restricted were not, however, the same for all of us. I missed having books around me and the chance to read and study. Others, accustomed to drifting off to the local pub for a pint after work in 'civvie street' found the restraints on that irksome in the extreme. Some loathed the lack of privacy, the ribaldry in the showers and the uncouth language from which there was no escape. Others adapted to all of that but simply could never understand the apparent need to do everything 'at the double' and increase their personal tempo appropriately.

Former urban dwellers seemed to be more unsettled at first than did those of us from rural or remote and thinly populated areas. They missed the services and entertainment facilities they had obviously got used to. The lads from the backwoods had perhaps learned to be more self-sufficient and had never experienced a plethora of services and social opportunities. A greater number than I expected, certainly in recruit training camp, actively and explicitly bemoaned the lack of sex. Allowing for the expected proportion of braggarts in this area of endeavour, again it seemed that many of the erstwhile city dwellers had not only greater sexual opportunity but also had the sexual habits of rabbits, far exceeding those of us from more 'protected' environments. In retrospect, it was noticeable that those who grumbled most about their enforced celibacy were those who also seemed to have a poor attitude to women as persons. There is perhaps some room therefore for qualifying the comments of Chambers and Landreth who perhaps over-estimated the proportion of virgins amongst National Service recruits.

There was the major adaptation that Servicemen had to make when called up of being flung suddenly into a wholly male environment. Later in their two years, there would be opportunities to mix with female Servicewomen and civilians, but for several months, with the exception of a few hours at weekends or on brief leaves, recruits would neither see, touch, nor speak with a female. The effect of this varied. For some, it led only to a preoccupation with sublimating their desires for female company into the habit of writing home or to girl friends more often and more fully to tell of their feelings and experiences. Letter writing played a much greater part in their lives than it ever had before. Some even waxed poetical and though most felt their words were very private, a few would be inclined to try out their efforts on the billet before sending them off to their girls SWALK. ('Sealed with a loving kiss!')

Many were of the opinion that the general coarsening of language and uninhibited swearing was in part attributable to the absence of the softening and moderating effect of having women around. It was always noticeable that, especially after we had been commissioned, when there were women officers in the Mess, even if some of them were every bit as verbally uninhibited as were the males, there was very much less of a tendency to be quite so vulgar.

A third effect of the absence of females was that there was an almost total absence of any discussion of human relationships as such. By and large, men are disinclined to focus their discussion on people in that way. They may heap opprobrium on those of their fellows who happen to incur their displeasure – such as our Drill Corporals – but that was usually in the form of affording a measure of emotional release from frustration rather than an analysis of relationships in any depth. Talk in the billet tended to focus very much on current activities or those in the recent past or near future. It was essentially commentary or description and, during training, very much concerned with what was engaging us at the time, from how to 'pull through' a rifle to the determination of a dew point or how to calibrate certain radar components.

At OCTU and later, there was rather more wide ranging talk (and rather less obscenity) when we knew that the establishment of certain points of view was necessary and when we were in a context which valued a reasonable standard of intellectual analysis. But even then, men were not disposed to reveal much of their inner selves to each other as they might have done with their girl friends or as a group of like-minded young women might have.

Perhaps by way of some sort of compensation for this, the level of trust and mutual interdependency one eventually came to feel for one's closer colleagues exceeded anything I have ever felt in any civilian job. Two factors seemed to militate in favour of this. The first was that there were often high levels of stress imposed on us both by people and events, which, though we were young, fit and resilient, might have broken us at times if we had not had a strong mutual support system. Second, we were all engaged in essentially similar tasks and activities, so we all had a very good grasp of what was involved in doing our jobs and what it would take to succeed at them. In most of industry and commerce, to say nothing of the variety of academic pursuits many of us had come from, there were more likely to be significant differences in the specific content and tempo of work undertaken by different individuals.

This element of common context seems to have had a binding effect whether National Servicemen were working as clerks in an office, patrolling a strip of jungle in Malaya, flying a night fighter or checking torpedoes on the deck of a destroyer. These loyalties eventually extended from the immediate small group to larger units, regiments, ships or squadrons and then to the particular Service. In certain circumstances, these very bondings could lead to such things as fights which would no doubt be seen as totally ludicrous or unreasonable by civilians detached from the military ethos. The form of these fights could vary from simple bar brawls in the case of lower ranks to complex and subtle conflicts at Staff Officer level when, for example, the year's appropriations and budgets were being argued at the highest levels.

One of the features of my own experience, as a National Serviceman, of progression from AC2 to, eventually, Flying Officer, was quite unexpected, almost insidious in its nature but real enough in retrospect. That was the marked change in attitude to Service life which paralleled that progression and which may, to some extent, have been reflected in the preceding chapters of this book.

In initial training there was no doubt that 'They' would not break 'Us'. 'They' represented everything that was disrupting our family lives, occupational careers, love lives, hobbies and interests. The sense of being oppressed by authority, just for its own sake, was overweening. But, as time and training progressed, these early resentments may not have entirely disappeared but they did diminish markedly. A sneaking regard for the professionalism and know-how of our instructors after we had escaped the mind-dulling rituals of recruit training began to replace the lightly suppressed scorn we had held for many of the DI Corporals and senior NCOs. There was also a recognisable end point to that training which would patently furnish us with new skills. The fact that the vast majority of us would never exercise most of these skills after we had left the Forces did not blind us to the fact that we had been trained to do something which we would never otherwise have achieved. Some did fall by the wayside and we all knew that the achievement had cost us something in both mental and physical effort and application. At that stage the 'Them'/'Us' boundary was already becoming less well defined.

Perhaps, compared to many National Servicemen, we were lucky in that we had been busy and fully engaged. Many saw only a humdrum, repetitive and un-taxing two years stretch out before them. That must have boded ill for personal satisfaction. It is little wonder that such men were irked by the necessity to spend all of two years, as they saw it, frittering away time.

The process for us, however, was continued at OCTU. By that time, 'We' were engaged in the detail of the business of actually becoming 'Them'. It actually became difficult not to identify with much of the ethos of the Service we were now so thoroughly immersed in. We were no longer simply a miscellaneous bunch of National Servicemen because we were totally integrated with Regular airmen of all non-commissioned ranks and of widely varying prior Service careers. The content of our day-to-day lives was indistinguishable from that of Regulars. Prior to that we had been easily recognisable as ephemera – two-year wonders who had no real identity with the RAF. Now, and even more when we were commissioned, we became representatives of the Service. We would be automatically committed to three and a half years part-time service in the Reserves even if we did not sign on for more than the minimum statutory period. It was indicative that, as the time for demobilisation from full-time service approached, several of us gave serious thought to the possibility of engaging for another year or two, if not more. Had it not been the case that so many of us had already undergone preparation in the form of academic study for other careers, several more would no doubt have settled for remaining in the RAF.

Many National Servicemen have remarked or written that they were glad of the chance to travel, especially abroad. For a proportion, that meant to a theatre of war such as Malaya or Korea but even for a significant number of these, the excitement and novelty of action was enough to compensate for the horrors and anxieties of combat. There are some written accounts which show that a period at the battle front was even preferable to mouldering in a humdrum job back at headquarters. Most of the National Servicemen that the writer met in Germany were glad of the opportunity to see parts of the world which they had only ever read about or seen on the films. Television was quite uncommon in the homes of many in 1951 and the upsurge in easy foreign travel for a large proportion of the population which came about in the sixties and later was as then unknown.

As for a posting to Germany, there were some differences in attitude to this depending on the age of the soldier or airman. Those who were, like many of the writer's age group, old enough to have remembered quite vividly living through the anxieties and privations of a wartime boyhood were perhaps more curious to observe at first hand what the Germans were like compared to how they had been depicted by the propaganda machine between 1939 and 1945. They also wanted to see what were the residual physical effects of the war, particularly of the awful bombings we knew urban Germany had been subjected to, more than did those Servicemen who, three or four years younger, had only sketchy or second-hand memories of the war.

The latter group tended, for example, to be more aware of the freedom offered by a foreign posting from hampering domestic attitudes and the restraints and prejudices they saw their home environment having placed on them. They tended to take the new Germany at face value. They would comment on the good beer and fractionally better summer weather, the better standard of barrack-room accommodation and so on. The older group (and these distinctions perhaps applied across the board to Servicemen generally, not only to National Servicemen) were somewhat more analytic and more wary of drawing over-quick conclusions about the host nation. Because National Servicemen were also posted abroad for shorter periods, they were also less likely to form longer-term affiliations with members of the indigenous population. Almost all National Servicemen tended to say that they would jump at the chance of a foreign posting if they were given the chance and, having enjoyed one, would talk about it as a highlight of their Service.

Quite a subtle effect of service abroad on National Servicemen was that it seemed to have, for many, the effect of extending their outlook on how the world beyond Kidderminster, Hebden Bridge or Perth might be. Many were recruited having travelled very little even in Britain. The parochialism of the northern Scot, for example, is much referred to. It has never been clear whether the reported headline in the Aberdeen *Press and Journal* after the loss of the *Titanic* was apocryphal or not. It read, 'Banff Man Lost at Sea'. Apart from having cycled alone round the whole of England and Scotland in three weeks in the summer of 1947, the writer himself had, for example, very little experience of the cities of England and none at all of Ireland or Wales when he was called up. Many with whom he shared billets and Messes were similarly naïve.

In the light of that, it is hardly surprising that a boat and train journey to and from Germany, a flight to Cyprus or Singapore or a temporary detachment to serve in the Kenyan bush was at the root of an enhanced self-confidence. Perhaps more importantly, it gave the chance for some sense of international issues to be grasped and for an awareness of the characteristics of other nationalities to grow and be assimilated into a man's wider understanding of the world. Such a process of growth was seldom articulated, even seldom noticed at the time. Many who experienced it, however, have remarked on some aspect of it subsequently. In a few instances, it may have endorsed already established prejudices but most considered that aspect of their Service life as perhaps the most valuable feature of it.

This writer would not place it quite as high as that so far as he himself was concerned. Our engagement in the more pressured activity of a formal NATO Exercise, coupled with the fact we were based on a temporary tented camp, reduced to a degree the potential for pleasurable and more relaxed exploration of the host country. Nevertheless, some of the episodes outlined in the preceding chapter will have demonstrated that there were occasions when our experience was enlarged and intensified in a way which would not have been possible had we remained in the UK. At a more trivial level, several of us who had some interest in languages, found that our use and understanding of colloquial German was enhanced. In general, there were wide differences among all National Servicemen who experienced a foreign posting in their interest in learning to communicate even in a limited way in the local language. Some with little or no tertiary education involving linguistic skills did remarkably well at trying to use German, Swahili or Malay, whereas others of whom, at first sight, one might have expected them to make full use of such an opportunity, were remarkably passive in that regard. To some extent the determining parameter was the amount of local 'fraternisation' through shopping, exploring the area during off-duty time and mixing socially with local girls.

A second influence deriving from being abroad in Germany which could be said to have extended my own understanding of international affairs (and I don't mean Kristina in the Münster Biergarten) was the experience of being operationally involved with airmen of other nationalities and the reality of coming face to face, although at a healthy distance, with the putative enemy of the day. Our squadrons regularly flew over the great German heath lands where Nato tanks and armour regularly trained and did practice firing. Our radar picked up patrolling USSR aircraft and the whole Exercise was on and over ground that had seen pitched battles as our forces raced to Berlin only a few years before. Although there was not a lot of discussion in the Mess or the crew rooms about the then political situation in Europe, it was inevitable that there would be some assessment of threat and counter threat in both our strategic and tactical thinking. This is not to say that such considerations did not engage us in our work in UK. It was just that without the sacred twenty-one miles of the Channel and a rather larger North Sea between us and any opposing forces, these thoughts did not have quite the same force and immediate relevance that they gained by our presence in Westphalia.

One of the most striking features of National Service for many of us who had higher education was that there was a tendency to what is now called 'dumbing down'. Neither in the barrack-room nor in the Officers' Mess was there any encouragement either explicit or by habit to engage in any detailed or protracted discussion of science, literature, philosophy or the arts generally. 'Serious' reading might be done in the privacy of one's own room were one an officer but round the bar in the Mess or in the NAAFI, talk was usually either trivial or focussed entirely on Service activities and personalia. The few occasions this writer found himself engaged in any extended discussion of, say, international events, scientific or socio-economic topics, were briefly in the billet with a few confidants with similar academic background. As an officer or cadet, such discussions in a more public setting were always with very senior officers of Staff College calibre. They were almost all highly able and widely read people who lived happily with the challenge of ideas as well as being on top of their Service job.

The opportunities for any National Serviceman who was not of commissioned rank to make contact in a social setting, which would allow of such conversation, were negligible. Even for a junior officer, such chances might occur only once or twice in a couple of years. Major permanent units such as Cranwell or Sandhurst would of course contain substantial libraries with the range of content comparable to most tertiary educational establishments in 'civvie street', but the average operational unit was less well-endowed.

National Service life was not geared to an academic tempo. It was scheduled in a very different way. Hours of work could be erratic at times, sometimes full of strange hiatuses, yet hectic and overfilled at others. Shift work, especially on operational units, was common, so that too broke up the natural rhythms which can be appropriate to sustained study. The life was more in keeping with activity rather than thought, with sport rather than study.

Servicemen, who by nature or inclination were solitary and ruminative of habit, almost all found the life much more trying than did mesomorphic, outgoing, even brash, young men. This has been intuitively noted by novelists like David Lodge and Leslie Thomas and described accurately by contributors to the documentary writings of Trevor Royle and of Chambers and Landreth.

The modes of adaptation which National Servicemen of widely differing characteristics and social background adopted to deal with the Service ethos were varied and interesting. First of all, it is worth remarking on the relatively small number who deliberately 'worked their ticket' by feigning chronic ill health, psychological disorder or physical incoordination of a gross nature. Several, in almost every intake, would at some stage declare their intention to try to do so but in due course the group pressure to see it through like the rest would prove stronger. In our 'square-bashing' flight we had our 'camel marcher' who really could not do otherwise and several others of that ilk are reported in the scientific literature who may have turned it on for the purpose and sustained it long enough to succeed in getting a discharge on medical grounds – or just because of general unsuitability! There were also some, such as epileptics whose medication was achieving only moderate control of their condition, who started having fits again when under severe physical or psychological stress.

By the time initial training ended, most conscripts had developed their own way of coping. For many, they treated it rather as habitual short-term prisoners and small time criminals in civilian life do, by settling down quietly to 'do their porridge'. Those were the ones who, within the first few weeks had drawn up a 'demob calendar'. These usually hung up on the inside of their locker and they would deliberately and with appropriate ritual, score off or blank out each day as it passed. A running total of 'Days still to do' was also kept. Towards the end of their two years they might even have it down to the hours to go and could tell anyone who asked how much Service time remained with great exactitude.

Some eventually developed an existing hobby or took up a new one in which their whole libido would be invested – a spare time pursuit which the daily work routine only got in the way of. This was not unlike the response of some workers in mass production factories after the war who were bored at work but who lived for their football or their racing pigeons. That sort of development was not usually possible until the Serviceman was posted to a steady job or to a unit where he was likely to remain for a significant period. Aero-modelling, snooker, photography, some form of sport, listening to or playing music were all observed as popular activities. Leslie Thomas, in *The Virgin Soldiers*, describes with great poignancy a habitual train-spotter, struggling in the jungle of Malaya.

Then there were the lucky ones who, never before having had a trade or skill, suddenly realised that there were opportunities in the

Services which might have a direct carry-over into later civilian life. It may never have been more than, for example, learning to drive, operate a telephone exchange or mend a radio set, but some of those were amongst the National Servicemen who eventually signed on for a longer term. Those who did not, nevertheless, found themselves writing home to ask their relatives about the job prospects when they came out. The bored and the feckless, reluctant soldiers and airmen, who did not share the experience but perhaps shared a billet with such new enthusiasts tended to be resentful. They would see their keener mates as turncoats and there would be occasional squabbles. One chap would be telling how his uncle in Bradford would be able to get him a job as a van driver when he came out while the sulky AC2 next to him might respond with 'Who'd want to stay in this bloody mob any longer than they had to anyway? I'm f****** fed up already. I'd go tomorrow if I could!' But these contretemps seldom lasted long and the squabblers would wander up to the NAAFI together for a pie and a pint.

Even amongst those of us who eventually were commissioned, there were divisions between those who became strongly tied in to the Service we were in and those who, while maintaining a decent level of attention to what their job involved, still retained some reserve about their commitment to it which would see them through any more than the two years. One close friend and contemporary of the writer's went straight into the Education Branch of the RAF, was busy and involved, thoroughly enjoyed it and signed on for another year of Service. Another (the writer's younger brother, in fact) also joined up for National Service as a private soldier in the Royal Artillery but he too was selected for a commission, survived the hazards of recruit training at Mons Barracks under the eagle eye of RSM Brittain and eventually finished up flying Air Observation Post light aircraft out of Middle Wallop – one of the 'pongos' we RAF chaps were so unfairly disparaging about when we were there. He too was one of those who became proud of his Regiment, glad to have had the new experience and went on to enjoy further years in the Territorial Army. Given that these cases are but anecdotal evidence rather than emerging from a proper statistical analysis, they do favour the writer's view that those who were most fully engaged with their duties as National Servicemen were those who felt it less of an imposition on their time.

Even for those who were irked by much of what they experienced in the course of their two years, there were many common features characteristic of their Service which have served to establish bonds between all National Servicemen for many decades after their Service had ended. Even the bonds between Regulars and National Servicemen who served in the same regiment, ship or squadron are for most more lasting and real than are many relationships between men in civilian life. It may bore the younger generation to tears to hear a couple of old codgers, say, in a train, who suddenly discover that they were both National Servicemen at such and such a base in 1950 or thereabouts. A conversation which may have been stilted and desultory up till then, suddenly takes off when the common experience is established and episodes and characters which they remember well are exchanged.

Such bonding is inevitably accompanied by the feeling that all those who came through National Service were mentally and physically tougher, broader in outlook, more democratic and more ready to be unselfish with their mates than were those who did not. Much of that feeling derives from the experience of early privation and stress which was so typical of the early training months where everyone had their faces rubbed in the dirt, as it were. The later *longueurs* which many felt then tend to be forgotten.

Only as the years have passed has a National Service Association been formed, and now it has a website on the internet! There was, after the end of National Service in the sixties, a feeling amongst many that while there were medals for service in the Forces serving at other periods, in and out of major wars, there was no similar recognition of those millions of young men who gave up two or more years of their lives in the service of their country. In the case of some, they gave up, not just years, but their lives themselves or their health and strength. That feeling gave rise to a movement which eventually originated a National Service medal. It was struck as a result of sponsorship by the Royal British Legion to mark National Service between the years of 1939 and 1960. The medal was struck so that it might be purchased only by those who performed National Service, both military and civilian, between January 1939 and December 1960, or their next of kin. The Poppy Appeal Fund is the beneficiary of the income from this.

The medal is therefore a memento rather than a decoration and may not be worn alongside officially recognised medals and decorations. Nevertheless, thousands of ex-National Servicemen applied for this and retain it with pride. It perhaps symbolises for many the half unconscious awareness that those two years were special in a unique way. Conscription had always been a hard principle for a British Parliament to cleave to. It came. It served its purpose and it has gone, perhaps forever. But those who were the conscripts may not at the time have heard the Press Gang at their doors, but would know it if they heard it again.

Several decades on from the event, the vast majority of ex-National Servicemen, when asked their views on their experience as conscripts for two years, will express some ambivalence about it. Commonly they will say something like, 'Well, in the end I'm quite glad

I did it though it often did not seem I'd ever be able to say that. Yes, there were quite a few good things about it!' Challenged again to say whether they'd like to do it again, most will have said 'No'.

Plate 19: National Service Medal (author)

The book *Called Up* by Chambers and Landreth is essentially one in which more than a dozen men who were National Servicemen have written of their experience and that is edited and presented with some commentary by the nominal authors. One or two of the chapters have been written by men subsequently to become better known to the general public by dint of their later journalism, authorship and radio or TV presentations. For example, Robert Robinson, responsible for Chapter 7 of that book, served eventually as a 2nd Lieutenant in the RASC in Kenya. He wrote:

'As a boy of nineteen I might very well have had a holiday in Dieppe, but only as a Serviceman of nineteen might I have lived in Africa. Only as that might I have seen my friend go mad, only as that might I have wielded command, might I have felt what it was like to be in the middle of a mutiny, or stopped a convoy to go behind a mango tree. This National Service had allowed me to know for certain one thing I had never known before: there was a 'me'.

Kenneth Smale, in Chapter 9, was a Sergeant Instructor in the RAEC.

'During the voyage home I had time to take stock of my experiences. Despite the many criticisms, I felt that National Service is what one makes of it. It can be a waste of time – or it can be profitable. I had travelled and done many of the things which had seemed beyond my reach. One does tend, I know, to forget the bad times and remember only the good – but, after all, is that a bad thing – if the good was worthwhile?'

Something of the same view was held by a clerk in the RAF, Peter Wiles, in Chapter 11.

'Yet it wasn't so bad. Looking back, that's precisely what I feel about it all. It was an education in getting on with people, an education which until then I had sadly neglected. It saved me from becoming a nasty little aesthete, without the humour or the stamina to achieve any of the things I dreamed of ... Looking back on my National Service, I think spontaneously of laughter. It is only because I have been driven to recollect my state of mind at the time I left school that I have brought to light certain less pleasant aspects of my life as a two-year warrior.'

Finally, from one of those who actually saw severe combat in the field, John Eason who was in the Black Watch in Korea and Japan. He wrote:

'Looking back now on my two years' National Service, I do not regret it – not even Korea. At times I loathed the Army, especially its obstinate stupidity. But I enjoyed its wonderful comradeship, which embraces men from all walks of life and I was glad to have the chance to travel halfway round the world and back.

Individually, National Servicemen may complain that they are wasting their time and that they could employ the two years more profitably. So they could – or rather, perhaps they could. But from the nation's point of view their service is vital, and I honestly believe that they are doing a tremendous amount of good for their country. Any man who will not give up two years of his life for his country should be thrown out of it.'

For himself, the writer has looked back on his service with a smile. What began as an irksome frustration of an academic career grew into an experience which is now recognised as having given him a unique enhancement of his ego-identity. This is almost certainly not an isolated effect on one man but something which most National Servicemen will have recognised in themselves to a greater or lesser degree. All will have been snatched from one life-style or psychological frame of reference and flung bodily into something, at once so alien but with so much in common for all who went through it, that it is not surprising that it came to be seen as a kind of complex and involuntary initiation for manhood.

As with many initiations, the initiates would carry a few lifelong scars, but the strength and self-confidence of which these were the badge are what underlie the bonds that those who were National Servicemen together immediately feel when the common background is revealed. As was earlier remarked, those bonds, not only between National Servicemen themselves but between National Service conscripts and ex-Regular Servicemen are still something which they all recognise as a background which can set them all apart from those who have never been anything but civilians. Of course there will be those among the latter who will look askance at such a separation and wax cynical about a group who could grumble so much about it when they were in it and yet brag about its beneficial effects when out of it. They may wonder too about the effects of the excessive masculine harshness and coarseness on the capacity for sensitive good citizenship and human relations.

What they will not necessarily know of will be the wide range of coping mechanisms which different personalities adopted to deal with such vicissitudes. They will not have heard of the laughter, the humour, the unselfishness, the accommodation of the bizarre, the frightening, the monotonous and the exciting which had to be made. It is true that ruminative self-scrutiny, introspection or emotional sensitivity was neither encouraged nor thought to be an adaptive mode for the National Serviceman to assume. The writer is himself all too aware that in writing this account, he has not dwelt to any extent on his own or anyone else's inner mental life. The plain fact was that few were prepared to reveal what that might have been – or even whether they allowed themselves much of an inner life!

Most, including the writer, would have harboured certain ambitions about what they might achieve, personally, occupationally or socially after National Service was over, but the exigencies of the moment nearly always precluded any extended articulation of these goals to others. It was almost as if parentheses had been placed around the two years in everybody's life. There might have been some talk about what happened before the brackets opened, so to speak, but less about what might happen after the closing of the brackets. The way in which things were talked of within the brackets was factual, direct, about action and adaptation rather than about feelings or emotions. There was simply no scope for indulging the latter. There were times when people might have been angry, irritated, frightened, depressed, euphoric, paranoid or even hallucinated. Apart from a brief remark or two to a close confidant that one felt like that from time to time, there was no pay-off either in luxuriating in the experience of one's emotions or talking to others about them. Actions always spoke louder than words. I have always been rather like one of Pavlov's 'phlegmatic dogs' anyway and it is probable that such temperaments are more adapted to the kind of experience which National Service supplied. The 'excitable dogs' suffered more.

One of the fundamental and long lasting benefits which accrued to me was the development of a resourcefulness and self-confidence which had come from my reactions to a wide variety of others in a relatively compressed period of time. By the end of the two years, I knew better what I could take – and what I could give (and I am not talking here of beneficence only). It had never occurred to me as a student, nor as a boy, that I was, in fact, physically and mentally stronger than most. As a child, my mother had tended, if anything, to encourage the view that I was 'delicate' and should not be subjected to all the 'slings and arrows of outrageous fortune'. She probably felt, being given to stereotypes, that her son should affect the wan and pallid air of what she took to be that of an intellectual.

It was only when my colleagues in the billet, and in the Mess, by their decisions and their reactions, made it clear that they saw me as reasonably tough in a variety of senses, and I myself, in a number of critical situations, found myself coping rather better than others equally stringently selected for the job, that this confidence and self-sufficiency became established. It is true that the relatively successful end to my undergraduate career had given me a foundation, but that was only about intellectual competence. It said nothing about the diverse skills necessary for living through day-to-day stresses in the way my Service experience had done.

Better still, the two years gave me an opportunity to mix with and to deal with, both as an officer and as an ordinary AC2, a more heterogeneous range of human beings than I had up to that time confronted. The good, the bad and the ugly all came my way. Psychopathy, paranoia, honesty, humour, hypochondriasis, selfishness, generosity and companionship flourished around me and I willingly shovelled all these grains of experience into my granary, later to be milled when my unconscious was running light.

For quite some time, perhaps months, after moving again into civilian life, I hankered after the thrills, the ribaldry, the fun and the foibles of the Service life. But by that time, the serious business of earning a proper living and pursuing the professional career I had always really aspired to, was becoming more pressing. So was Janet, who could by now have papered her walls with two years of regular but none too literate letters. So I came home and began to consider taking a wife. The prospective candidate, for her part, was more concerned to find me a real job. New rules of engagement were pending!

Bibliography

Chambers, Peter and Landreth, Amy (1955) *Called up: The Personal Experiences of 16 National Servicemen,* Allan Wingate, London

Forty, George (1980) *Called Up: A National Service Scrapbook,* Ian Allen Ltd, London

Gelb, Norman (1986) *Scramble: A Narrative History of the Battle of Britain,* Michael Joseph, London

Lodge, David (1962) *Ginger, You're Barmy,* McGibbon and Key, London

Marwick, Arthur (1984) *Britain in our Century,* Thames and Hudson, London

Royle, Trevor (1986) *The Best Years of their Lives: The National Service Experience 1945-63,* Michael Joseph, London

Thomas, Leslie (1966) *The Virgin Soldiers,* Constable & Co Ltd, London

Wesker, Arnold (1962) *Chips with Everything,* Blackie and Son Ltd, Glasgow and London

Woodrup, Len (1993) *Training for War Games,* The Book Guild Ltd, 25 High Street, Lewes, Sussex

The Author

Dr David Findlay Clark OBE DL MA Ph.D. C.Psychol., F.B.Ps.S. ARPS

Recently retired from working as a consultant clinical psychologist in private practice, Dr Clark is a son of the manse who was brought up in Banff and educated at Banff Academy and Aberdeen University. He is still a Clinical Senior Lecturer in the Department of Mental Health there though no longer active in teaching.

After a period of National Service in the RAF (from AC2 to Flying Officer) which became the source of much of the material in this book, he worked first as an industrial psychologist at Leicester Industrial Rehabilitation Unit of the then Ministry of Labour before becoming a clinical psychologist in the NHS. He has taught and researched at the Universities of Leicester and Aberdeen in the course of his work within a number of hospitals in the NHS, eventually retiring from the NHS in 1990 as Director of the Grampian Health Board's Area Clinical Psychology Services. For his work in that context he was awarded an OBE in 1989 and, having been active in one or another form of public service for most of his life, became Deputy Lieutenant of Banffshire in 1992.

He has been a Consultant for the WHO in Sri Lanka and has also been invited to lecture on his research in India, Canada and the USA. He is the author of a textbook, *Help, Hospitals and the Handicapped* as well as a contributor of chapters in several other major texts and over thirty professional research papers in learned and technical journals.

Latterly he has taken to less academic forms of journalism by writing magazine articles and another book, *One Boy's War*. He writes now as an additional activity to his pervasive hobby interests in photography, painting and drawing, music and golf. He lives with his wife, Janet, in Banff, and has two married daughters and four grandchildren.

Glossary

AC2	Aircraftman 2nd Class
AI	Air Interception
AOC	Air Officer Commanding
AVM	Air Vice Marshal
CO	Commanding Officer
DF	Direction Finding
DI	Drill Instructor
ETA	Estimated Time of Arrival
FFI	Free from Infection
GCA	Ground Controlled Approach
GCI	Ground Control Interception (Unit)
GD	General Duties (the flying branch of the RAF)
IFR	Instrument Flying Rules
KFS	Knife, Fork and Spoon
KRs	King's Regulations (now QRs, Queen's Regulations)
LAC	Leading Aircraftman
MHz	MegHertz (radio frequency)
MP	Military Police
MO	Medical Officer
MT	Motor Transport
NAAFI	Navy, Army and Air Force Institution
NATO	North Atlantic Treaty Organisation
NCO	Non-Commissioned Officer
NF10	Night Fighter Mark 10
OCTU	Officer Cadet Training Unit
OQs	Officer-like Qualities
PBX	Private Branch Exchange
PC	Permanent Commission
PI	Practice Interception
PO	Pilot Officer
POM	Potential Officer Material
PPI	Plan Position Indicator (radar display tube)
PTI	Physical Training Instructor
QFE	Barometric Pressure Settings on an Altimeter for Airport Level

QNH	Barometric Pressure Settings on an Altimeter for Sea Level
R/T	Radio Telephony
RAEC	Royal Army Educational Corps
RAMC	Royal Army Medical Corps
RDF	Radio Direction Finding
REME	Royal Electrical and Mechanical Engineers
ROC	Royal Observer Corps
RSM	Regimental Sergeant Major
RTB	Return to Base
RTO	Rail Transport Officer
RTU	Returned to Unit
SAC	Senior Aircraftman
SADO	Senior Administrative Officer
SNCO	Senior Non-Commissioned Officer
SWO	Station Warrant Officer
TAF	Tactical Air Force
Tx/Rx	Transmit/Receive (switches on a radio)
VFR	Visual Flying Rules
VHF	Very High Frequency (radio waves)
WAAF	Women's Royal Auxiliary Air Force
WingCo	Wing Commander
WO	Warrant Officer